Political Communication in Direct Democratic Campaigns

Challenges to Democracy in the 21st Century Series

The series 'Challenges to Democracy in the 21st Century' was initiated by the Swiss National Center of Competence in Research *NCCR Democracy,* an interdisciplinary research program launched by the Swiss National Science Foundation and the University of Zurich in 2005. The program examines how globalization and mediatization challenge democracy today (www.nccr-democracy.uzh.ch).

SWISS NATIONAL SCIENCE FOUNDATION

Series Editor: **Hanspeter Kriesi**, University of Zurich, Switzerland

Democracy faces substantial challenges as we move into the 21st Century. The West faces malaise; multi-level governance structures pose democratic challenges; and the path of democratization rarely runs smoothly. This series examines democracy across the full range of these contemporary conditions. It publishes innovative research on established democracies, democratizing polities and democracy in multi-level governance structures. The series seeks to break down artificial divisions between different disciplines, by simultaneously drawing on political communication, comparative politics, international relations, political theory, and political economy.

Series Editorial Board:

Marc Bühlmann, University of Berne, Switzerland
Claes de Vrese, University of Amsterdam, the Netherlands
Frank Esser, University of Zurich, Switzerland
Herbert Kitschelt, Duke University, USA
Sandra Lavenex, University of Lucerne, Switzerland
Jörg Matthes, University of Zurich, Switzerland
Gianpietro Mazzoleni, University of Milano, Italy
Wolfgang Merkel, WZB-Berlin, Germany

Titles include:

Hanspeter Kriesi
POLITICAL COMMUNICATION IN DIRECT DEMOCRATIC CAMPAIGNS
Enlightening or Manipulating?

Maija Setälä and Theo Schiller (*editors*)
CITIZEN'S INITIATIVES IN EUROPE
Procedures and Consequences of Agenda-Setting by Citizens

Challenges to Democracy in the 21st Century
Series Standing Order ISBN 978–0–230–30487–1 (hardback)
and 978–0–230–30488–8 (paperback)

You can receive future titles in this series as they are published by placing a standing order. Please contact your bookseller or, in case of difficulty, write to us at the address below with your name and address, the title of the series and one of the ISBNs quoted above.

Customer Services Department, Macmillan Distribution Ltd, Houndmills, Basingstoke, Hampshire RG21 6XS, England

Political Communication in Direct Democratic Campaigns

Enlightening or Manipulating?

Edited by

Hanspeter Kriesi
Chair in Comparative Politics, Department of Political Science,
University of Zurich, Switzerland

First published 2012 by
PALGRAVE MACMILLAN

Palgrave Macmillan in the UK is an imprint of Macmillan Publishers Limited,
registered in England, company number 785998, of Houndmills, Basingstoke,
Hampshire RG21 6XS.

Palgrave Macmillan in the US is a division of St Martin's Press LLC,
175 Fifth Avenue, New York, NY 10010.

Palgrave Macmillan is the global academic imprint of the above companies
and has companies and representatives throughout the world.

Palgrave® and Macmillan® are registered trademarks in the United States,
the United Kingdom, Europe and other countries.

ISBN: 978–0–230–30489–5

This book is printed on paper suitable for recycling and made from fully
managed and sustained forest sources. Logging, pulping and manufacturing
processes are expected to conform to the environmental regulations of the
country of origin.

A catalogue record for this book is available from the British Library.

Library of Congress Cataloging-in-Publication Data

Political communication in direct democratic campaigns : enlightening or
manipulating? / [edited by] Hanspeter Kriesi.
      p. cm.
   Includes index.
   ISBN 978–0–230–30489–5 (hardback)
      1. Communication in politics. 2. Political campaigns – Press coverage.
   3. Mass media – Political aspects. I. Kriesi, Hanspeter.
JA85.P6524 2011
324.7′3—dc23   2011021107

10 9 8 7 6 5 4 3 2 1
21 20 19 18 17 16 15 14 13 12

Printed and bound in the United States of America

Contents

Tables

Figures

Preface and Acknowledgements

This book is the result of a joint project of three groups of researchers at the University of Zurich – two groups of communication scientists and a group of political scientists. The three cooperated together in the framework of the Swiss research program on the Challenges of Democracy in the 21st Century. As all those who have already tried it know, interdisciplinary research is not easy, even if the researchers involved come from neighbouring disciplines as did our three teams. Each discipline has its own concepts, approaches and disciplinary culture, which not only influence the way its practitioners prefer to work, but also affect such details as the way they present their results. Political communication is an area of research located at the crossroads of political science and communication science, and it is quite obvious that its study should give rise to the kind of cooperation as the one this book is based upon. However, more often than not, even in this particular field, studies remain confined by disciplinary boundaries. It was the Swiss research program on democracy – the National Centre of Competence in Research (NCCR) Democracy – which made this interdisciplinary effort possible. It provided the opportunity for us to develop an integrated approach to political communication – a common language and a common approach to its study, which we hope will be of some interest to the students of political communication from different disciplinary origins.

This book is a study of political communication in Swiss direct-democratic campaigns. It is predicated on the assumption that direct-democratic campaigns constitute an especially useful setting for studying political communication. Compared to electoral choices, direct-democratic choices have the considerable advantage that the object of the choice is closely circumscribed. It is an issue-specific choice, which is presented to the voters in a binary format; that is, the voters' attention is focused on a straightforward task. Given its binary format, a direct-democratic campaign usually pits two coalitions against each other. Moreover, such a campaign usually has a clear beginning, and typically ends with the vote, and it consists of a narrowly circumscribed time interval, which is characterized by an exceptional intensification of political communication. In other words, a direct-democratic campaign comes close to a natural experiment in a quasi-laboratory setting. Swiss direct democratic campaigns are of particular relevance because, apart from providing a quasi-experimental setting for the study of political communication, they have the additional advantage that the Swiss setting constitutes the paradigmatic case for direct democratic votes – the setting that is currently emulated by an ever-increasing number of countries.

In its 1996 Christmas issue, the *Economist* had this vision: 'The coming century could see, at last, the full flowering of the idea of democracy.' It suggested that the 'half-finished thing' of democracy in the twentieth century could grow to its full height; it could grow to include the people in the political decision-making process. We believe that, in many ways, such a development could benefit from the experience of the Swiss with direct-democratic procedures, and we think that it is of particular relevance to learn how political communication works in this paradigmatic case.

Our research and the preparation of this book have benefited from the support of many colleagues. In the framework of NCCR Democracy, we have been closely supervised by a group of experts who provided constructive criticism and support. In particular, we would like to thank Robert Entman and Adrienne Héritier for their helpful advice. At different occasions, we have presented our ideas and preliminary results to colleagues who provided us with their comments and critiques. Among them are the group of colleagues around Christopher Green-Pedersen at the University of Aarhus (Rune Slothus, Rune Stubager, and Peter Mortensen), James Druckman, Hans Mathias Kepplinger, Jan Kleinnijenhuis, and Paul Sniderman. We are also very grateful to all the politicians, campaign managers, public officials, journalists, and newspaper editors who were willing to give us some of their precious time to answer our questions. We would like to thank the Swiss Federal Chancellor, Oswald Sigg, for the support he lent to our study. We are equally grateful to the members of our three survey samples who have been willing to answer our detailed questions in up to three panel waves. The cooperation of all these people has allowed us to put together a truely exceptional data set, without which we would not have been able to implement our integrated approach. Last but certainly not least, we would like to thank the Swiss National Science Foundation and the University of Zurich, who jointly finance NCCR Democracy, of which this study is a part.

Contributors

Laurent Bernhard is a postdoctoral researcher at NCCR Democracy. He received his PhD in political science from the University of Zurich. His main research interests are direct democracy and comparative political economy. He is currently working in a research project on the debates about the issue of unemployment in six Western European countries.

Heinz Bonfadelli is a full professor at the Institute for Mass Communication and Media Research, University of Zurich. His research interests are in the fields of media effects and knowledge gap research.

Urs Dahinden works as a full professor for Communication and Media Science at the University of Applied Sciences in Chur and as a senior lecturer at the University of Zurich, Switzerland. His research interests are in the field of health communication, political communication, new information and communication technology and empirical research methods. Recent publications focus on the effectiveness of health campaigns in mass media and in online media.

Thomas N. Friemel is a senior teaching and research associate at the Institute of Mass Communication and Media Research at the University of Zurich. His research focuses on media use, media effects, interpersonal communication and the application of social network analysis in communication science.

Matthias A. Gerth is a PhD student at the University of Zurich, IPMZ-Institute of Mass Communication and Media Research, and project assistant at NCCR Democracy. His recent work focuses on issues of media management, media marketing, local media markets and political news coverage.

Regula Hänggli is a senior research associate at NCCR Democracy and a head assistant in comparative politics at the University of Zurich. Her current research deals with framing, political communication and opinion formation, topics on which she has recently published in *Political Communication and European Political Science Review*.

Hanspeter Kriesi holds the Chair in Comparative Politics at the Department of Political Science of the University of Zurich. Previously he has taught at the universities of Amsterdam and Geneva. His wide-ranging research interests include the study of direct democracy, social movements, political parties and interest groups, public opinion, the public sphere and the media. He is the director of NCCR Democracy.

Rinaldo Kühne is a PhD student at the Institute of Mass Communication and Media Research, University of Zürich. His research focuses on the process of public opinion formation, effects of emotions, media effects and empirical methods.

Jörg Matthes is Assistant Professor in Political Communication and Political Behaviour at NCCR Democracy and the Institute of Mass Communication and Media Research, University of Zurich. His research focuses on public opinion formation, political communication effects, media content, advertising research and empirical methods. He is section chair of the Methods division of the German Communication Association and associate editor of *Communication Methods and Measures.*

Patrick Rademacher is a research consultant in a strategy consulting firm specialized in the content industries. Earlier he was a post-doc and PhD student at the IPMZ-Institute of Mass Communication and Media Research of the University of Zurich, and project assistant at NCCR Democracy. His work focuses on issues of media management, online economics, media brands and political news coverage.

Christian Schemer is a post-doc at the Institute of Mass Communication and Media Research, University of Zürich. His research focuses on the process of public opinion formation, effects of emotions, media effects and empirical methods.

Gabriele Siegert is Professor of Communication Science and Media Economics at the University of Zurich, Director of the IPMZ-Institute of Mass Communication and Media Research and Vice-Dean of the Faculty of Arts. Her research focuses on media economics, media management and advertising. Recent publications deal with the comparison of advertising markets, commercial audience research or media brands.

Werner Wirth is Professor of Communication and Empirical Media Research at the Institute of Mass Communication and Media Research, University of Zürich. His research focuses on media effects, entertainment, media and emotions, interactive media and empirical methods.

1
Political Communication: An Integrated Approach

Hanspeter Kriesi

An integrated approach to political communication

This book is about political communication in a democratic polity. It analyses the communication processes in Swiss direct-democratic campaigns and their effect on the information processing or opinion formation of the citizen public. In other words, it deals with the formation of the will, the particular moment that precedes choice, in which the voters ponder different solutions before settling on one of them (Manin 1987: 345).

Political communication is at the heart of the democratic process because this process presupposes – among other things to be sure – that the citizens have an 'enlightened understanding' of the choices at stake. As Robert Dahl (1989: 112), one of the foremost democratic theorists of our time, has pointed out, in a democratic polity, each citizen ought to have adequate and equal opportunities for discovering and validating the choice on a matter to be decided that would best serve his or her interest. This book views the democratic process from the perspective of campaign-specific public debates involving politicians, journalists, and media owners, as well as the public audience of voters, and it asks to what extent such debates contribute to the citizens' 'enlightened understanding'. By focusing on political communication and the information processing by campaigners and voters, this book echoes the deliberative turn taken by democratic theory, which is replacing a vote-centric approach with a talk-centric one. It adopts the view underlying deliberative theory that 'voice rather than votes is the new vehicle of empowerment' (Chambers 2001: 231).

Under contemporary conditions, political communication is essentially mediated or media-centred communication. While traditional forms of assembly-based communication or face-to-face communication in direct encounters between campaigners and citizens continue to exist, present-day political communication could not occur without various uses of media (Entman and Bennett 2001: 1). In particular, answering the question about the extent to which public debates contribute to an enlightened understanding on the part of the citizens needs to take into account the role of the media, and the way politicians use the media in their attempts to reach out to voters.

Entman and Bennett (2001: 471f.) have distinguished two approaches to the study of political communication, the one focusing on the characteristics of communication processes through which messages and political information are constructed by political actors and the media, and the other mainly concerned with individual responses to persuasive messages about particular choices. The first approach focuses on what we could call the production of political communication; the second, on its receiving end. Seldom are these two approaches joined in a single research endeavour. Jacobs and Shapiro (2000: 55) argue that the 'full interconnectedness of elite politics, media coverage, and public opinion has been neglected by pundits and scholars alike'. This is unfortunate, because approaches focused on one type of actor only are incomplete. The analysis of political actors and their communication strategies is incomplete because it does not take into account the essential role of the media in the transmission of politicians' messages to the public audience of voters. The media-centred analysis is incomplete because it neglects that political input drives the mass communication process. Similarly, analysis centred on the public audience and its reactions to elite communications is incomplete because it overlooks that politicians' strategies for handling media coverage and public opinion set the context for possible communication effects on public opinion.

The two approaches to the study of political-communication processes are intimately related to two more general views of the democratic political process – a supply-side view and a demand-side view. The demand-side view approaches the political process from the voters' perspective. According to this view, voters' preferences constitute the key determinants of the democratic process. The voters are the principals, and the elected representatives, their agents. In a democratic system, politicians have to be responsive to voters' demands and preferences because the voters hold them accountable for the policies they adopt, and sanction them if they do not take their preferences into account. This view underlies some of the most influential theories of the democratic process today – theories which consider the voters' preferences as given and as imposing binding constraints on politicians' manoeuvring space. Examples are provided by both the most well-known theories of political sociology (for example, Lipset and Rokkan 1967 and their followers) and the most influential theories of the rational choice tradition (e.g. Downs 1957 and his followers).

The supply-side view, by contrast, attributes more autonomy to political elites. From the point of view of this alternative vision, the citizens' vote is a reaction of the voters to the terms proposed by the elites. Manin (1995: 290) has formulated this vision most pointedly by positing that, in politics, there is no demand which is independent of supply. For the supply-side vision, political communication and information processing both by decision-making representatives and voters becomes crucial for the democratic process. According to this vision, politicians can be principals as well as agents. On the one hand, this vision recognizes that ensuring accountability requires that voters are provided with the information that will enable them to evaluate the responsiveness of the representatives who make political decisions in their name, and allows them to impose electoral sanctions on representatives who do not prove to be responsive. On the other hand, this vision also recognizes that the relevant information is to a considerable extent controlled by the very politicians who are held to be accountable by the voters.

The supply-side vision insists that it is the political actors who set the agenda, that is, who provide the alternative options for the voters' choice; who promote the particular problem definitions, causal interpretations, moral evaluations, and/or treatment recommendations for the issues at stake; and who mobilize voters to make a choice in favour of their own preferred option. This is the conception of democracy put forth by Schattschneider (1975 [1960]: 138), who defined it as 'a competitive political system in which competing leaders and organizations define the alternatives of public policy in such a way that the public can participate in the decision-making process...Conflict, competition, organization, leadership, and responsibility are the ingredients of a working definition of democracy.'

Agenda control or agenda-setting is a first key instrument of the politicians. As Schattschneider (p. 66) has pointed out, 'the definition of the alternatives is the supreme instrument of power', and he famously observed (p. 69) that 'organization is the mobilization of bias. Some issues are organized into politics while others are organized out'.

In addition, politicians may also attempt to influence the criteria by which the voters come to evaluate the different options. The determination of the standards (the issues or attributes of issues) that people use to make political choices is also referred to as 'priming'. Priming has received strong and consistent support since it was first analysed in a series of U.S. network-television news experiments (Iyengar and Kinder 1987).

Moreover, shaping voters' information processing implies a struggle not only for *what* people talk or think about and the kind of evaluation criteria they apply, but also for *how* they think and talk about political issues (Pan and Kosicki 1993: 70). Most information is uncertain, and information is often ambiguous, that is, subject to differing interpretations or perspectives. This means that influencing voters' information processing is concerned not only with the salience of some issues and evaluation criteria, but also with their meaning, as well as with the voters' positioning with respect to them. The more recent approach of *framing analysis* also refers to the salience of issue attributes, but it expands beyond the analysis of salience and tackles the way political actors attempt to influence the public's interpretation of political issues. Frames are defined as 'central organizing ideas that provide coherence to a designated set of idea elements' (Ferree et al. 2002: 105; Dahinden 2006: 87). As 'central organizing ideas', frames emphasize certain interpretations of policy issues to the detriment of others; they resonate with certain issue-specific positions at the expense of others, and they provide reasons for defending one policy-specific position rather than others. By appropriately framing an issue, political actors attempt to construct the meaning of the reality in question in a way that supports their own point of view.

The processing of information involved in the 'formation of the will' may enlighten the public by clarifying the implications of the issues at stake for its underlying value preferences, but it may also manipulate the public into adopting issue-specific positions inconsistent with its underlying value preferences. Far from being enlightening, the deliberation in a given campaign may have 'pathological effects' (Stokes 1998), that is, it may lead people to hold beliefs that are not in their best interests (Przeworski 1998). Deliberation may result in 'ideological domination', as Gramsci (1971) suggested a long time ago. Whether or not, in a given campaign, deliberation has enlightening or manipulative consequences is an empirical question.

In the present study, we explicitly attempt to integrate the analysis of the strategies of the political and media actors with the analysis of their impact on the opinion formation of the citizen public. Figure 1.1 summarizes the general design of our study: It highlights the three types of actors involved in the political-communication process – the political actors, the citizens, and the news media – and it links the political-communication process to the procedures of representative and direct democracy. Citizens elect politicians and, in direct-democratic procedures, vote on some specific policies that have been decided upon by politicians. The public debate,

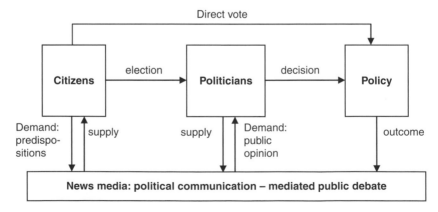

Figure 1.1   An integrated approach to the study of political communication

which accompanies these decision-making processes, is mediated by the news media, and fed by the citizens' 'demands', the politicians' 'supply', and the outcome of the policies which they have adopted. The debate produces public opinion, which is closely monitored by the politicians, and provides the citizens with the politicians' supply and information about the outcome of the policies. The implications of this schematic outline will become clearer in the following sections, which discuss the three types of actors and the relationships among them in more detail.

Political actors

Combining the demand-side view with a supply-side view of the democratic process amounts to an integrated approach which allows for the possibility that the 'popular will' is, in part at least, subject to the influence exerted by political elites. This is not to assert that the popular will is 'largely not a genuine but a manufactured will', as Schumpeter (1942 [1962]) suggested in one of his devastating formulas. But it is to acknowledge that the democratic vote is influenced by the politicians' supply, and that it is the product of political-communication processes, which politicians use to influence their voters' choice.

This is not necessarily problematic. On the contrary. In the contemporary version of democracy, 'representatives must, in practice, exercise some degree of independence, discretion, and judgement as they respond to public preferences' (Jacobs and Shapiro 2000: 303). Responsive leaders use rhetoric, that is, the art of persuasion, to sway public opinion, but they use it in a way which facilitates public discussion, and they are held in check by a public that is capable of assessing the validity of their talk. The use of rhetoric becomes problematic when it is designed to impose politicians' preferred policies on voters whose preferences do not correspond to those of their representatives. In this particular case, which is described by Jacobs and Shapiro (2000), politicians resort to 'crafted talk' in order to simulate responsiveness and to induce voters to accept policies which they would not have accepted had they not been deceived by the politicians' rhetoric. The key question, of course, concerns the conditions under which leaders use their manoeuvring space to improve their responsiveness to the voters, rather than to strive, as they also might, for 'simulated' or 'instrumental responsiveness'.

We would like to suggest that 'responsive leadership' requires the combination of three closely related preconditions. First, it depends on the *competitiveness* of the political process. As Bartolini (1999: 450) has observed: 'Elections make politicians accountable on a regular basis, but only competitive interactions make them responsive.' Competitiveness in this context is not only a question of party competition, but also of a viable civil society more generally: a civil society consisting of multiple private and public-interest associations articulating a large spectrum of different interests and points of view, as well as of a myriad of informal, heterogene-ously composed groups discussing the arguments proposed by the political elites.

Second, 'responsive leadership' requires *an attentive public*. An attentive public implies the less-than-full participation of all citizens. Citizens need not necessarily all be fully informed, nor do they all need to be fully involved in politics. It suffices that they monitor the political process (Schudson 1998) and keep the scores (Stimson 2004). Monitoring or scorekeeping citizens scan (rather than read) the informational environment so that they may be alerted if something goes wrong, and they often use heuristic shortcuts (rather than elaborate arguments) to make up their political minds.

Third, *the independence, resourcefulness and plurality of the news media* constitutes a crucial precondition for the presence of an attentive public. The combination of these three requirements defines the liberal representative model of the public sphere. This model is distinct from more radical nor-mative models (the participatory, discursive, and constructionist models), which set more demanding standards with respect to citizens' involvement in the public debate, and place a high value on their 'empowerment' (Ferree et al. 2002: 205–231). The three conditions, in other words, define a mini-mal set of conditions that have to be fulfilled for the public debate to attain the required quality.

To the extent that political elites are subject to competition and monitored by independent and resourceful media and an attentive public, plebiscitory rhetoric and crafted talk risk being exposed by political adversaries and the news media. As Sniderman and Theriault (2004: 158) point out, 'in a prop-erly democratic polity opposing camps campaign on behalf of competing ways of understanding what is at issue'. And they suggest that the clash of political arguments, 'far from overwhelming or perplexing or blinding the political judgements of ordinary citizens, may be a condition of the possi-bility of their exercising it.' We shall see in this volume that the Swiss direct-democratic campaigns provide ample evidence for this claim.

The media

As already pointed out, under contemporary conditions, communication between the political elites and the citizens is typically not direct, but is mediated by a third party – the news media. Political communication is no longer party-centred, but *focused on the news media*. Research has demon-strated that the public does, indeed, form its impressions about the politi-cal world from the news media (Graber 2001; Zaller 2003). The increasing role of the media has been discussed mainly as a US American develop-ment in the past, but European systems have observed similar trends more recently (Swanson and Mancini 1996; Hallin and Mancini 2004). These trends go beyond the fact that political communication has increasingly become 'media-centred'. They refer to a more fundamental change in the relationship between politics and the media, which has been summarized by the concept of 'mediatization' (Mazzoleni and Schulz 1999). This concept implies that the media have become an autonomous force in politics which is no longer dependent on governments, political parties or interest groups, and that they have come to follow their own professional and commercial logic (that is, they have increasingly come to follow their own rules of selecting, interpreting and constructing political news messages), and, even more importantly, the media are increasingly imposing their logic on political actors (who not only have to adapt to this logic if they want to succeed, but to adopt it outright as well). As a result, in the public sphere political actors and the media interact in complex ways which cannot simply be instrumentalized by one of the actors involved.

In many ways, *commercialization* is the driving force behind the media's increasing autonomy from politics. News content is a product, the creation and distribution of which depends, not primarily on the needs of politicians, but on the market value attached to the attention and tastes of media consumers, the technologies affecting the cost of information generation and transmission, and the values pursued by journalists and media owners. As argued by Hamilton (2004), consumers' desires are the key exogenous determinants of the production of news. And, unlike politicians, who seek a conduit for serious information, audiences mainly seek, as Entman (1989) suggests, entertainment over information. Competition drives news organizations to maximize profits, so the media play more to the audience than to the source.

Focusing on the consumers, however, leaves out some other important players, such as advertisers, investors and owners. McManus (1995) offers a market-based model of news production that is not consumer driven. As he argues, consumers, in fact, find themselves in an asymmetrical relationship with media firms. On the one hand, this asymmetry results from the fact that news is most often not an experience, but a credence good – a good you buy on faith because you as a consumer may not be able to establish its quality, even after consumption. Consumers, in other words, are vulnerable to opportunism on the part of the media firm, much more so than investors, advertisers, and sources, even if brand names sometimes help them evaluate quality after a product gains a reputation. On the other hand, and even more importantly, individual investors, advertisers and sources exert much greater influence over the media corporation than an individual consumer, and they also have a greater stake in the outcome of transactions with the media corporation than the consumer. The individual consumer is the least powerful and the least interested stakeholder in news production. To the extent that it increases their profits, rational investors are expected to take advantage of the consumers' inability to recognize quality news and of the low reward for reading or viewing it. This implies that the media may lower their news-production costs without losing their viewers/readers by providing 'soft' or low-quality news.

Our general approach to conceptualizing the relationship between political actors and the media is the actor-centred political-process model as it has been introduced by Wolfsfeld (1997). Following his lead, we believe the best way to understand the role of the news media is to view it as part of a larger contest among political antagonists for the control of the public agenda and the public's interpretation of specific policy issues. Given the crucial role of the news media in reaching out to the citizen public, the struggle for attention and for the meaning of political issues becomes a struggle for the control of the news agenda and for the framing of the news.

In this struggle, the relationship between political actors and the news media is one of mutual dependence: Political actors need the media to reach the public, while the media need input from political actors for their news production. As Wolfsfeld (1997: 13) puts it, their relationship is one of a 'competitive symbiosis', 'in which each side of the relationship attempts to exploit the other while expending a minimum amount of costs'. Or, as Gans (1980: 116) pointed out in an often-cited quote: 'The relationship between sources and journalists resembles a dance, for sources seek access to journalists, and journalists seek access to sources.' But, significantly, Gans went on to stress that this relationship was likely to be an asymmetrical one, too: 'Although it takes two to tango, either sources or journalists can lead, but more often than not, sources do the leading.' Wolfsfeld's (1997: 3) key hypothesis makes the same point: The political process is likely to be the driving force in this relationship. The reasons he provides for this hypothesis are numerous, but most importantly, he suggests that the news media are much more likely to react to political events than to initiate them. We shall see that this is also the case in the campaigns we study here.

The audience or the citizen public

The supply-side vision of representative democracy assumes as a matter of course that the media-centred communications of the political elites have an impact on the citizen public. Zaller's (1992) influential theory about the nature and origin of public opinion is most in line with such a supply-side vision. His theory aims at showing how variations in the elite discourse affect both the direction and organization of public opinion. Since the political elites mainly communicate to the public through the news media, the question of whether the elites have an impact on the citizen public essentially comes down to the question of whether or not the mass media have an impact on public opinion (Zaller 1996: 21).

In line with the supply-side vision, Zaller argues that perhaps the most fundamental question is whether the public is given any choice at all. For, in the absence of choice, the public can do little more than follow the elite consensus on what should be done. When elites divide, so does the public.

Zaller emphasizes the role of elite-supplied information in shaping mass opinion, but he allows for two key intervening variables which modify the impact of the elites' communications at the micro-level of individual members of the public – the individuals' fundamental values and ideological orientations, that is, their predispositions, and their political awareness. In Zaller's theory, *predispositions* take the place of preferences. We shall adopt this terminology. Predispositions mediate people's responses to elite information.

As is pointed out by Sniderman et al. (2001), Zaller's theory is rather ambiguous about the degree to which predispositions are open to influence by situational factors, such as elite messages. For our present purposes, we start from the assumption that citizens make their choices as a result of the combined effect of predispositional and situational factors, but that the precise impact of the two types of factors depends on the particular context of the choice. Whereas the fundamental predispositions of the citizens are unlikely to be available to elite influence in the short run, the widespread lack of political information, the complexity of political issues, and the corresponding difficulty for citizens to connect their predispositions to the political choices at hand make them more or less susceptible to communication effects, depending on situational factors. Thus, as Zaller (1992) has argued, the citizens' opinion formation will, among other things, heavily depend on the familiarity of the issues at stake, and on the intensity and balance of the information flows.

The conventional view on the effect of mass communication on public opinion has been highly sceptical about the extent of possible effects. The 'minimal effects paradigm' of political communication has for a long time pervaded – or, according to Bartels (1993a: 267), even embarrassed – political communications research. More recent studies, however, have challenged this minimal effect view of political communication. Indeed, in their review of the literature, Iyengar and Simon (2000) maintain that political campaigns do matter and can be pivotal. Similarly, several recent studies (Nadeau et al. 2001; Farrell and Schmitt-Beck 2002) provide evidence for substantial and systematic campaign effects on citizens' voting behaviour. However, earlier expectations that campaign messages manipulate easily persuadable voters have been abandoned. Increasingly, campaigns are viewed as playing a key role in citizens' information processing, providing voters with the necessary information for making a choice in line with their pre-existing preferences (Finkel 1993; Gelman and King 1993; Stimson 2004; Arceneaux 2006; Andersen et al. 2005).

This is in line with Lazarsfeld et al.'s (1968 [1944]) landmark investigation of the 1940 presidential elections, which already found that presidential campaigns are generally ineffective at persuasion. Rather their functions are to *reinforce* early deciders and to *activate* the latent predispositions of the initially uncommitted. Despite dramatic changes over the last half century in the technology of campaigning, their conclusions have stood up rather well. Reviewing the evidence, Kinder (1998: 186) suggests that 'as large-scale, expensive experiments in political persuasion, American presidential campaigns are a bust'. And he provides three sets of explanations for their failure to persuade (Kinder 2003: 368–371; 1998: 186): one answer is that the campaign of one side is *'neutralized'* by the campaign of the other side so that the net effect is small, although the total effect, as Zaller (1996) has attempted to show, may be very large. A second answer explains the lack of persuasion effects by the *strength of political predispositions* – a key element of demand-driven models. If anything, campaigns serve to reinforce the impact of these predispositions by providing the voters with cues which allow them to connect their predispositions to the choices at hand. In this sense, campaigns essentially have an 'enlightening effect' (Gelman and King 1993). Finally, if strong partisans are essentially unmovable because they are so deeply committed, other potential voters are difficult to per-suade because they are *not paying attention*. Neutralization, resistance and indifference constitute the three principle obstacles to persuasion.

Kinder (2003: 371) mentions, nevertheless, two openings for persuasion: On the one hand, there is what he calls *low-information persuasion*, which closely resembles the mechanisms of Zaller's model – generally uninformed and little-interested citizens may be susceptible to persuasion by simple cues provided by elites. On the other hand, there is an opportunity for what he calls *persuasion over the long haul*, public opinion may change in response to new information and changing conditions – for the most part large-scale historical events such as the Depression and World War II, or major catastrophes such as the accident at Tschernobyl. Political persuasion, in other words, is contingent on circumstance. As Stimson (2004: xvii) insists, change in public opinion happens when people care, and when the chan-ging tide of public opinion starts rolling, he adds, it is most unwise to stand against it, which is to suggest that, even over the long haul, politicians are well advised to adapt to public opinion rather than to attempt to shape it.

Direct-democratic campaigns as the setting for the study of political communication

Political communication cannot be studied in the abstract. The answer to the question, to what extent do public debates contribute to the enlightened understanding of the citizens crucially depends on the specific characteristics of the media system, the political system and of the issue-specific subsystem in which the debate takes place. The characteristics of the context in which the public debate is embedded may be more or less favourable for its quality and its capacity to contribute to the enlightened understanding of the citizen audience. The public debates we will be studying in this book are set in Switzerland, specifically, they are set in the context of Swiss direct-democratic campaigns. We shall make an attempt to conceptualize the key context characteristics in more general analytical terms so as to allow for a comparison with other contexts and to draw more generally applicable conclusions.

We believe that political communication and its effects are best studied in the framework of a political campaign. In the preface to the second edition of their classic study, *The People's Choice*, Lazarsfeld et al. (1968 [1944]: xxi) suggested that 'a disciplined and limited kind of dynamic research, focused on social events and developments lasting several months or, at most, several years' holds the greatest promise for the future development of the social sciences. Among the examples of such promising research they included the systematic analyses of political campaigns, which was, of course, what they had done in their own research. Campaigns can be conceived of as series of communication events conducted by political actors in order to influence voters in the run-up to elections (Nimmo 1970: 10).

For the study of political communication and its effects, institutionalized political campaigns such as elections have two great advantages: First, they are of limited duration, with a (more or less) clear beginning and a clear end, and second, they typically involve an important intensification of political communication. Usually, the flow of political communication on many (and perhaps most) important matters is relatively stable over time, which makes it, as Zaller (1996: 48) observed, "all but impossible to detect the extent to which citizens are responsive, in a dynamic sense, to the flow of political communication'. Political campaigns, by contrast, introduce sharp changes in the flow of political communication, which allows for studying its impact. Institutionalized campaigns such as election campaigns have the additional advantage that their coming is known in advance, which makes it possible to obtain a baseline of public opinion before they start.

Electoral campaigns are by no means the only ones. Another type of institutionalized campaign that shares the advantages of electoral campaigns is the *direct-democratic campaign*. Just as electoral campaigns in majoritarian (but not in proportional electoral systems), direct-democratic campaigns typically give rise to the confrontation between two opposing camps. The presence of two competing camps guarantees competing information flows, and the bipolar (as contrasted to multipolar) character of the competition keeps the information flows within manageable proportions. Moreover, this type of campaign has the additional advantage of being *issue-specific*. This implies that the campaign is much more focused than an electoral campaign, which allows for a more detailed study of the communication strategies and their impact on the voters. In many ways, a direct-democratic campaign comes close to a natural experiment in a quasi-laboratory setting. Thus, far from being simply marginal political events in a minor state, Swiss direct-democratic campaigns provide a unique opportunity to study the impact of political communication in a natural setting.

The setting of Swiss direct-democratic campaigns has the additional advantage that it constitutes the paradigmatic case for direct-democratic votes – the case that is currently emulated by an ever-increasing number of countries. In its 1996 Christmas issue, the *Economist* had this vision: 'The coming century could see, at last, the full flowering of the idea of democracy.' The 'half-finished thing' of democracy in the twentieth century could grow to its full height; it could grow to include the people in the political decision-making process. The *Economist* expected the move in the direction of a democracy in which voters directly participate in political decision-making to 'put down its roots only in places where the soil is ready', that is, mostly in countries around the North Atlantic. Scarrow (2001), who looked at institutional change in these countries, came, indeed, to the conclusion that institutions are changing to accommodate more direct citizen participation. She found widespread institution reforms favouring direct democracy. For countries where such reforms take root, the Swiss experience can provide highly relevant information.

Research on direct democracy has intensified in recent years, and there is now an impressive amount of scholarly work in this area. When reviewing this literature (Lupia and Matsusaka 2004; Smith and Tolbert 2004; Kirchgässner et al. 1999), it becomes apparent, however, that the political supply-side has only received scant attention. Most studies are either concerned with the citizens' opinion-formation processes or with the effects of direct-democratic institutions on the economic performance of a country. Moreover, to the extent that they exist, studies of direct-democratic campaigning are mostly confined to the United States and almost exclusively consist of single case studies (see Bernhard 2010). We choose a comparative design with three Swiss direct-democratic campaigns which differ systematically with respect to their familiarity and complexity. Two of these campaigns concern the domain of immigration policy: the referendum by the left against the revised asylum law, which was voted on 24 September 2006, and the initiative 'for democratic naturalizations', launched by the populist right and submitted to the voters on 1 June 2008. The third campaign concerns fiscal matters. It was also launched by a referendum from the left – the referendum against the revision of the corporation tax, on which the Swiss voted on 24 February 2008.

Exaggerating only a bit, we can take the three campaigns to represent three rather ideal-typical choice situations. First, the asylum campaign stands for a campaign on a familiar issue of low complexity, an easy choice situation, where most voters' minds were essentially made up before the campaign even started. Second, the naturalization campaign stands for a campaign on an unfamiliar issue of low complexity, an intermediate choice situation, where most voters' had first to familiarize themselves with the issue, but where learning about the issue was easy. Third, the corporate tax campaign stands for an unfamiliar and complex issue, a difficult choice situation, where many voters, even at the end of the campaign, had a hard time knowing what the choice was all about.

The choice of direct-democratic campaigns as a field of reserach comes, however, with a price attached. The institutional specificity of such campaigns may limit the generalizability of our findings. First, the direct-democratic campaign does not take place in a vacuum. It is embedded in a larger political debate that was going on before the start of the campaign and that continues beyond the direct-democratic vote. In the Swiss context in particular, the direct-democratic campaign comes at the end of a protracted political process, which means that the opinions of a large part of the public may have already been made before the outset of the campaign.

Second, there are theoretical reasons to believe that such campaigns are not particularly conducive to deliberative quality (Chambers 2001). Direct-democratic votes introduce an extreme form of majoritarianism, and any rule that permits a majority to prevail raises the possibility that the majority will not listen to a minority once sufficient votes exist to return a verdict. Even in situations where there is no clear majority, referendums invite participants to approach the debate strategically rather than discursively, that is they create an incentive to find arguments that will sway only the needed number of voters. Moreover, the direct-democratic campaign is brought to a close by a vote. In the vote, as Manin (1987: 359) points out, 'the process of the formation of the wills is finished'. The vote signals closure and irreversibility. As a result, a direct-democratic debate tends to be led in zero-sum terms, may polarize, heighten distrust, exacerbate misunderstandings, and not give rise to mutual recognition and increased thoughtfulness. Direct-democratic campaigns, in other words, give rise to quite specific political communication processes, which means that our results may not be readily generalizable to other settings.

This problem is compounded by the fact that we study direct-democratic campaigns and their effects only in a single country – Switzerland – and that we study only a limited selection of three campaigns. The specificities of this particular country – the institutional characteristics of its direct-democratic procedures, the peculiarities of its party system and its media system, as well as the aspects of its wider national economic, cultural and political context – constitute so many constraints for generalizing what we shall find in our study.

We attempt to uncover the general mechanisms at work in political communication and to show how they ultimately shape the voting choices of citizens in a democratic decision-making process. This is not an entirely impossible undertaking, because Swiss direct-democratic campaigns do not differ fundamentally from electoral campaigns in Switzerland or in other Western democracies. As a matter of fact, the direct-democratic procedures that have been institutionalized in Switzerland complement, and are embedded in a representative model of democracy. Accordingly, just as in representative democracy, political elites and the organizations they represent constitute the driving force in the process of the citizens' opinion formation in such direct-democratic campaigns (Budge 1996; Kriesi 2005).

Overview of the contents of the book

This volume is divided into three parts. The first part includes two additional chapters which discuss the context conditions for the political communication processes analysed in this volume as well as the design of our study. In our attempt to flesh out the general mechanisms at work in the campaigns we are studying here, we take great pains to situate the political communication processes in the specific context. In Chapter 2, we present in more detail the specific institutional context of Swiss direct-democratic campaigns, the general structuration of the choice by the overall make-up of the systems of interest intermediation (parties, interest associations and the media), as well as the issue-specific context of the three campaigns which constitute the object of our study. In Chapter 3, we explain how the integrated approach has been implemented. We present the overall design of our approach; outline the methods of data collection, which include interviews with political and media actors, content analyses of documents produced by the political actors and of media coverage, and panel surveys in the French and German speaking part of Switzerland. We illustrate the logic of our integrated approach using the example of the way the arguments provided by the politicians to defend their positions in a given campaign are, in turn, taken up by the media and the voters. Finally, we introduce the logic of the longitudinal analysis.

The six chapters of Part II present the political actors and their strategies and the media actors, as well as the relationship between the two. Chapters 4 to 6 deal with three aspects of the politicians' strategies. In Chapter 4, we start out with the process of coalition formation in the political elites, which follows a specific logic in direct-democratic campaigns. There is little room for bargaining, there are no designated leaders, and both the number and the type of potential coalition partners are large. The chapter argues that coalition formation is decisively shaped by the belief systems of the actors involved and discusses the pivotal role of the moderate right, whose coalitional decisions heavily depend on the issue in question – it may join forces either with the left or the conservative right. As we shall see, the implications of these coalitional decisions are of great importance for the dynamics of the campaign and the eventual outcome of the vote. In Chapter 5, we take a closer look at the messages political actors tend to select, and we highlight three strategic choices in crafting the message: First, and most importantly, politicians have to choose one or several substantive frames capable of steering the attention of the media and the public to their own cause and away from the cause of their opponent. Second, they have to decide whether and how to use the opponents' frames. Third, they have to decide about whether they want to focus on the contest or on the substantive content of the debate – on politics or on policy. The analysis reveals that the politicians encountered in our three campaigns mainly focus on their own substantive frames, but that they also react defensively to the substantive frames of their opponents. Chapter 6 moves on to the diffusion of the political actors' campaign messages by focusing on the targeting, timing and choice of appropriate communication channels. Targeting deals with the question of what segment of the population politicians focus on. Basically, there are two promising strategies: appealing to one's own constituency (mobilizing), and appealing to undecided voters (chasing). As far as timing is concerned, the analysis is restricted to the decision on when to launch the campaign. Finally, adopting the concept of the action repertoire in social movement research, we introduce the notion of a communication repertoire, and we distinguish between direct and indirect channels based both on the actors' own organization and on the media. As will be shown, the communication strategies of political actors involved in direct-democratic campaigns crucially depend on the availability of specific resources.

The next three chapters address the media actors, their strategies and the processes that influence the frames applied by journalists. In Chapter 7, we highlight the role of media organizations in political campaigns. Starting from the basic assumption that media are a crucial actor in democratic societies, we discuss whether the commercialization of media organizations challenges their contribution to the functioning of democratic society. To deal with this question more precisely, we ask whether Swiss media organizations are mainly market-driven or follow normative journalistic standards in covering political campaigns. Our results show only little evidence for the commercialization of Swiss media organizations. Chapter 8 moves on to the campaign coverage by the media. We find that the intensity and style of the media coverage varies in different types of media, but only marginally in the three campaigns. We analyse the coverage in terms of actor type and camp. The results indicate a striking bias between pro arguments and contra arguments in the media coverage. In all three campaigns, one camp was covered significantly more frequently than the other. In Chapter 9, we take a closer look at frame building, that is, at the processes that influence the frames applied by journalists in direct-democratic campaigns. Derived from research on media attention, agenda-setting and issue-specific discourses, we consider two factors to be central in frame building: the frames in the media input and the power of the speakers. Issue type (familiarity), political institutions and external events are investigated as contextual factors. In general, our analysis confirms that the input of the political actors plays a decisive role in Swiss direct-democratic campaigns. It is the political actors who introduce the most important frames into the public discourse and who counter frame the adversaries' arguments. In addition to the frames in the media input, the campaign-specific power of a speaker is important, too.

Part III turns to the impact of the three campaigns on the opinion formation of the voters. Four chapters deal with various aspects of opinion formation. In Chapter 10, we begin by analysing to what extent the three campaigns have activated pre-existing political predispositions, and how the activation process varies from one campaign to the other. In particular, we analyse the role of the combination of partisan predispositions and issue-specific predispositions. We find that all three campaigns have had massive effects. They all reinforced and activated previously held predispositions. Conversion turned out to be very important in the referendum on the corporate tax reform – our most complex and unfamiliar issue. Chapter 11 focuses on the role of voter learning during referendum campaigns. The basic question is: Do all citizens gain knowledge distributed by the media in an equal way? The expectations based on knowledge-gap theory are largely confirmed: Existing knowledge gaps increase during the campaigns because citizens with a higher educational and/or social status are politically more interested, have a higher level of basic knowledge, use the information-rich print media more frequently, are more attentive to media information, and are more integrated in interpersonal communication networks.

The last two chapters in Part III analyse the role of arguments and emotions for the voting decision. Chapter 12 asks what kinds of voters are susceptible to being swayed by certain types of arguments. The fundamental idea of this chapter is that arguments and ideology interact, that is, that some arguments will be more powerful in predicting voting behaviour for voters on the left, while other arguments exert a stronger impact on voters on the right. Findings in the naturalization and the asylum campaign suggest that such interactions tend to occur towards the end of the campaign. We conclude that the interaction of arguments and ideological predispositions depends on the extent to which arguments can be linked to ideological positions. Chapter 13 investigates the impact that emotions exert on voting intentions in political campaigns. Affective influences on voting intentions may occur either directly or indirectly, that is, mediated by political cognitions of voters. Based on reasoning chains models of political attitude formation and change, we demonstrate that direct emotional effects on vote intentions are more pronounced for the highly complex corporate tax reform, but less so for the immigration issues. By contrast, we find that affective influences on vote intentions are mediated by the arguments for and against the proposal when the issue is moderately complex. Chapter 14 summarizes and discusses the implications of our results.

2
The Context of the Campaigns

Hanspeter Kriesi and Laurent Bernhard

Direct-democratic campaigns take place in an institutional and issue-specific context. Political institutions define the rules of the game of the direct-democratic process, and as such they are, as Sniderman (2000: 69) points out, the 'organizers of political choices'. They organize the choices for political and media actors, and for voters. They do so by imposing constraints and opportunities on the communication strategies of the strategic actors, which, at the same time, pre-structure the fundamental options available to voters. It is very important to keep in mind that, in politics, 'citizens are presented with an organized set, or menu, of choices' (Sniderman and Bullock 2004: 338). Direct-democratic choices under contemporary conditions do not differ in this respect from electoral choices in representative democracies. The format of the choice is given, and so are the alternatives on the menu from which citizens can choose. In this chapter, we present the specific institutional context of Swiss direct-democratic campaigns, the general structuration of the choice by the overall make-up of the systems of interest intermediation (parties, interest associations and the media), as well as the specific context of the three campaigns which constitute the object of our study. We begin with the institutional setting, and then move on to the intermediary systems and to our three campaigns. For the presentation of the campaigns, we proceed in three steps. First, we briefly introduce the stakes and the coalitional configurations involved in the respective policy domains. Next, we discuss the political processes that, in each case, have preceded and pre-structured the issue-specific campaigns. Finally, we situate the three campaigns within the context of all direct-democratic campaigns that have taken place at the federal level since the early 1980s, in order to provide the reader with a general idea of their representativeness for Swiss direct-democratic campaigns.

Swiss direct-democratic institutions

Direct-democratic institutions come in different varieties, and each has a different logic attached. One version is the *populist*, unmediated form of direct democracy, which best corresponds to the practice in the member states of the United States. When the populist and progressive reformers of the late nineteenth century introduced direct-democratic procedures in the United States, they did so, above all, to restrict the power of political parties and their political machines, which were in control of the state parliaments at the time (Cronin 1989: 50–57; Smith and Tolbert 2001: 740, 2004: 112ff.; Bowler and Donovan 2006). In the United States, the popular initiative, still today, is primarily used by social movements and interest groups to circumvent the state parliaments controlled by the parties. This is possible because popular initiatives are submitted to a popular vote without the intervention of the state governments and their parliaments. By contrast, the Swiss variety of direct democracy is closely linked to the procedures of representative democracy, and it is much more organized and more tightly *controlled* by the political elites. Both government and Parliament have an important role to play in the preparation of the proposals submitted to the voters.

Broadly speaking, we can classify Swiss direct-democratic institutions according to two criteria[1]:

- The source of a proposition: elite or citizens
- The initiation of the vote: required by the constitution or demanded by the citizens

Combining the two criteria allows us to classify the three basic direct-democratic institutions at the federal level – the popular initiative, the compulsory referendum and the optional referendum (Table 2.1).[2] According to the *source* of the proposition, we can distinguish initiatives from referendums: Initiatives are propositions 'from below', formulated by organizations representing groups of citizens, while referendums concern propositions 'from above', that is, legislative acts proposed by the government and adopted by Parliament. Accordingly, initiatives and referendums follow entirely different logic. The *initiative* has an agenda-setting function. It launches a public debate on a given issue and puts the issue on the political system's agenda. An initiative qualifies for a vote if it is signed by 100,000 citizens (roughly 2 per cent of the current number of citizens) within a period of 18 months. The text of an initiative has to be thematically focused on a single issue, and it may not conflict with international

Table 2.1   Classification of direct-democratic institutions

	Source of proposition	
Required by	**Government**	**Citizens**
Constitution	Compulsory referendum	–
Citizens	Optional referendum	Popular initiative

law. Otherwise, there are hardly any requirements to be fulfilled. In contrast to the practice in the United States, the government and the Parliament discuss the text of the initiative before it is submitted to the popular vote, and provide it with a voting recommendation that almost always recommends its rejection.

A *referendum*, by contrast, concerns a legislative act originating from the government and intervenes only after the members of the political system have taken their decision on a piece of legislation. It comes in two basic versions which can be distinguished on the basis of our second classification criterion: Referendums are required either by the Constitution (in the case of constitutional amendments) or by a group of citizens (in the case of regular legislation). Constitutional amendments are subject to the *compulsory* referendum, while regular legislation is subject to the *optional* referendum. Constitutional amendments are quite frequent in Switzerland, where the Constitution has been, on average, amended more than twice a year since the beginning of the 1980s. Such amendments are adopted only if they obtain a double majority – a majority of the people and a majority of the Swiss cantons, that is, the country's member states. Regular legislation, once adopted by Parliament, passes into law by default if a referendum is not required by a group of citizens within three months after its adoption by Parliament. However, if a group of at least 50,000 citizens sign a petition for a referendum, the legislative act has to be submitted to a popular vote. Legislative acts voted upon in an optional referendum require only a simple popular majority to pass into law.

All three instruments have in common that they imply an *issue-specific choice*. They also have in common that they all imply a majoritarian logic in the popular vote. They all confront the voters with a *binary choice* – either in favour (pro) or against (con) the issue-specific proposition at stake. Moreover, this choice is generally a choice between, on the one hand, the position of the government and the majority of Parliament, and, on the other hand, the position of some challengers and the minority of Parliament. But the reader should note that 'pro' and 'con' have different meanings in popular initiatives and in referendums. Since the government and Parliament typically reject popular initiatives, the choice in favour of an initiative is almost always a choice in favour of the challengers, while the choice in favour of a legislative act submitted to a referendum is always a choice in favour of the government. This difference in the meaning of a yes vote has important implications for the challengers' chances to impose themselves against the majority position. Challengers generally have a hard time imposing themselves anyway. For the sponsors of an initiative, however, the fact that they have to mobilize for a yes vote implies an additional disadvantage – one which they share with the sponsors of initiatives in the United States: They have to lead a 'status quo modifying campaign', while the challengers in a referendum vote may lead a 'status quo preserving campaign' asking the citizens to vote 'no'. As is well known, 'status quo preserving campaigns' are more easily won than 'status quo modifying campaigns' (Gerber 1999).

The structuration of the choice: the systems of interest intermediation

The extended political process that precedes the popular vote, not only in the case of referendums, but also in the case of initiatives, serves to *pre-structure* the configuration of the political actors involved in a given direct-democratic campaign. The preceding political process is bound to have included a lot of bargaining, and to have led to the formation of issue-specific parliamentary, and even pre-parliamentary, coalitions, which constitute the point of departure for coalition formation in the direct-democratic campaign. Given the key role of the *political parties* in the political process preceding the vote, the *party system* constitutes a crucial element of the institutional setting, which serves to pre-structure the direct-democratic coalition formation. Similarly, given that interest groups 'capable of launching a referendum' are already co-opted in pre-parliamentary decision-making, and that they are key players in direct-democratic campaigns, the system of interest associations has to be taken into account as well. Third, given the media-centred character of political communication, we should also take into account the main characteristics of the Swiss media system.

The party system

As far as parties are concerned, Switzerland has a *multiparty system* that, in principle, offers countless possibilities for coalition formation in direct-democratic campaigns. In practice, however, these possibilities are reduced to only a limited number. There is a tendency in such a multi-polar party system, as Sniderman (2000: 83) correctly guesses, to collapse into a functionally bipolar one. This is not only a result, as he believes, of the irresistible attractions of structural simplicity. Such a reduction is also induced by the structural conditions of a direct-democratic vote, where the voter, as we have just seen, ultimately only has a binary choice. Moreover, the structure of the system is less complex than it initially appears. In spite of its exceptional degree of fragmentation, the Swiss party system essentially has a *tri-polar structure*, which is typical of Western European party systems (Kriesi et al. 2008). It is divided into the *left* (the Social Democratic Party (SP), the Green Party, and some minor parties), the *moderate right* (including the liberal Free Democratic Party [FDP], the Christian Democratic Party [CVP] and the minor Liberal Party of Switzerland [LPS]), and the *new populist right* (the Swiss People's Party [SVP] and some minor parties).

In the peculiar Swiss system of government – a grand coalition composed of the four major parties (SP, FDP, CVP, and SVP), which represents all three

poles, even a governing party may oppose the government on specific policies. In some cases, all four parties of the Swiss grand coalition government
jointly support a parliamentary proposal, and the challenge is launched by
one of the minor parties. Typically, however, the governmental coalition
splits, and either the left or the new populist right opposes the governmental coalition (Kriesi 2005: 26–34). In other words, typically, the governmental coalition is composed of either the moderate right and the new populist
right (*centre-right coalition*) or the moderate right in alliance with the left
(*centre-left coalition*). Roughly two-thirds of the 230 federal votes that took
place between 1981 and 2007 were characterized by either a centre-right
(44 per cent) or a centre-left (19 per cent) coalition. In the more recent past,
these two types of coalitions have become even more predominant – they
make up 50 per cent and 22 per cent, respectively, of the federal votes that
have taken place since 2000, compared to 45 per cent and 12 per cent of
the votes in the 1980s. While the left has always been in the minority in
Swiss politics, and, therefore, has always assumed to the challenging role,
the increasing number of centre-left coalitions reflects the increasingly
oppositional stance of the Swiss People's Party, which has been the cham-
pion of the new populist right since the 1990s. The remaining coalitional
configurations either concern a general partisan consensus (16 per cent), the
challenge of only minor parties from the left or the right (11 per cent), or
deep governmental splits, where two of the four major parties join forces in
opposing a parliamentary proposal (10 per cent).

In the controlled version of direct democracy that exists in Switzerland,
the partisan coalitions have been shown to play a key role in determining
the outcome of the vote (Kriesi 2005). Two detailed case studies, one of a
vote on abortion, and the other of two votes on the Swiss relations with
the European Union (EU), also show that the parties' standing in the media
is reinforced during direct-democratic campaigns (Höglinger 2008; Tresch
2008). In addition, these studies indicate that direct-democratic campaigns,
more generally, provide windows of opportunity for weak political actors.
Such campaigns allow peripheral political actors (including minor parties)
to get access to a public audience that far exceeds their usual reach. Direct-
democratic campaigns may, however, also weaken parties to the extent that
they induce intra-party conflict (Ladner and Brändli 1999: 286). It is, indeed,
not uncommon for cantonal sections of Swiss parties to take a different
stance from their national parties, which complicates the coalitional structure of a direct-democratic campaign. Given that Swiss parties traditionally
have been rather loose federations of cantonal sections, there is always a
possibility that some cantonal sections *may deviate* from the positions taken
by the national parties in a given campaign. However, the number of deviating sections has usually been quite limited and confined to the parties of
the moderate right, which are less cohesive than the polar opposites on the
left and on the populist right.

The system of interest associations

If parties are key players in the more mediated form of direct democracy as it is practised in Switzerland, they are not the only actors involved in direct democratic campaigns. The Swiss experience, indeed, also provides evidence that direct democracy fosters competition between parties and a variety of *interest groups*. Since Swiss parties typically lack financial resources, interest groups become key sponsors of campaign efforts. In previous studies, it proved, however, difficult to separate the impact of parties from that of interest groups in direct democratic campaigns (Kriesi 2005: 63; 2006: 607). The relative importance of parties and interest groups in direct-democratic campaigns varies according to *policy- or domain-specific conditions*. Policies are made in domain-specific subsystems, which, in addition to political parties, include a large number of actors whose composition varies from one policy domain to the other. From the point of view of direct-democratic campaigns, it is particularly important whether or not a domain concerns broad, diffuse constituencies and/or some narrower interests. Donovan et al. (1998) distinguish between campaigns in which a narrow group challenges another narrow group (*interest-group contests*), broad groups challenge narrow interests (*entrepreneurial contests*), a narrow group challenges a broad, diffuse group (*client contests*), and where a broad group challenges another broad group (*majoritarian contests*). *Narrow interests* include the key *economic interest groups* and *trade unions*, but also a range of more specialized interest groups (such as professional associations) and experts (scientists, policy analysts, consultants, journalists, and so on). Broad, diffuse constituencies, by contrast, are organized by political parties, but also by *citizens' interest groups* or 'social movement organizations'. The latter include organizations of the new social movements of the seventies and eighties that have become more or less institutionalized interest groups (ecological organizations, human rights and aid organizations, consumers' organizations, pacifist groups, or women's associations). In addition, broadly based groups also include more traditional organizations, such as churches, pressure groups defending traditional interests, and, last but not least, offices of public administration.

The media system

The Swiss *media system* has traditionally been of the democratic corporatist variety which prevails in Northern continental Europe (Hallin and Mancini 2004: 67f.). It has been characterized by the limited development of media markets, an important degree of political parallelism (strong ties between the media and the political world), the development of journalistic professionalism (journalistic standards supporting norms such as proportionality, elite domination, detachment, civility, and closure), and a considerable degree of state intervention. The strong forces of convergence towards the liberal model have made themselves felt belatedly in Switzerland, too, but they have not yet gone as far as in other countries. Thus, in Switzerland, the process of the 'disembedding' of the press, that is, of its increasing autonomy from politics, started late, and, although it is largely completed by now (Blum 2003: 369; 2005: 124, Imhof et al. 2008), there are still some ties between political and media actors. Even in the absence of an explicit political parallelism, editorial policies of key newspapers remain tinted by political preferences, as media bias theory suggests (Oliver and Maney 2000: 468–69).

Moreover, the Swiss media landscape is still shaped by the extraordinary importance of the press, and most advertising money is spent on newspapers. In the context of direct-democratic political campaigns, too, the press is still the most important source of information for citizens (Marcinkowski 2006: 398; Trechsel and Sciarini 1998; Kriesi 1994) because, among other reasons, political radio and TV ads are prohibited in Switzerland. Most importantly, the Swiss media system is linguistically segmented. It is structured along the lines of the four linguistic regions of the country – German, French, Italian and a tiny Romanch-speaking region (Meier and Schanne 1994: 36–48). This linguistic segmentation concerns both the electronic media and the press. In particular, it also characterizes the structure of public radio and television, which continue to dominate the supply of political information programs in the electronic media (Imhof et al. 2008). The national radio and television organization is structured into independent units which are organizationally rooted in the linguistic regions, such that each region has its own public radio and TV programmes. This linguistic segmentation is reflected in the users' habits: The overwhelming majority of the Swiss exclusively follow the programmes of their own linguistic region, in addition to the programmes of foreign stations of the same language (Kriesi et al. 1996; Tresch 2008: 33).

The number of media outlets – as measured by the number of available newspapers and their circulation in proportion to the population (4.6 million German, 1.5 million French, and somewhat less than a half million Italian speakers) – is larger than in other Western countries (Dahinden and Trappel 2005: 397). There is still an important, fragmented, regional and local press. The largest among the regional papers reach 40 per cent (*Berner Zeitung*), 50 per cent (*Aargauer Zeitung*), or even close to 60 per cent distribution (*St. Galler Tagblatt*) in their regions. Two elite daily newspapers (*Le Temps* in the French-speaking region, and *Neue Zürcher Zeitung* in the German-speaking part of the country) reach 140,000 and 300,000 readers per copy; two news magazines (*Bilanz* and *Weltwoche*, both German-speaking) have 200,000 and 350,000 readers, respectively; two tabloid newspapers (*Le Matin* and *Blick*) have 270,000 and 670,000 readers, respectively. In addition, there are four major Sunday newspapers, including two elite papers (*NZZ am Sonntag* and *Sonntagszeitung*, both German-speaking), with 480,000 and 770,000 readers each, and two tabloids (*Le Matin Dimanche* and *Sonntagsblick*) with 520,000 and 900,000 readers, respectively.[3] However, in line with the forces of convergence, the Swiss press has more recently also undergone a striking process of concentration and of 'tabloidization' (Imhof et al. 2008). A small number of popular/tabloid/gratuitous papers with a high coverage have come to play an increasingly important role within the media systems. One of the free papers (*20 minutes*) has, in fact, become the most widely read Swiss newspaper by far, with 490,000 and 1,370,000 readers in the two major language regions, respectively.

The stakes and coalitional configurations in the relevant policy domains

Now that we have reviewed the general context conditions, we now turn to our specific cases – two campaigns related to optional referendums, and one for a popular initiative. Two campaigns concern the domain of immigration policy: the (optional) referendum by the left against the revised asylum law, which was voted on 24 September 2006, and the initiative 'for democratic naturalizations', launched by the populist right and submitted to the voters on 1 June 2008. The third campaign concerns fiscal matters. It also relates to an optional referendum launched by the left – the referendum against the revision of the corporation tax, on which the Swiss voted on 24 February 2008. Table 2.2 situates these three campaigns in terms of the institutional instruments, policies, and coalitional configurations involved. In this section, we briefly introduce the stakes and the coalitional configurations in the respective policy domains. In the next section, we shall turn to the specific pre-structuring of the choices by the preceding issue-specific debates and decisions in the government and in Parliament.

Table 2.2 Classification of three campaigns in terms of institutions and policy domains

	Policy domain	
Instrument	Immigration policy	Fiscal policy
Optional referendum	Asylum law (centre-right coalition)	Corporation tax (centre-right coalition)
Initiative	Naturalization initiative (centre-left coalition)	–

The populist Right's drive for a restrictive immigration policy

The domain of *immigration policies* has become increasingly prominent in national Western European politics as a result of the processes of globalization and denationalization (Kriesi et al. 2006, 2008). Without going into the details here, let us just note that, as part of these global processes, immigrants from ever more distant and culturally remote shores are coming to Western Europe and posing a threat to the traditional way of life and the economic life chances of some groups in the indigenous population. All over Western Europe, the new populist right has begun to mobilize these indigenous groups in the name of a more restrictive immigration policy. Immigration policy represents a case of 'majoritarian contests' in terms of the typology introduced by Donovan et al. (1998), where one broad group challenges another broad group. And, as the new populist right mobilizes in the name of the interests of the indigenous population, the parties of the left constitute the main protagonists in the defence of immigrants' rights and the promotion of a liberal immigration policy (Koopmans et al. 2005). In addition, labour unions and broader-based citizens' interest groups, such as churches and religious associations, human rights and aid organizations, along with some more specialized pro-migrant and anti-racist groups, join the mobilization on behalf of the migrants' interests in particular, and of human rights interests in general. Economic interest groups other than labour unions tend to keep a low profile in this domain.

What is particular about the Swiss situation in this policy domain is that the direct-democratic institutions provide the two adversarial camps with an institutional opportunity to mobilize their constituencies – an opportunity which they lack in other countries. In Switzerland, the populist right uses the initiative to promote more restrictive immigration policies, while the left uses the optional referendum to prevent restrictive modifications of existing policies. Thus, there have been no fewer than 16 votes on immigration-related propositions since the beginning of the 1980s – these have mainly been votes on the initiatives of the populist right and on referendums launched by the left. The initiatives of the populist right are aimed at a general restriction of the number of foreigners (2), a restriction of illegal immigrants, asylum-seekers, or of naturalizations while the seven referendums of the left concerned either the asylum law (4) or the immigration law (3). The three remaining votes referred to the facilitated naturalization of second- and third-generation immigrants – constitutional changes proposed by the government and an optional referendum launched by the populist right against the modification of the law on the sale of real estate to foreigners. The two propositions we have selected for our study represent the two typical cases in this policy domain – a referendum against the asylum law launched by the left, and an initiative in favour of a more restrictive naturalization policy launched by the populist right.

With the left and the populist right diametrically opposed over immigration policy, the *moderate right* takes a pivotal position, which it uses for variable alliances. It tends to ally itself with the left in its opposition to the initiatives of the populist right, but to support the more restrictive legislation promoted by the populist right. Although the populist right has so far not been able to impose its radical demands in this policy domain, the pressure exerted by its initiatives and by its constant mobilization has not failed to impress the moderate right, which has consented to a series of legislative measures restricting the scope of immigration. The moderate right has also adopted these respective positions in our two cases, with important implications for the outcome of the vote. It sided with the populist right in the case of asylum law, but allied itself with the left against the naturalization initiative of the populist right.

Neo-liberal tax reforms

Our third case – the vote on the corporation tax – constitutes a stark contrast to the field of immigration policy. It concerns the classic confrontation between the left and the united right over a class-based economic issue. In terms of the typology of Donovan et al. (1998), it constitutes an 'entrepreneurial contest', where a broad group (the left) challenges a narrow interest group (the business community). The reason this issue has come up on the Swiss policy agenda is also related to the processes of global competition. Switzerland has traditionally offered comparatively low taxes to the business community. Since the 1990s, in the context of intensifying international competition for the localization of capital investment, the federal government proceeded to alleviate the fiscal charges for particularly sensitive parts of the economy, that is, the mobile production factors. More generally, as in other countries, the question of fiscal reform has become a major battle ground for the neo-liberal camp in Switzerland. Fiscal reform has operated on the tax side as it has on the expenditures side, and there have been a series of votes at the federal level concerned with general fiscal reform.

While neo-liberal reformers attempted to revise the tax code everywhere, it was only in Switzerland that they had to take into account the direct-democratic operation of the system. Indeed, since the general architecture of the highly complex federalist fiscal system, including the right to levy specific taxes, is part of the Constitution, any modification of this architecture implies a compulsory referendum. Therefore, there have been no fewer than 31 votes on fiscal matters at the federal level since the beginning of the 1980s. Three-quarters of these votes were the object of compulsory referendums. The majority concerned the general architecture of the fiscal system (18) or transportation taxes (9). Only four, including our present case, more directly concerned the question of the fiscal charges for the mobile production factors.

The pre-structuring of the choices in the three campaigns

The case of the asylum law 2006

As already indicated, the referendum which led to the vote in September 2006 was launched by the left against the tightening of the law adopted by the government and the centre-right Parliamentary majority. On 24 September 2006, the voters accepted the tough new asylum law by two-thirds majority of 67.7 per cent. This result did not really come as a surprise. It was almost identical to the results of two related previous votes, in April 1987 and June 1999. The vote on the asylum law was accompanied by a vote on the reform of the immigration law, which was also accepted, by a similarly impressive majority. Both reforms had been discussed in Parliament in spring 2004. Compared to the government's proposal, both bills had been toughened during the parliamentary debates, under the pressure of the populist right (SVP), with the moderate right's support. The latter's support was mainly motivated by the close outcome of the vote on the SVP's radical asylum initiative in 2002. Although the initiative was rejected, it obtained no less than 49.5 per cent of the popular vote and the support of 12.5 cantons, which made the moderate right receptive to the SVP's far-reaching demands.

Among other elements, the new asylum law stipulated that asylum requests from refugees who had already been accepted by another state would not be considered. It also prohibited social assistance for refugees whose requests had been legally rejected. In addition, the new law introduced more restrictive rules for refugees without proper identification; it adopted a so-called airport procedure allowing for rapid decisions at the refugees' point of entry, and it allowed for the possibility of exchanging information with refugees' home countries. Finally, more drastic coercive measures (various forms of detention of asylum-seekers) were adopted, and the duration of the existing measures was extended. Since these coercive measures concerned not only refugees, but all immigrants without a residential permit, they were included in the reform of the immigration law. It is worth mentioning that the United Nations High Commission for Refugees (UNHCR) and the Council of Europe voiced concern about this reform.

While the new asylum law was a clear case of retrenchment, the new *immigration law* had more the character of a compromise solution. In addition to the already mentioned reinforcement of coercive measures, and the introduction of a 'dual system' for the labour market that made it much more difficult for foreigners from outside of the European Free Trade Association (EFTA)/EU to get a job in Switzerland, the law also introduced some advantages for immigrants, such as facilitated access to residence permits for well-integrated immigrants, reintegration aid for immigrants returning to their home countries, and measures facilitating family reunions. The latter were, however, watered down to such an extent – the right to residence permits was restricted to children under the age of 12 – that they could no longer be considered a relevant advantage for immigrants.

Immediately after the adoption of the two bills in Parliament, the *Social Democrats* (SP) and the *Greens* announced that they were going to launch a referendum against the asylum law. The coherence of the left (and as it turned out of the opposing camp as well) was taxed by the fact that the Greens, in collaboration with two specialized aid organizations (Forum for the Integration of Migrants [FIMM], and *Solidarité sans frontières*), constituted the ad hoc Committee for a Double No (K2N) that linked the referendum on the asylum law to a referendum on the new immigration law. While the Greens attacked both laws, a majority within the SP, at first, wanted to concentrate on the asylum law. It was considered an easier target because it was a pure case of retrenchment. Together with a policy-specific citizens' interest group – the Swiss Aid for Refugees, or SFH (*Schweizerische Flüchtlingshilfe*), the SP formed an ad hoc committee against the asylum law – Coalition for a Humanitarian Switzerland, or KHS (*Koalition für eine humanitäre Schweiz*). Only when Ruth Dreyfuss, a highly respected former Social Democratic member of government, decided to head a competing committee that challenged both laws, the SP ended up collecting signatures against both laws as well.

In addition to this opposition, the governmental centre-right coalition faced a serious problem of internal cohesion, because a *third force* – the ad hoc committee of the so-called *Bourgeois coalition* (BK), composed of actors close to the governmental centre-right coalition but opposed to the reform proposal – constituted itself and mobilized quite intensely for the referendum against the asylum law (but not for the one against the immigration law). Surprisingly, this third force was led by an outsider who did not belong to the political elite, but to the business elite. It strongly appealed to *religious organizations* and was supported by both the Protestant Church and the Catholic Church leadership, which had gotten involved in the campaign before. Under the impact of the mobilization by this third force, the pivotal moderate right fragmented to some extent. But in this case, its fragmentation was limited to the French-speaking part of the country. In the German-speaking part, it remained solidly attached to the defence of the two bills.

Eventually, the campaign against the two proposals mobilized a large number of organizations in addition to political parties: These mainly include domain-specific organizations that support refugees and foreigners, as well as religious organizations. They mainly argued that the new asylum law violated the Swiss humanitarian tradition. On the government side, the number of organizations was more limited and included the usual allies of the moderate right – the business interest associations, in a minor role, and some domain-specific organizations that were defending the Swiss national tradition. The main argument by supporters of the new law was that the rampant misuse

a) Pro-campaign

b) Contra-campaign

Figure 2.1   Ads of the two camps in the asylum case

Notes: English translation: Stop Misuse | Asylum and Immigration law | 2 x No | The new Asylum law | is inhuman, | gets the wrong persons, | promotes illegality, | produces red tape, | asks too much of the cantons, | in short: costs a lot and | its of no use.

of the right to asylum should be stopped. Figure 2.1 (a & b) provides typical examples of posters and ads the two sides used during the campaign.

The case of the naturalization initiative 2008

On 1 June 2008, the naturalization initiative of the Swiss People's Party (SVP) was voted down by 63.6 per cent of the voters. Unlike the outcome of the voting in our first case, the clarity of this verdict came as a big surprise and constituted a conspicuous defeat for the SVP, for whom this vote had been the most important test of its new opposition politics.

To understand the thrust of the SVP's initiative for democratic naturalizations, one needs to know that local municipalities play a key role in the naturalization process in Switzerland. Moreover, it is important to keep in mind that naturalization has never been a completely administrative procedure in this country, but has always involved political elements as well. In fact, the procedure varies greatly between cantons, and even within cantons from one locality to the other (Helbling and Kriesi 2004; Helbling 2008): individual naturalization decisions can be taken by general assemblies of local citizens, by local parliaments, local executives or local naturalization committees. Until a Federal Court decision in 2003, such decisions could even be taken by popular votes at the ballot box. In reaction to an infamous vote in the city of Emmen, where a series of applicants to Swiss citizenship from the former Yugoslavia were denied Swiss citizenship in a popular vote, the Federal judges decided to outlaw popular votes on naturalizations. They argued that the rejection of naturalization requests required a justification, and that such a justification was not possible in a direct-democratic vote. The popular vote had only been used in a limited number of places, but it could be shown that the rejection rate of naturalization applicants in these places was much higher than in the rest of Switzerland (Helbling and Kriesi 2004).

It was in reaction to this decision by the Federal Court that the SVP launched its popular initiative in 2004. The initiative proposed that the voters in a given municipality should be able to decide on the kind of procedure they wanted for naturalizations – in particular, whether they wanted to vote at the ballot box on individual naturalizations. Moreover, the initiative stipulated that it should not be possible to appeal in court against local rejections of naturalization requests. The initiative, in fact, demanded that the act of naturalization should become an exclusively political act, decided by the country's citizens – and not by an administrative procedure. It was submitted in November 2005 with the required number of signatures.

The government rejected the initiative, arguing above all that it violated international law, in particular the European Convention on Human Rights, UN Pact II, and the UN Convention against racism. The debate in Parliament on the initiative was rather controversial, since several members of the moderate right felt a good deal of sympathy for the proposal. Eventually, the Parliament decided by a clear majority to reject the initiative. But it provided the populist right with a substantial concession by elaborating an indirect counter proposal to the initiative in the form of a modification of the law on civic rights: This proposal stipulated that naturalizations in general local assemblies would still be possible. In the event that the initiative should be rejected, this counter proposal was to enter into force. The main arguments against the initiative insisted on the guarantee of a fair naturalization procedure in accordance with the rule of law. Discriminatory decisions should be ruled out.

In the campaign, the populist right confronted the moderate right and the united left. The moderate right was not able to prevent some of its members from joining the other side. Although only two cantonal sections of the liberals (FDP) deviated from the party line, some prominent Liberal figures joined a committee for 'Reinforcing citizens' rights' in support of the SVP's campaign. The SVP's campaign was also supported by a committee of the radical right under name 'Security for All' that spent a lot of money in support of the initiative. Other conservative-nationalist organizations supported the initiative as well. The SVP's campaign mainly warned against 'mass naturalizations' and reused its well-known ads from a previous 2004 campaign on the naturalization of second- and third-generation immigrants (see Figure 2.2). Arguments concerning the security were mainly used by

a) Ad of the populist right in support of its initiative

b) Ad of the moderate right's contra campaign

Figure 2.2 Ads of the two camps in the naturalization case

Notes: English translation: Stop Mass Naturalizations | Yes for the Naturalization initiative | "Fairness instead of arbitrariness" | No to the Naturalization | initiative on 1 June 2008!

the radical right, with reference to some well-known acts of violence by young criminals of foreign origin.

On the government side, the left formed a united front, including the Social Democrats, the Greens and the Christian Socialist Party, as well as the peak associations of the social-democratic and the Christian unions, associations of second-generation immigrants, and some specialized aid organizations (FIMM and *Solidarité sans frontières*) that had already mobilized against the asylum law. The moderate right, by contrast, formed two separate committees – one composed of the Liberals, the other by Christian Democrats, Green liberals, and Evangelicals (see Figure 2.2 for an example of the latters' campaign ads). The initiative's opponents also found the vocal support of no fewer than 70 professors of constitutional law, who, in large ads, warned against the discriminatory implications of an acceptance of the initiative. The peak economic interest associations did not get involved in this campaign – except, surprisingly, for the association of small businesses and trade, which joined the supporters of the initiative.

The case of the corporation tax 2008

The outcome of the third vote was also unexpected. Given the generally favourable attitude of the Swiss voters with respect to the neo-liberal tax reforms, it came as quite a surprise that, on 24 February 2008, the revised corporation tax was accepted in a popular vote by only the barest possible majority of 50.5 per cent. The reform had three components. Its core element was a reduction of the tax on dividends for large shareholders – a measure meant to alleviate the double imposition of dividends, which Switzerland practises as one of the last member states of the Organization of Economic Co-operation and Development (OECD). The second component referred to the possibility of introducing an alleviation of the cantonal tax on capital, while the third component provided special measures for ownership succession in private, non-incorporated companies.

The reform constituted a political compromise between the business community, the cantons, and the parties of the right. To improve the competitiveness of the Swiss economy, the business community wanted to do completely away with the double imposition of dividends, but it had to take into account the needs of the cantons, which had proven to be a formidable adversary in the previous vote on the tax package of 2004. Thus, with respect to the double imposition of dividends, the reform did not go all the way to suppress the tax on dividends entirely, but proposed to reduce the tax to 50 or 60 per cent for investors holding at least 10 per cent of the shares in company or private property. The government had proposed reducing the tax for all shareholders, but Parliament had introduced the qualification of the 10 per cent, which was already in force in several cantons, in order to limit the loss of tax revenue for the cantons. Restricting the measure to large share holders allowed to win over the cantons to support the new law.

Of the 26 cantons, 17 had already introduced such a reduction for their own taxation. As a result of this restriction, the law mainly favoured the owners of the myriad small and medium-sized companies who had invested their money in their own firms. The whole package was designed to strengthen these small and middle-sized firms, which are often considered to constitute the backbone of the Swiss economy.

The second component of the law also carefully took into account the tax autonomy of the cantons. It introduced the possibility (but not the obligation) for cantons which levy a tax on profits to suppress their tax on capital, leaving the details of the procedure up to cantons. Finally, the law introduced alleviations for personal companies in a period of transition. This train of measures was intended to facilitate the transfer of a company from one generation of owners to the next, or to alleviate the fiscal burden for the self-employed who wanted to close down their business.

The left considered this reform unnecessary and unfair, since it privileged the income from capital over the income from labour. The Social Democrats decided to launch the referendum against the law in order to give a strong signal against the 'race to the bottom' in tax competition. They were supported by the Greens, the two peak labour unions, and by two organizations of the global justice movement – Attac Switzerland and the Berne Declaration. The Social Democrats were in charge of the contra committee during the campaign. The challengers focused mainly on the first component of the reform, which they considered a unilateral favour for the wealthy. They, somewhat far-fetchedly, also argued that the reform constituted a danger for the health of the Swiss old-age pension scheme (see Figure 2.3 for an illustration of their propaganda).

Under the leadership of the Christian Democrats (CVP), the parties from the right (FDP, CVP, LPS, SVP, and the Green Liberals) formed a joint committee to defend the reform. The three major peak business interest associations (Economiesuisse, the association of small businesses and trade, and the farmers' association) all came out strongly in favour of the reform. The pro-alliance emphasized that the reform supported the backbone of the Swiss economy, the small and medium-sized companies and that it would enhance the investment and growth of the whole economy (see Figure 2.3).

The representativeness of three campaigns

How do our three campaigns compare to federal campaigns in general? We are able to put them into perspective with regard to four criteria – their importance, familiarity, complexity, and intensity, as well as the overall balance or asymmetry of the resources of the two camps. With respect to the criterion of importance, assessed by a sample of citizens both for the country as a whole and for their own personal situation, we have information

a) Pro camp

b) Contra camp

Figure 2.3   Ads of the two camps in the corporate tax case

Notes: English translation: Strengthen small firms and trade | The 300,000 small and medium sized firms (KMU) constitute the heart of the swiss economy. They employ two thirds of the workforce. But it is exactly these firms which are disadvantaged by the tax code. | Small firms' Yes tax reform | I am not stupid | Damaging the old age pension? | No to tax gifts for large shareholders.

on all the federal votes since 1993. For the other criteria, our information extends back to the beginning of the 1980s.[4]

In terms of *importance*, the public considers the two immigration propositions of much greater importance than the corporation tax. As is shown in Table 2.3, both immigration issues are attributed an above average importance for both the country as well as the personal situation of the citizens.

However, the two cases do not belong to the most important propositions ever submitted to the voters. The corporation tax corresponds to a proposal of average importance for the country, and of less than average importance for the citizens' personal situation. Since most Swiss do not hold any shares, it is not surprising that the citizens in general did not consider this an important issue for their personal situation.

The corporation tax, however, constitutes one of he most *complex* objects that have ever been submitted to the voters. Complexity is measured by the share of voters who had difficulties in taking a decision on a given proposal. Almost two-thirds of the voters had difficulties in taking a decision on the corporate tax, compared to an average of not much more than a third. In fact, since the early 1980s, only four other propositions have been considered more difficult than the corporation tax – three agricultural issues voted in 1995, and an institutional proposition concerning the introduction of a 'constructive referendum' voted in 2000. Both the corporate tax and the naturalization initiative were highly unfamiliar issues, as is indicated by the rather large shares of voters who were still undecided at the beginning of the campaign, also reported in Table 2.3. Unfortunately, we do not have any comparable information for other federal votes with regard to this criterion. The lack of familiarity of the corporation tax and of the naturalization initiative suggests that, in these two case, the campaigners enjoyed a greater amount of latitude than for the asylum issue.

The indicators for the *intensity* and the *balance/asymmetry* of the campaigns are provided by a count of the advertisements in a selected number of six major newspapers – three each in German- and French-speaking Switzerland – over the last four weeks preceding the vote. These indicators are, of course, only proxies of what we ideally would like to measure, but, given that the campaigners mainly use newspaper ads to sway the public, they provide a rather good idea of the intensity and the balance or one-sidedness of a given campaign (Kriesi 2005). Table 2.4 presents the relevant

Table 2.3 Relative importance and difficulty of the three proposals: indicators based on VOX-surveys

| | Importance | | | |
	Collective	Personal	Complexity	Familiarity
Asylum	7.7	6.8	38.0	14.3
Naturalization	7.7	6.6	27.0	35.7
Corporation tax	6.5	4.8	61.1	28.7
Overall average	6.7	5.3	37.0	
Maximum	8.5	7.3	65.8	
Minimum	4.3	2.5	8.1	
Number of cases	143	143	226	

Table 2.4 Campaign spending on the three proposals: number of ads in selected newspapers

	Intensity: total count	Pro	Con	Advantage Pro
Asylum	127	62	64	−2
Naturalization	106	83	10	73
Corporation tax	370	366	4	362
Overall average (225)	97	46	52	−14
Average optional referendums (68)	107	68	39	29
Average initiatives (86)	114	40	74	−34

figures. As becomes immediately apparent from this table, the corporation tax gave rise to the most intense campaign of the three. Moreover, this campaign was most imbalanced, since the government's side enjoyed a tremendous advantage with respect to its challengers. Advantages such as this one have, indeed, been extremely rare in Swiss direct-democratic campaigns. In fact, since the early 1980s, there have been only three other campaigns on optional referendums, where the government's camp enjoyed a comparable advantage, all three of which concerned highly intense campaigns. In the case of the corporation tax reform, the resources for the defence of the government's reform came mainly from the business interest associations, which signals the singular importance the business community attributed to this particular reform. Given the lack of familiarity with this issue and the implied latitude of the campaigners, we expect, of course, that the great investment of the pro-side in this campaign should have largely paid off.

By contrast, in terms of intensity, the immigration issues gave rise to average campaigns. While the asylum campaign was quite balanced, and can be considered a typical campaign for an optional referendum, the campaign for the naturalization initiative had a one-sided character, too. In this case, however, the balance was in favour of the challengers from the populist right. In this respect, the naturalization initiative is typical of the initiatives launched by the populist right, which, with one exception, have all enjoyed an advantage in terms of the resources invested in ads. However, the initiatives of the populist right themselves are quite atypical in this regard, since initiatives from other quarters, especially initiatives from the left, usually face much more resourceful campaigns of the government's side, and tend to be greatly outspent by their adversaries.

Table 2.5 Overall preconditions for the three proposals, in terms of familiarity, intensity, and balance

Intensity	Balance	Difficulty	
		High	**Low**
High	Pro	Corporation tax	
	Symmetric Con		
Average	Pro Symmetric Con		Naturalization Asylum

Given the familiarity of the public with the immigration issues, and given its proven support of rather restrictive immigration policies, the defenders of the liberal position can be expected to have faced an uphill battle in both cases.

Table 2.5 summarizes the general preconditions for the three campaigns. As the table suggests, the immigration issues share rather similar contextual preconditions which are diammetrically opposed to the preconditions of the corporation tax. The only difference between the immigration cases is that the populist right enjoyed a clear advantage in terms of resources on the naturalization initiative, but not on the referendum against the asylum law. We should also keep in mind, however, that initiatives generally have a more difficult time to pass than optional referendums, and that the populist right could no longer count on the support by the moderate right in this particular case. In other words, the battle is likely to have been less predetermined in the initiative's case than in the case of the asylum law.

Conclusion

We have focused on the essentials in this chapter, what the reader needs to know about the Swiss context to be able to situate our three campaigns. In the space of this short chapter, we are, of course, not able to introduce all the details of the Swiss political system, which is often difficult for the uninitiated to understand. But we believe that the reader now has a pretty good idea about the context in which we have to situate the results that we present based on our study. In Parts II and III, we present our results. Before we turn to these results, however, let us briefly give you an idea of the distinguishing characteristics of our integrated approach to the study of campaigns.

Notes

1. To be sure, there are other criteria to classify direct-democratic institutions, for example, the criterion of whether or not the direct-democratic decision is binding. Since all Swiss votes are binding, this particular criterion is not very pertinent in our present context.
2. For each one of these three types there are different subtypes, but for our purposes it will be sufficient to distinguish among the three general categories.
3. The source for this information: http://www.wemf.ch/de/print/machBasic.php.
4. The data on the importance and the complexity of the proposals come from the VOX-surveys that are regularly held after Swiss direct-democratic votes (see http://voxit.sidos.ch/). They correspond to aggregations of individual responses. The data on the intensity and balance of the campaigns are based on our own work (for more details, see Kriesi 2005).

3
Design of the Study: An Integrated Approach

Regula Hänggli, Christian Schemer, and Patrick Rademacher

In the recent decades different complementary approaches to capturing the effects of political campaigns have been offered (for an overview see Brady and Johnston 2006; Goldstein and Ridout 2004, Iyengar and Simon 2000). Without doubt, one of the strongest approaches to investigating the effects of mediated political campaigns is the analysis of *longitudinal data* from panel designs (e.g. Bartels 2006). However, even studies relying on panel data are plagued with the problem of drawing causal inferences about campaign effects because little is known about the content of the press releases, the political advertisements or the news media. This shortcoming is addressed in the present study by using an *integrated* approach. We explicitly attempt to integrate data collection and data analyses of the strategies of political and media actors an analysis of their impact on the opinion formation of voters. Figure 1.1 in Chapter 1 illustrates the integrated design of the present study: It highlights the three types of actors involved in the political communication process – politicians, the news media and citizens – and the decisions and processes taking place at the site of each one of these actors, as well as the sets of reciprocal processes linking each pair of them.

In our integrated approach, we followed the pioneering idea of Lazarsfeld et al. (1944) and the advice of Bartels (2006: 134): 'Because campaigns are dynamic phenomena, good campaign studies must be dynamic too'. Thus, whenever possible, we conducted data collection and data analysis in a longitudinal fashion. With this integrated panel design, we can cover the whole campaigning process. Direct-democratic campaigns have a clear beginning and a clear end, which allows the drawing of causal inferences about direct-democratic campaign effects: One can start collecting data before the direct-democratic campaign takes off, and can investigate the longitudinal variation in the strategies of the political actors, in the content of the news media and political advertisements, and in the longitudinal variation in voters' political attitudes. In addition, direct-democratic campaigns are relatively short. This means that only few external events are likely to intrude into the campaign and intervene with the observed changes. The integrated approach allows examining also reciprocal processes.

In this chapter we attempt to provide the general reader with enough information about the integrated approach, the methods of data collection, and the methods of data analysis to assess their strengths and limitations. For details in the context of the underlying methodology, the interested reader should contact the authors.

Data collection

Taking the integrated approach into account in the design of our study, we collected data focusing on the political actors, the media actors, and the public. For political actors, we used a double strategy of data collection: interviews with the campaign managers of *all* key collective actors and a content analysis of the campaign material produced by these actors and of their political advertisements. The relevant organizations were identified on the basis of various sources: the parliamentary debates, the campaign for the collection of signatures, voting recommendations, the press and websites more generally. We used cross-checks with the persons we interviewed to complete the set of relevant actors. Data concerning the media organizations were also collected via a double strategy: interviews with representatives of the most important media organizations in Switzerland and a corresponding analysis of the media content. Public opinion is captured by means of three panel surveys in the French- and German-speaking part of Switzerland. In all surveys, the first panel wave was fielded before the campaign started, and the final survey took place after the date of vote. The computer assisted telephone interviews (CATI interviews) were conducted by a single company.

Most importantly, we developed all instruments (i.e. questionnaires, code books) in co-ordination with all members of the study. Furthermore, we improved our measures successively from one campaign to the other, for example, by shortening measurement scales. Such improvements notwithstanding, we made sure that issue-unspecific instruments were kept comparable across the different campaigns.

Expert interviews with political and media actors

The interviews considering the strategies of political actors were conducted with the campaign managers of all relevant political organizations which took part in the campaign. Table 3.1 gives an overview of the number and type of organizations interviewed. We distinguish five types of actors: ministers (responsible members of the Swiss Federal Council) and the administration; political parties, economic interest groups, including unions; ad hoc campaign committees; and, finally, citizens' interest groups including church organizations. In the case of the asylum law, we had 46

Table 3.1 Number and type of political organizations interviewed, by campaign

	Asylum law		Naturalization		Corporate tax	
	Contra	Pro	Contra	Pro	Contra	Pro
Parties	10	6	10	3	7	5
Citizens' interest groups	14	2	7	3	3	0
Economic interest group	4	3	4	1	3	10
Ad hoc committees	5	0	1	1	0	0
Minister	0	2	3	0	0	2
N per camp	33	13	25	8	13	17
Total N	46		33		30	

different interlocutors. Thirty-three organizations belonging to the challengers' camp, which illustrates that the campaign against the asylum law mobilized a large number of collective actors, especially parties and citizens' interest groups. In the naturalization case, we interviewed 33 organizations, again, a much larger number from the contra camp (25) than from the pro camp (8). Half of the conversations were held with parties and citizens' interest groups from the contra camp. In the tax reform campaign, the economic interest groups were particularly active. Overall, we interviewed 30 organizations in this case, 17 on the pro side, of which 10 were economic interest groups. The number of actors varies in each campaign since the organizations do not have enough resources to campaign every time. The involvement of an organization not only depends on the importance of the issue for the organization, but also on the number of important issues on the agenda in a given year.

Our research team deliberately did not focus on the leaders of the organizations. Rather, the campaign manager – that is, the person acting in the background who was responsible for the direct-democratic campaign – was better suited to answer our questions about the campaign strategies. We conducted two face-to-face interviews with each campaign manager – one at the outset of the campaign, and one after the citizens' vote. This design was motivated by the fact that questions relating to expectations are preferably asked prior the vote, whereas evaluation questions only make sense after the end of the campaign. The Swiss campaign managers were very cooperative. With one exception, we had no problem obtaining interview partners. In the one exception, the campaign manager was at the same time also a very powerful politician at the same time. He did not give a reason for refusing the interview. However, we were able to interview another key campaign manager from the same party, and we obtained all the necessary information. Thus, we can conclude that, in Switzerland, it is no problem at all to conduct interviews with the campaign managers. It was, however, difficult to garner information about the campaign budget. In Switzerland, people speak only confidentially about money. We did receive some honest answers about the monetary aspect of the campaigns, but some campaign managers refused to mention any amount at all, some spoke only in vague terms about the budget, and a few lied about the amounts they spent, as our checks based on secondary material indicate. To ensure we had reliable information about the monetary aspect, we measured the size and number of political advertisements – one of the key budgetary items in a Swiss direct-democratic campaign. Based on the total size of political advertisements, we calculated the money the political actors spent on advertisements.

We recorded the interviews and took notes. Immediately after the interviews, we wrote minutes in which we summarized the main statements. The detailed record was used only for clarification. We did not transcribe the interviews and accepted that the minutes already include some interpretation of the two interviewers. This pragmatic way of using the minutes is sufficient to answer our research questions and allowed us to conduct and analyse a total of no less than 218 interviews. It would not have been possible otherwise. The modal duration of an interview was about 60 minutes.

The interviews relied on two structured questionnaires containing more than 200 closed-end and open-end questions. In the first interviews we started with questions about the issue at hand, the importance of the referendum or initiative, the motivation, goals and expectations of the organization involved. Then, we spoke about the content of the campaign (the message, arguments, and policy aspects), the relationship to the media, and the campaign strategy (responsibilities, organizational structure, action repertoire, negative campaigning, timing, targeting). In addition, as already indicated, we wanted to know more about fund-raising and spending. Finally, we ended with questions about the partisan and issue-specific predisposition of the campaigners. In the second interview we spoke about the influence of the political actors and the coalitional structure, and asked whether and how the organizations had changed their strategy over the course of the campaign. The most important part of the interview was reserved for the evaluation of the campaign (the strategic elements, content, and result). We ended with questions about the media, the costs of the campaign and some general questions about the organization and the campaign manager.

Concerning the media actors, we conducted interviews with representatives of the most important media organizations in Switzerland for each campaign, focusing on print media and Public Service TV.[1] We made sure that the selected media covered all relevant media types: high-quality elite newspapers (which we call 'Elite'), free newspapers ('Free'), news magazines ('News Magazine'), regional newspapers ('Regional'), tabloid newspapers ('Tabloid'), Public Service TV news ('TV news'), and a Public Service TV show ('TV show').[2] Since we assumed that the chief editors as well as the financial heads of media organizations are responsible for the outcome of journalistic products – and therefore ultimately for the quantity and quality of content and coverage – we interviewed both professional groups. Table 3.2 gives an overview of the interviews we conducted over the three campaigns (for a more detailed overview at the level of the media outlet, we refer the reader to Appendix 1).

Almost all the experts we contacted to request an interview, agreed to participate in our study. Moreover, a large majority of the experts were willing to participate in all three campaigns. In the case of the asylum law, we had 28 different interlocutors. In the naturalization campaign, we conducted interviews with 35 experts. In the tax reform campaign, we interviewed 37 experts.[3] In each campaign, two-thirds of the experts were representatives of media organizations in the German-speaking part of Switzerland and a third were of media organizations in the French-speaking part of Switzerland. The same ratio applies with regard to the professional groups, where two-thirds of the experts were (representatives) chief editors and a third were (representatives) financial heads of media organizations.

Table 3.2 Number and type of media professionals interviewed, by campaign

	Asylum law		Naturalization		Corporate tax	
	Editor	Finance	Editor	Finance	Editor	Finance
Elite	4	2	4	2	4	2
Free	2	2	4	2	4	3
News magazine	0	0	2	1	2	1
Regional	7	3	7	3	7	4
Tabloid	2	1	3	2	3	2
TV news + TV show	3	2	3	2	3	2
N	18	10	23	12	23	14
Total N	28		35		37	

N: In a few media organizations, the interviewed expert held simultaneously the post of chief editor and financial head. In these cases, the expert is counted only once as 'chief editor'. In some media organizations, the financial head was responsible for two or more media outlets. For both these reasons the number of interviewed financial heads is lower than the number of interviewed chief editors.

In the asylum law and the tax reform campaigns, the interviews consisted of a one-hour, face-to-face interview before the vote as well as a 15-minute telephone interview after the vote. For the face-to-face interviews we handed a copy of the questionnaire out to the experts so they could follow the questions, and if necessary, fill in their answer or check the appropriate response. To motivate the experts to participate a third time, we reduced the length of the interview in the naturalization initiative. We first conducted a 15-minute telephone interview, and then asked the media experts to fill in a 30-minute online questionnaire, both after the vote. All interviews were digitally recorded and transcribed by using the software NVivo.

As only little was known about the strategies and processes of issue selection and construction by (Swiss) media organizations in the context of political campaigns, we conducted the guideline-based expert interviews for the asylum law campaign as an explorative study. We used the insights from this first campaign to generate a structured and standardized questionnaire for both the naturalization campaign and the tax reform campaign, containing mostly closed-end, but also some open-end questions. For all three campaigns, the questionnaires consisted of the same sections. In the first section we wanted to learn how the experts perceived the influence of the Swiss media on the public (agenda setting), as well as on other media (intermedia agenda setting). Next, we asked the experts about the editorial positioning of their media and whether they typically take a stand in political campaigns. In the third section, our questions dealt with the experts' ideas about their audience. Then we dealt with journalistic quality and quality management in the editorial department, spoke about the relation between political public relations (PR) and the news department, and, finally, we addressed the financial and human resources available in media organizations to cover political campaigns. Having standardized the questionnaire after the asylum law campaign, we also addressed the campaign-specific issues at stake in a seventh section for the naturalization campaign and the tax reform campaign.

Content analysis of campaign material and media content

In all three campaigns, we conducted a content analysis of the campaign material, directed at the media (press releases, speeches from media conferences, or public statements produced by the political actors), of political advertisements and the media's news reporting. All material was coded with the same codebook, which consists of three levels – the levels of the article, the political actor or journalist, and the argument.

The first level of the codebook refers to the *article*. By article we mean a document such as a press release for the campaign material, a news article, or a political advertisement in the newspaper. At the article level, we coded formal information, such as the date, name of the newspaper, title, position, length, section, article type, the use of an image, and information about the content, such as the cause for the report, intermedia agenda setting, relevance, source, number of point of views, difficulty of phrases, presence or absence of a lead, degree of objectivity, and emotionality and emotion. For some purposes, the article is the appropriate level of analysis. Looking at an article as a whole allows us, for instance, to ask what percentage of articles quote a particular organization (see Chapter 8) or to capture the intensity of the campaign (see Chapter 2).

The second level refers to a *political actor* or a *journalist* who uses an argument. At this level, we coded such information as the organization, institution or party the political actor or journalist is associated with, her name or regional provenance, or her position. The third level of the codebook refers to the *argument*. An argument is defined as a verbalization of a specific point of view. In each document – press release, newspaper article, TV news programme, and so on – we coded all the arguments provided by/reported for each the relevant actors (organizations or their individual representatives) in our study. We coded them in great detail. In particular, for each argument, we used two different codes – one for its offensive and one for its defensive use. Then, we summarized the arguments in a limited number of abstract categories (=frames), which we created on the basis of our reading of the specific controversy in a given campaign. The arguments are one of the core elements of our research, because they allow for linking together the different actors – politicians, journalists, and voters.

For the media's news reporting, we selected the most important elite newspapers, free newspapers, news magazines, regional newspapers, tabloid newspapers, Public Service TV news and Public Service TV shows in both the German-speaking and in the French-speaking parts of the country (see Appendix 1). For the asylum law, the coverage of the media was analysed over a period of 16 calendar weeks. This campaign started earlier than the other two campaigns because the issue was important to many organizations on the contra side and they tried to frame the issue before the summer holiday had started. The other two campaigns were shorter. Thirteen calendar weeks before the respective vote were analysed in both. In the naturalization initiative, the attention paid to the first 100 days of a newly elected member of the Federal Council delayed the beginning of the campaign. Only when the event punctuating the end of these first 100 days had past, did the campaign and the media coverage start in earnest. The vote about the tax reform took place in February. February votes usually imply shorter campaigns because they do not start until after the Christmas break. In all three campaigns, we covered the direct-democratic campaign from start to finish.

Table 3.3 shows the total number of articles and arguments which were produced and coded.[4] The most newspaper articles and documents directed towards the media were found for the asylum law campaign. However, the number of arguments was smallest in this case. In other terms, the average

Table 3.3 Total number of articles and arguments coded by campaign and channel

Number of articles	Asylum law	Naturalization	Corporate tax
Media coverage	992	947	740
Media input	92	69	88
Political ads	371	327	434
Number of arguments			
Media coverage	3906	4774	4406
Media input	1061	782	1056
Political ads	1818	1625	1110

length of a media article was shorter. It contains about four arguments per news article. In the tax reform campaign, the articles were longer than in the two other cases. About six arguments were coded in each article.

In the asylum law campaign eight different students coded the material. At the argument level, Cohen's Kappa for intercoder *reliability* is 0.61, which is not high, but is acceptable. We consider it acceptable because we checked all the arguments after the coding and corrected for coding errors. In addition, for the analysis, we summarized the detailed codes for arguments to broader categories (frames), which are less error prone. In the other two campaigns, the coding was done by ten students. The reliability of the coding in the naturalization initiative and the tax reform is assumed to be the same or even slightly better because the instructions, support and coding scheme were improved, and four of the coders stayed with the coding team.

Panel study

For each campaign, we conducted a panel study. The structure of the questionnaire remained comparable across the three campaigns, and differed only in thematic focus. Cognitive pre-tests preceded the main studies to ensure that the questionnaires were not too long and were consumer friendly in terms of comprehension. Three independent samples were recruited by random quota. In order to minimize dropout, the interviewees received an incentive for their participation. Table 3.4 lists the relevant information pertaining to the panel studies. As can be seen in this table, in the study about the asylum law campaign, participants were interviewed three times, whereas there were only two waves of interviews in the other two studies. The first interviews always took place before the campaign started. The final wave was started after the vote.

Although our samples are representative in terms of participants' sex, age, and residence, three aspects impair the representativeness of our results. First and most problematic is the bias in terms of education. That

Table 3.4   Details of three panel studies

Study details (issues, panel waves, date of interviews)	N	% Female	Mean age (SD)
Panel Study I: Asylum law			
Wave I (7/4–7/20/2006)	1725	52.2	48.5 (17.1)
Wave II (8/28–9/2/2006)	1415	53.7	49.3 (17.0)
Wave III (9/25–9/30/2006)	1094	54.6	50.4 (17.1)
Panel Study II: Corporate tax			
Wave I (1/9–1/23/2008)	1251	50.3	50.2 (16.3)
Wave II (2/25–3/7/2008)	1001	50.4	50.2 (16.4)
Panel Study III: Naturalization			
Wave I (4/7–4/25/2008)	1251	51.3	48.5 (16.8)
Wave II (6/2–6/20/2008)	999	50.2	49.6 (16.7)

Table 3.5   Results and participation rates: comparison of official outcomes with outcomes of our study

Campaign	Results: per cent in favour		Participation rate	
	Official[a]	Our study	Official[a]	Our study
Asylum law	67.8	61.3	49.2	87.5
Naturalization	36.0	27.7	45.1	79.9
Corporate tax	50.4	52.6	39.0	86.2

[a] Official results without Ticino (Italian-speaking part of the country) that was not covered by our surveys.

is, the lowest educational levels are under-represented in our data. Second, there is also systematic panel attrition. For instance, less-educated and younger people are more likely to drop out of our samples. These biases, along with a leniency bias, may have produced over-reporting in voting turnout (see Table 3.5). Because of this bias we do not analyse participation as a dependent variable in the present study. The panel studies come much closer to the official outcomes of the vote. Still, for all results we are careful when generalizing our findings to the population level. Apart from parameter estimates at the population level, there are no hints that would prevent us from drawing conclusions about structural relations between variables, even if these are affected by panel non-random missingness or panel mortality attrition.

In all three panel studies, the structure of the questionnaire remained the same, only the thematic focus changed. Most of the constructs in the questionnaire were assessed repeatedly. The first part of the questionnaire captured participants' interest in the campaign, interpersonal communication, and information-processing strategies. Subsequently, we asked for the knowledge or salience and the approval of the arguments. The knowledge and approval of arguments are of pivotal interest in the present studies. For each panel wave in the three studies, respondents were asked whether they knew the specific arguments and the extent to which they agreed or disagreed with those arguments. Table 3.6 shows the

Table 3.6   The most important arguments by camp and campaign

Pro camp	Contra camp
Asylum law	
The abuse of asylum policy must be stopped.	The humanitarian tradition of Switzerland must be maintained.
The execution of asylum politics must be more efficient.	The rights of asylum seekers have to be protected.
Switzerland is too attractive to asylum seekers.	Foreign people contribute to the social and cultural quality of Switzerland.
There are already too many foreigners in Switzerland.	
Tax reform	
This tax reform advances SMEs.	This tax reform makes the tax system even more complicated.
This tax reform advances the competitiveness of the Swiss economy.	Tax relief for major shareholders is unfair.
This tax reform advances investments and creates new jobs.	This tax reform harms old age and survivors insurance (AHV).
Double taxation is unfair.	A clear signal against excessive manager salaries is needed.
	This tax reform means unacceptable tax loss for the federal government and the cantons.
	All shareholders should get a tax discount.
Naturalization	
Mass naturalization has to be stopped.	This initiative brings discriminatory and arbitrary naturalization decisions.
Civil servants should not be allowed to decide about naturalizations.	Naturalization candidates are generally well integrated.
The people should decide about naturalizations.	Naturalizations have to be in accordance with the rule of law.
There are too many foreigners in Switzerland.	This poll damages the image of Switzerland.
Each municipality should itself decide which authority is responsible for naturalization.	The rights of the foreigners have to be protected.

most important arguments proposed by the pro and contra camp by each campaign.

After the argument block in the questionnaire, respondents in the first study were asked to report their emotional reactions towards asylum seekers, towards foreigners in general in the second study, and their affective reactions in the context of the corporate tax debate in the third study. Subsequently, the attitudes about the specific issue, people's voting intentions and the intended (or actual) participation were gauged. In all three surveys, issue-specific predictors were assessed, such as values, authoritarianism, threat perceptions.

A quite important measure was the use of or reliance on different communication channels and mass media. In order to link the panel study with the content analysis of the news media, we asked what specific medium (TV and newspaper) the interviewees used to keep informed about the issue during the campaign. Additionally, we measured the reliance on other sources (e.g. radio, websites, or campaign advertising). Finally, we asked for general political interest, party identification, ideological left–right self-positioning, trust in government, and demographics (e.g. religion, occupation). Sex, age, education, and residence were asked right at the beginning of the interview. These questions ensured that our quota would be completed. The time to complete the CATI interviews was about 20 to 30 minutes.

Illustration of the integrated approach in data collection

Let us illustrate the integrated approach with an example, the arguments. The arguments provide the most important link between all relevant actors in the political campaign. In all our instruments, we included questions about the very same arguments. First, we asked the political and media actors about the importance of each argument in their campaign and their position on this argument. For instance, they were asked about the importance of the argument 'the abuse of asylum policy must be stopped' and about how much they agreed with it. In the content analysis, we coded how often the argument 'the abuse of asylum policy must be stopped' was mentioned in the campaign material and in the news media and whether it was approved or not. Finally, in the panel survey, we asked the survey respondents whether they were aware of the most important arguments and whether they agreed with them. Thus, our interviewees were asked whether they had heard the argument 'the abuse of asylum policy must be stopped' and how much they agreed with it. This procedure was applied to all arguments that were deemed important in the campaign-related discourse. Such a concerted approach in data collection enables us to trace the flow of arguments from political actors via mass media reporting to the public.

Data analysis

The analysis can be done longitudinally. Except for the interviews with the media actors, we can rely on data containing repeated assessments of constructs in the course of three different campaigns. Our approach to monitoring the content of the mass media continuously, to assessing the strategies of political actors and to gauging public opinion by interviewing the same individuals before and after the campaign has several strengths (e.g. Finkel 1995; Halaby 2004; Singer & Willett 2003; Woolridge 2002). First, repeated measures permit the direct analysis of dynamics and change at different levels. For instance, by integrating prior public opinion as an explanatory variable, we can run more rigorous tests of opinion change within the public. The same holds true for the dynamics of the campaign covered on TV or in the press.

Second, based on panel data, we can establish causal priority among variables. Several studies in the field have failed to provide convincing evidence for causal order among variables because they were only able to rely on cross-sectional data. Thus, to gain a more thorough insight into the order of causes and effects of variables, panel data are an important prerequisite. Third, with retests of the same measures over time we can address the issue of reliability more appropriately. However, given that we measured most of our constructs with several items, the reliability of constructs can also be established in measurement models. Fourth, given that the campaigns had not started yet when we fielded the first wave of the panel, we do not confound previous knowledge with early campaign effects. For instance, most of our respondents in the first interview did not know that they would have to cast their vote several weeks later. Even if our respondents differ in knowledge about a specific campaign issue, this effect is not due to the specific campaign but rather to inter-individual differences in political awareness.

Conclusion

Our integrated approach is characterized by the close cooperation between political scientists and communication scholars. We all focused on the same objects of investigation (the three campaigns), and shared the same instruments. Nevertheless, we did not completely abandon the division of labour between the two disciplines. In what follows, the political scientists mainly focus on the presentation of political actors' strategies, while the communication scientists mainly address media strategies. It is in the analysis of the impact of the campaigns on the public that the two join forces most productively, by highlighting different aspects of the impact of political communications on the citizen public.

Appendix 1 Media analysed

			Expert interviews			Content analysis		
Type	Media	Language	Asylum law	Naturalization	Tax reform	Asylum law	Naturalization	Tax reform
Elite	*Le Temps*	French	x	x	x	x	x	x
	Neue Zürcher Zeitung	German	x	x	x	x	x	x
	NZZ am Sonntag		x	x	x	x	x	x
	Sonntagszeitung		x	x	x	x	x	x
Free	*20 Minutes*	French	x	x	x	x	x	x
	le matin bleu			x	x		x	x
	20 Minuten	German	x	x	x	x	x	x
	Punkt CH			x	x	x	x	x
News magazine	*L'Hebdo*	French		x	x		x	x
	Weltwoche	German		x	x		x	x
Regional	*24 heures*	French	x	x	x	x	x	x
	Tribune de Genève		x	x	x	x	x	x
	Aargauer Zeitung	German	x	x	x	x	x	x
	Basler Zeitung		x	x	x	x	x	x
	Berner Zeitung		x	x	x	x	x	x
	Die Südostschweiz					x	x	
	Die Südostschweiz am Sonntag						x	
	Neue Luzerner Zeitung		x	x	x	x	x	x
	Sonntag (AZ)						x	x

Continued

Type	Media	Language	Expert interviews			Content analysis		
			Asylum law	Naturalization	Tax reform	Asylum law	Naturalization	Tax reform
	St. Galler Tagblatt					x	x	x
	Tagesanzeiger		x	x	x	x	x	x
Tabloid	Le Matin	French	x	x	x	x	x	x
	Le Matin Dimanche						x	x
	Blick	German	x	x	x	x	x	x
	Sonntagsblick		x	x	x	x	x	x
TV News	le journal	French	x	x	x	x	x	x
	10-vor-10	German					x	x
	Tagesschau		x	x	x	x	x	x
TV Show	TSR Infrarouge	French	x			x	x	x
	Arena	German	x	x	x	x	x	x
	SF Rundschau	German					x	x

Notes

1. The role of the Internet in the campaigns is being analysed by Patrick Rademacher in his doctoral thesis.
2. The daily newspapers selected were those with the highest total audience for German-speaking as well as French-speaking Switzerland. Concerning TV, we concentrated on Public Service TV, as commercial and privately owned TV plays only a marginal role in Switzerland. We did not analyse media from the small Italian-speaking part of the country.
3. In the naturalization and the corporate tax campaign more media outlets were included to increase the validity of the qualitative results based on the interviews with media actors. The quantitative results with regard to the content analyses should not vary, as there were not many articles in these new included media outlets.
4. In Chapter 9, we arrive at a different total of arguments because we dropped letters to the editor, TV shows, news magazines, newspapers not analyzed in all three campaigns, and non-arguments.

4
Coalition Formation

Laurent Bernhard and Hanspeter Kriesi

Unlike in the literature on representative democracy, hardly any attention is paid to the process of coalition formation in the context of direct democracy. To our knowledge, Manweller (2005); Bowler & Hanneman (2006); and Kriesi (2005, 2006) are the only studies which explicitly address this issue. In this chapter, we take a closer look at the process of coalition formation in the context of Swiss direct-democratic campaigns. We argue that in these campaigns, the conditions for coalition formation are quite different from those obtaining in representative democracy. This has major implications for the way coalitions are formed and have to be examined.

In a representative democracy, coalition formation takes place at different stages of the political process. It may occur before elections, in the formation of pre-electoral coalitions (Golder 2006); it takes place in the process of government formation; and it is pervasive in parliamentary logrolling. At each stage, the process is characterized by a certain number of features that distinguish it from coalition formation in direct-democratic campaigns. First, there is *no room for bargaining*. The proposal submitted to the vote is issue-specific and has been definitely packaged at earlier stages of the process – either by its sponsors or by a parliamentary majority. The issue specificity is not an accidental characteristic, but is usually constitutionally prescribed (Clark 1998: 467). As we argue below, in their mediated form, direct-democratic processes do not preclude logrolling at previous stages of the political process. However, at the stage of the popular vote, there is no room left for bargaining. Moreover, the choice is highly pre-structured by the fact that there usually are only *two options* – support or rejection of the proposal. Once the proposal is submitted to the vote, the potential coalition partners have only the choice of taking or leaving it. In addition, each direct-democratic vote is a rather *unique* event that is hardly connected to other votes, even to those that take place at the same time. This leaves little room for possible side payments among the actors involved. Our argument is that direct-democratic institutions follow a binary logic on any given issue-specific proposal, which strikes at the roots of bargaining (Barry 1975: 485f.).

Second, there is *no institutionally designated leader* who is charged with the task of forming a coalition in favour of or against the proposal. As far as Swiss practice is concerned, the government tends to adopt a low-key approach. Rather, leadership is expected to vary as the case arises. Third, the number of potential coalition partners is, at least potentially, much larger than in representative democracy. This is because the big political parties are not the only relevant actors. Besides minor parties and public administrations, various economic and citizens' interest groups are likely to take part in direct-democratic campaigns. Therefore, the high number of actors stemming from different backgrounds increases the complexity of the coalition-formation process. Fourth, direct-democratic coalitions resemble pre-electoral coalitions to the extent that they have an influence on the outcome of the vote. Indeed, the main objective of these coalitions is to influence the final result (Kriesi 2006). From the perspective of the political elite, direct-democratic votes are fundamentally unpredictable (Papadopoulos 1991), as the decision-making competence is delegated to citizens. In addition, the large number of actors involved tends to increase uncertainty about the outcome and to decrease the possibility of control by any single actor.[1]

Against the background of these specificities of direct-democratic campaigns, the problem of *size* is posed in terms that are clearly opposed to those in representative democracies. According to the literature on government formation, actors will form coalitions just as large as the minimum necessary to obtain control over the government, that is, they will form 'minimal winning coalitions' (Riker 1962). Both sides involved in a given direct-democratic campaign, however, face a strong incentive to secure the support of as many allies as possible. Therefore, we assume that they will try to maximize the size of their coalitions. In line with this reasoning, it is well established that the coalition size strongly increases the chance of success at the polls (Kriesi 2005: 65). As a consequence, we do not expect to see 'minimal-winning coalitions', but rather oversized coalitions which include actors of different types and political orientations. However, increasing the number of coalition partners introduces the problem of *heterogeneity*, or the 'extension dilemma', which is familiar to social movement strategists (Jasper 2006: 127f.): 'the further you reach out your team or alliance, the more diverse it will be and the less unified'. To deal with this problem, we expect political actors to split into *component coalitions*.

In this chapter, we argue that the coalition structure is decisively shaped by the *belief systems* of the actors involved. We focus on the pivotal role of the moderate right. In cultural issues, its decision to join either the left or the new populist right is expected to depend on pragmatic considerations regarding the issue at stakes (secondary beliefs). Given its intermediate stance on cultural issues, the moderate right will not have close ties to its coalition partners during these campaigns. Rather, it will form a separate component coalition. By contrast, in the economic domain, the moderate right is expected to coalesce with the new populist right, thereby producing a classical left–right opposition. The coalition on the right is expected to be based on shared core and secondary beliefs, thus constituting a 'natural alliance'. As a consequence, the major right-wing forces should closely work together and therefore find themselves in the same coalition component.

The Swiss direct-democratic context

The extended political process preceding the campaign before the vote serves to *pre-structure* the configuration of the actors involved in the campaign. Although in the final stage of the direct-democratic vote, bargaining is no longer possible, the preceding political process is bound to have included a lot of bargaining and led to the formation of issue-specific parliamentary, and even pre-parliamentary, coalitions, which constitute the point of departure for the coalition formation in the direct-democratic campaign. The government and the parliamentary majority always are part of one of the two camps facing the challenger coalition in the campaign. More specifically, in the case of a referendum, challengers of the proposal adopted by Parliament face the opposition of both the government and the parliamentary majority. In the case of a popular initiative, its sponsors usually have to face the opposition of the two as well, since they almost always reject the popular initiatives. In the context of referendums, however, the government coalition pleads for a reform by issuing a 'yes' recommendation to the citizens.

The positioning of political parties provides a useful baseline for the analysis of direct-democratic coalition formation in Switzerland. As has been outlined in Chapter 2, Switzerland is characterized by a tri-polar party system, consisting of the left, the moderate right, and the new populist right. The role of the moderate right is of crucial importance, as it takes a *pivotal position* between the left and the new populist right. It joins forces with either the left or the right to constitute centre-left or centre-right coalitions. The moderate right's strategic decision to join one or the other camp has been shown to be of crucial importance with respect to the outcome of the vote (Kriesi 2005, 2006).

If parties are important players in the more mediated form of direct democracy, as it is practiced in Switzerland, they are not the only actors involved. In addition to the parties, *interest associations* take part in the campaigns. The configuration of associations on both sides is determined by the interests related to the issue at stake. Economic and social policies typically mobilize the business interest associations and the unions, while policies more related to the cultural dimension of the political space – issues such as immigration, or questions related to cultural liberalism – bring in organizations connected to the new social movements (such as human rights groups, ecological organizations, pacifist groups, or women's associations), religious organizations, or professional associations. The interest groups play a crucial role during the campaigns because they provide the *resources for mobilization*. Swiss political parties are typically poor organizations, and thus heavily rely on the financial and logistic support by interest associations for the organization of direct-democratic campaigns.

Contrary to parties and interest associations, the *government* is expected to accomplish its campaign involvement with a certain restraint. According to this traditional view, which is derived from the specific informal rules of *concordance* and *collegiality* (see Kriesi 2009), the role of the authorities consists in informing the citizens about the issues at stake rather than in engaging in propaganda manoeuvres. To fulfil this task, the government is allowed to defend its standpoint on radio and TV during prime time and to present its arguments in a ballot pamphlet which is sent to each citizen.

Since there are no institutional leaders in direct-democratic campaigns, *ad hoc committees* are constituted on either side for the purpose of coordinating the various campaign activities of the political organizations involved. Committees usually perform the function of meta-organizations that regroup a wide range of actor types. Alternatively, important actors may take it upon themselves to coordinate the alliance partners on their side of the campaign.

Coalition structure

The way the coalitions are formed crucially depends, as we argue, on the belief systems of the political organizations. Within the institutional constraints, we expect the coalition formation of the relevant actors to be primarily based on the actors' shared beliefs, and less on their short-term strategic considerations. This is in line with the advocacy coalition framework (ACF) (see Sabatier and Weible 2007: 192ff.). The expected importance of beliefs in coalition formation does not imply that the actors are value-rational in their political orientations. It only means that, when forming coalitions, actors pursue policy-specific goals that are in line with their core interests and principles.

Following the ACF, we propose to conceptualize a three-tiered hierarchical structure of beliefs. At the broadest level are *deep core beliefs*, which are not policy specific. They involve fundamental values, general normative assumptions about human nature and about the proper role of government. The traditional left–right scale operates at the deep core level, as do traditional scales of political values. As far as the latter are concerned, we typically find *two dimensions* in Western Europe – an economic and a cultural one (Kriesi et al. 2008). The *economic* dimension refers to the classic opposition between state intervention and market solutions that has constituted the core of the opposition between left and right. The *cultural* dimension had its roots in religious confrontations. Under the impact of secularization, the transformation of the class structure, and globalization, it has, however, acquired an entirely new meaning. The cultural dimension is now opposing liberal and cosmopolitan values on the one side, and authoritarian and protectionist/traditional values on the other. Moreover, with the opening up of the European nation states the cultural dimension has become ever more prominent in the mass publics and in electoral competition.

At the next level are *policy core beliefs* which are applications of deep core beliefs that span the entire policy subsystem. The final level consists of *secondary beliefs*. They are relatively narrow in scope and address specific aspects of the policy in question. In particular, they refer to the specific characteristics of the proposal submitted to the vote. Actors of the political elite have well-developed political ideologies, which impose constraints on their political belief systems (Converse 1964: 227–230). This means that their secondary beliefs are embedded into their policy cores, which in turn are embedded into their deep core beliefs.

Political actors may join a given coalition for different reasons. Basically, there are four possible types of alliances on either side (see Table 4.1). Actors who share both core and secondary beliefs constitute a *natural alliance*. Based on the highly constrained character of the belief systems of political elites, we expect above all to find this kind of coalition. Second, actors who share neither core nor secondary beliefs, but who still take the same position with regard to the proposal constitute an *unnatural alliance*, or what Ossipow (1994: 39) calls an *objective coalition*. Such an alliance does not result from any explicit compact, but comes about by an aggregation of actors or component coalitions of actors who campaign independently of each other in pursuit of a common goal. Such actors find themselves on the same side of a campaign, but for entirely different reasons. They do not agree with respect to the specific aspects of the proposal, and these disagreements are rooted in different policy core beliefs and/or deep core beliefs. On the opponents' side, the proposal may go too far for some, not far enough for others; on the supporters' side, different actors may support different aspects of the proposal.

The third type refers to actors who share secondary beliefs, but for different deep core or policy core reasons. One group of actors may support a given proposal for cultural considerations, while, for another group of actors, the same proposal mainly speaks to their economic interests. In this case, the leaders of the two groups may explicitly form partial, or *component,* coalitions that cater to their specific target groups, in order to deal with the

Table 4.1 Coalition types based on shared beliefs

Secondary beliefs	Core beliefs	
	Shared	Not shared
Shared	Natural alliance	Pragmatic alliance
Not shared	Ideological alliance	Unnatural alliance

problem of heterogeneity implied by the different core beliefs. Contrary to the previous type, the component coalitions are likely to cooperate in this case. They constitute a *pragmatic alliance*. The final combination – actors who do not agree on secondary beliefs, but share the same core beliefs – may at first sight be highly unlikely. But it may still happen that, for ideological reasons, actors stick together even though they do not agree on various aspects of the proposal. They constitute what an *ideological alliance*. Such actors are likely to constitute a common component.

As far as the coalition formation is concerned, the positioning of the moderate right in the context of the tri-polar configuration of the Swiss political system is of particular importance. In line with Kriesi (2005, 2006), we hypothesize that the coalition structure depends on the issue at stake. In the economic domain, the *deep core, policy core, and secondary beliefs* of the moderate right are quite similar to those held by the new populist right. Therefore, classic left–right oppositions should prevail as long as economic aspects are submitted to a vote. In addition, because of shared beliefs, we expect the two parts of the right to closely collaborate with each other. As a result of these natural alliances, the most important actors (CVP, FDP, and SVP) should appear in the same coalition component. In cultural issues, however, the moderate right finds itself cross-pressured, between the libertarian values of the left and the authoritarian claims of the new populist right. As the moderate right takes an intermediate stance, its deep core beliefs do not serve as a guide to its positioning. Rather, its choice to either join the left or the new populist right is expected to be decisively shaped by its *secondary beliefs*, thereby giving rise to 'pragmatic alliances'. Since the moderate right distinguishes itself from the actors at the extremes by taking an intermediate stance on cultural issues, it won't have close ties to its coalition partners during these campaigns. Independently of the decision to form a centre-left or centre-right coalition, the moderate right will therefore form a coalition on its own.

Data and method of analysis

This chapter draws on interviews that have been conducted with 109 campaign managers of political organizations that took part in the Swiss direct-democratic campaigns under scrutiny. To identify the *coalitions* and their possible *components* on both sides, we rely on *network analysis*. In our second interviews with the key campaign managers, we presented them with the original list of organizations we had selected. We asked them to indicate the organizations on the list with whom they had closely collaborated during the campaign. After they had gone through the list, we asked them to indicate the three organizations with whom they had collaborated particularly closely, and finally, we asked for the one organization of the three, with whom they had most closely collaborated. This kind of procedure is very much inspired by earlier work on political elites and their involvement in specific policy domains (e.g. Knoke et al. 1996; Kriesi 1980; Kriesi & Jegen 2001; Laumann & Pappi 1976; Laumann & Knoke 1987). A collaborative relationship is indicated by a '1' in the adjacency matrix, a particularly close relationship by a '2', and the closest collaborative tie by a '3'. Isolated actors, that is, organizations that are not connected to others at all, have been removed.

To study coalition structures on the basis of this type of data, we draw on *block-model analysis*, which allows for distinguishing between structurally equivalent groups of actors (our coalitions) on the basis of an analysis of the cooperative relationships. A block model consists of two elements (Wasserman and Faust 1999:395): (1) a partition of actors in the network into discrete subsets called positions, and (2) for each pair of positions, a statement of the presence or absence of a tie within or between the positions. We make use of the CONCOR algorithm, which applies successive splits to the network. The first split is expected to generate the two opposing camps. Subsequent results will reveal the structure of the coalition components. Because there was a limited number of observations, we will present the results of the 4-block solutions.

The *deep core beliefs* are operationalized in two ways: We measure the self-positioning of the key campaigners on a left–right scale (indicator DCB1), which gives us a most general indication of their ideological position. In addition, we obtain two measures for their political values (indicators DCB2). For this purpose, we confronted the respondents with seven choices about the Switzerland they desired. Three choices refer to classic *economic* values (state-intervention in the economy versus market competition, large income differences versus small income differences, solidarity versus self-responsibility), and another set of three choices refers to *cultural* values (opening up to the world versus independence, equality of chances for foreigners versus better chances for the Swiss, modernity versus tradition). A seventh, more neutral item – reforms versus status quo – was introduced, as well. A factor analysis of these seven items reveals the expected two dimensions, with the economic dimension clearly constituting the first factor; and the cultural dimension, the second. The reform/status quo item is mainly associated with the economic dimension, and not with the cultural one. This reflects the notion that, nowadays, reformers mainly come from the neoliberal camp, while the left has a tendency to privilege the preservation of the achievements of the past. The economic dimension essentially distinguishes a pro-market from a pro-state position, while the cultural dimension refers to the distinction between a traditional, culturally protectionist position and an open, multicultural position.

The *policy core beliefs* are also operationalized by means of four different scales measuring issue preferences. With respect to the two immigration proposals, the corresponding indicator is based on the actors' degree of *xenophobia*. This scale is composed of a set of five items referring to perceived individual/collective economic, cultural, and safety threats due to immigration (see Sniderman et al. 2004). Concerning the corporate tax reform, we make use of a measure that is labelled *economic stakes*. It consists of six items, three of them being related to the degree of approval of the economic status quo; and the remaining ones, to assessments of to what extent the principle of equality are currently fulfilled in Switzerland. As expected, all these items form a single factor for each campaign. We use these factor loadings (PCB) as indicators for the policy core beliefs.

For the operationalization of the *secondary beliefs*, we use twelve key *issue-specific arguments* that have been formulated over the course of each campaign. Respondents could indicate their opinion about these arguments on a five-point scale, ranging from 1 'do not agree at all' to 5 'totally agree'. For each campaign, the positioning with respect to these arguments constitutes a single factor (SB) on which we rely to measure the political organizations' secondary beliefs.

Finally, there is a measure for *power*, which allows us to specify the average influence of the main coalitions involved. Power is operationalized by a reputational indicator and is based on a set of questions referring to the list of all organizations involved (Kriesi et al. 2006). In the second interview, the respondents were first asked to name all organizations on this list which, from their point of view, had been particularly influential during the campaign. Next, they were asked to name the three most influential organizations; and, finally, the most influential one. For each actor, a summary indicator counts the number of times a given organization was mentioned by the respondents in reaction to these questions, with similar weights attached as for the cooperative ties: mentions as 'most influential' are coded as '3', mentions among the 'three most influential' as '2', and mentions as 'influential' as '1'. The values of the indicator range from 0, for an organization that has never been mentioned as influential, to 3 times the number of respondents, for an organization that would have been considered to be the most influential actor by all of them. We rely on the absolute power level by adding up, for each coalition, the values obtained for their respective member organizations.

Results

The opposing camps are internally connected by multiple ties, but are hardly at all linked to each other. With the exception of the campaign on the revised asylum law, there are no collaborative ties between the two at all. In line with this observation, the first split applied by CONCOR produces the supporters' and the opponents' coalitions, respectively. The second split divides ideologically heterogeneous camps in terms of beliefs, and homogeneous ones in terms of power. In the case of the naturalization campaign, three blocks seem to be appropriate, since two blocks are densely connected to each other. For this reason, we decided to collapse them into the moderates' component coalition. Table 4.2 presents the various blocks involved in each campaign as well as their camp affiliations, the overall power, and the number of organizations they contain.

In line with the first hypothesis, the organizations belonging to the moderate right distinguish themselves clearly from the left and from the new populist right when it comes to cultural issues. As expected, the moderate right forms a separate component coalition regarding the two campaigns on immigration. In the case of the asylum law, its main forces (CVP, FDP and some economic interest groups) joined the new populist right in the 'yes' camp. As is shown in Figure 4.1, the belief systems of the moderate right sub-coalition clearly are different from those of the new populist right (here, labelled as the conservative right). With respect to all four beliefs indicators, the moderate right takes an intermediate stance. As

Table 4.2   Overview of the component coalitions by campaign

	Position	Government coalition	Power	N
Asylum law				
1. Left	Contra	No	234	20
2. Third force	Contra	No	245	11
3. Moderate right	Pro	Yes	147	8
4. Conservative right	Pro	Yes	95	4
Naturalization				
1. Left	Contra	Yes	131	14
2. Moderates	Contra	Yes	123	9
3. Conservative right	Pro	No	119	6
Corporate tax				
1. Core left	Contra	No	103	7
2. Satellite left	Contra	No	12	6
3. Satellite right	Pro	Yes	64	11
4. Core right	Pro	Yes	161	6

far as the cultural values (DCB2) and the xenophobia (PCB) are concerned, the factor loadings of the moderate right even point in the direction of their adversaries. It is only at the level of the secondary beliefs which delineate the approval to issue-specific arguments (SB) that the moderate right comes closer to the new populist right. Therefore, the alliance between these two components follows a 'pragmatic' logic. This result also is in line with our theoretical expectations.

To combat the naturalization initiative launched by the SVP, the moderate right coalesced with the left, from which it structurally distinguished itself. The second opponents' component coalition is not confined to the moderate right, however. Since this block includes centrist parties as well as religious organizations, it regrouped moderate forces. The 'moderates' block is considerably different from the left with respect to the left–right scale (see Figure 4.2). In terms of secondary beliefs, the two opponents' coalitions are on the same wavelength, however. Therefore, this type of alliance can again be considered as a 'pragmatic coalition'.

The campaign against the asylum law mobilized a large number of organizations, in addition to political parties: These mainly include domain-specific organizations which support refugees and foreigners, as well as religious organizations. The *left block* is composed of twenty organizations which regrouped themselves into two ad hoc committees. The Greens,

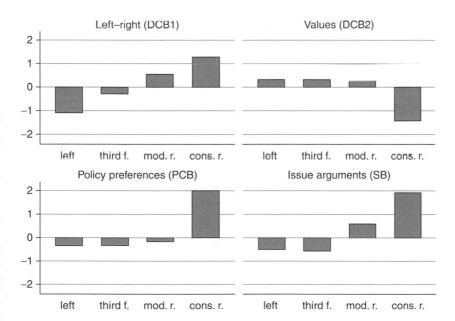

Figure 4.1   Beliefs in the asylum law campaign by component coalition

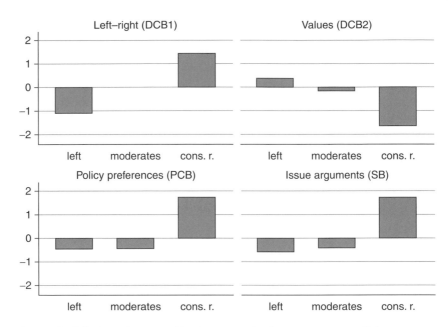

Figure 4.2   Beliefs in the naturalization campaign by component coalition

in collaboration with two specialized aid organizations (FIMM-Forum for the Integration of Migrants, and *Solidarité sans frontières*), constituted the *Committee for a Double No (K2N)* that linked the referendum on the asylum law to a referendum on the new immigration law. Together with a policy-specific citizens' interest group – the Swiss Aid for Refugees (SFH *Schweizerische Flüchtlingshilfe*) – the Social Democratic Party formed an ad hoc committee against the asylum law – the *Coalition for a Humanitarian Switzerland* (KHS-*Koalition für eine humanitäre Schweiz*).

The governmental centre-right coalition had to face a problem of internal cohesion, because the *third force*, composed of people close to the governmental centre-right coalition, but opposed to the governmental proposal, constituted itself and mobilized quite intensely against the law. Surprisingly, this coalition was led by an outsider, Markus Rauh, who did not belong to the political but to the business elite. It appealed to *religious organizations* and was supported by both the leadership of both the Protestant Church and the Catholic Church, who had already planned to get involved in the campaign. Under the impact of the mobilization by this third force, the pivotal moderate right fragmented to some extent. But in this case, its fragmentation was limited to the French-speaking part of the country.

The number of organizations participating in the campaign on the government side was more limited, and included the usual allies of the moderate right – the business interest associations, in a minor role, and some domain-specific organizations defending the Swiss national tradition. On the supporters' side, the two coalitions – the moderate right and the new populist right – seem to have led their campaigns quite independently. In fact, in this particular campaign, the major parties of the moderate right (FDP and CVP) chose not to cooperate with the populist right. Typically in the case of a centre-right coalition, the FDP and CVP usually form a joint committee with the SVP, with one of them taking the leading role, but in the present case, each party led its own campaign. The FDP attempted to distance itself from the SVP by focusing on its own liberal migration concept, while the CVP adopted a low-key approach, since the proposal not only gave rise to internal tensions, but also caused conflicted with the Catholic Church. The SVP, by contrast, was very active and, in fact, dominated the campaign. Its professionally organized campaigning team leads a permanent electoral campaign, of which direct-democratic campaigns on issues related to immigration are an integral part (Kriesi 2005b: 268).

In the case of the naturalization initiative, the challenging organizations were much more numerous than the supporters. Basically, these organizations originate from two different backgrounds. The *left block* is composed of the usual suspects, that is, the Social Democratic Party, the Greens and the unions (Swiss Federation of Trade Unions, Unia, and Travail Suisse). In this campaign, they were supported by domain-specific organizations such as *Solidarité sans frontières*, FIMM, and Second@s plus. The Green Party was put in charge to coordinate the campaign activities of the left. The Social Democratic Party kept a rather low profile in this campaign, concentrating its efforts to combat a constitutional amendment on health care which was being submitted to a vote at the same time.

The second opponents' component coalition regrouped *moderate forces*. Since this block includes centrist parties (Evangelical Party and Green Liberals) as well as religious organizations (the Catholic Church and the Evangelical Church), it is not confined to the moderate right. Detailed analysis confirms that the ties between Liberals and the Christian Democrats were not as close as one would initially expect (see Chapter 2). The Liberals primarily worked with the federal authorities (the Federal Ministry of Justice and Police and the Federal Office of Migration), while the Christian Democrats coalesced with the Green Liberals and the Evangelical Party, and to a lesser extend, with the religious groups. It is worth mentioning that the Federal Ministry of Justice and Police has been designated the most influential actor of the con side.

Among the organizations that were interviewed in the context of the naturalization initiative, only seven of them supported the proposition.

It is not surprising that the Swiss People's Party (SVP) is widely considered to be the most powerful actor. It was under its leadership that the proposal was launched and the campaign conducted. The SVP was backed by some conservative organizations which include Pikom, *Pro Liberate* and Security for All (Sifa, *Sicherheit für alle*). Most importantly, dissidents from moderate right parties formed a committee in favour of the initiative. Its members exclusively stemmed from the German-speaking part of Switzerland.

On the *economic dimension*, the campaign on corporate taxes corresponds to the expected opposition between the left and the right. On both sides, these blocks are divided into a core and a satellite, where the latter is internally less connected than it is to the core. The major forces closely worked together. As a consequence, the component coalitions are not structured along ideological lines. Figure 4.3 shows that the blocks of the right are quite homogeneous in terms of beliefs. This result confirms the 'natural alliances' hypothesis between right-wing organizations in the economic domain.

In the case of the corporate tax reform, the actors of both camps are divided in terms of power. The three major right-wing parties (CVP, FDP and SVP) as well as the most important economic interest group, *Economiesuisse*,

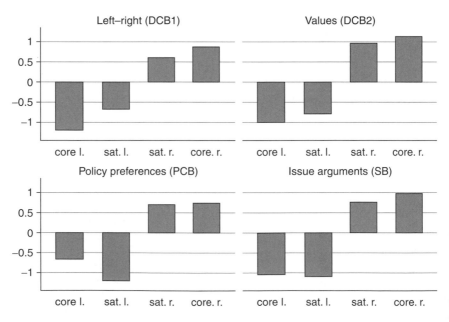

Figure 4.3 Beliefs in the corporate tax campaign by component coalition

a business association which represents the biggest Swiss companies, as well as the Federal Finance Department belong to the core component coalition (as opposed to the peripheral 'satellite' block). On the supporters' side, *Economiesuisse* performed the task of financing and coordinating the various campaign activities. It is therefore not surprising that *Economiesuisse* turned out to be the most powerful actor in this campaign. It closely collaborated with the main bourgeois parties (SVP, FDP, and CVP) as well as with the Federal Finance Department. The Christian Democrats were considered to be the most influential party on the pro side. This was because they took the lead on party-related matters. The satellite block of the supporters' side comprises some minor economic interest groups and parties (such as the association of small businesses and trade, the Swiss Farmers' Association and the Liberal Party).

The core block of the actors aligned on the opponents' side is primarily composed of the Social Democratic Party, the Greens, the Swiss Federation of Trade Unions, as well as Attac and the Berne Declaration, the two organizations of the global justice movement. Among the opponents of the corporate tax reform, the Social Democratic Party has been considered the most influential actor. This is not surprising, given the fact that the SP played a very active role in this campaign and, de facto, took the lead in the 'no' campaign. The satellite group, for its part, is composed of some minor parties (Evangelical Party, Christian Social Party), unions (*Travail Suisse*), citizens groups (AVIVO, Association for the Elderly, Displaced Persons, Widows and Orphans, a communist seniors' organization), and a French-speaking sub-satellite.

Conclusion

Coalition formation in direct-democratic campaigns follows a singular logic. In these campaigns, there is little room for bargaining, there are no designated leaders, and the number of potential coalition partners is large. We have argued that coalition formation is decisively shaped by the belief systems of the actors involved. The analysis of our three campaigns confirms the importance of this. In the two immigration campaigns, the binary logic of the vote forced the moderate right to join one of the two camps, despite all the substantive distinctions the actors wished to make.

The heterogeneity caused by the moderate right manifested itself in the formation of rather independent component coalitions, each of which was based on distinct sets of beliefs. The moderate right's coalitions with the conservative right (asylum law) and with the left (the naturalization initiative) followed a purely pragmatic logic. With respect to the economic domain, we showed that the prevailing coalition between the moderate right and the new populist right is based on shared beliefs. Consistent with our hypothesis, in this domain, coalition formation resulted in natural alliances.

Note

1. However, compared to pre-electoral coalitions, the issue specificity of the campaign may, given knowledge about the distribution of the issue-specific popular preferences, reduce the uncertainty of the outcome.

5
Construction of the Frames

Regula Hänggli, Laurent Bernhard, and Hanspeter Kriesi

In this chapter we look at how political actors craft their messages in terms of framing. Frames are 'central organizing ideas that provide coherence to a designated set of idea elements' (Ferree et al. 2002: 105). A frame is like 'a picture frame, it puts a border around something, distinguishing it from what is around it'; it is a 'spotlight' that attracts our attention to certain aspects of an issue, and directs it away from other aspects (Gamson 2004: 245). According to Entman's (1993: 52) influential definition, to frame is to selectively emphasize/evaluate certain aspects of a perceived reality and to make them more salient, 'in such a way as to promote a particular problem definition, causal interpretation, moral evaluation, and/or treatment recommendation for the item described'. In other words, to frame is to actively construct the meaning of the reality in question. For instance, in the case of capital punishment, the issue can be defined in terms of 'innocence frame' that accentuates imperfections in the justice system, or in terms of the 'morality-based frame' that focuses on the question whether it is right or wrong to kill when punishing (Dardis et al. 2008; Baumgartner et al. 2008). In strategic framing just as in any kind of strategic action, there are as Jasper (2006: 171) points out, 'few rules...but many choices'.

In order to win a campaign, we argue that political actors face three strategic choices (Hänggli and Kriesi 2009). First, they have to choose one or several substantive frames capable of steering the attention of the media and the public to their own cause and away from the cause of their opponents (Substantive Emphasis Choice). Second, political actors have to decide about the amount of attention they want to pay to the opponent's substantive frame(s) as compared to their own frames and whether they want to use their opponents' frames offensively or defensively (Oppositional Emphasis Choice). Third, political actors have to decide how much priority they want to give to their own substantive frame(s) as compared to the campaign contest (Contest Emphasis Choice). These three choices are by no means exhaustive. There are many choices, as indicated in Jasper's quote. However, we do suggest that all actors involved in strategic framing are implicitly or explicitly confronted with at least these three choices. Let us explain each one of them in more detail.

First, the strategic actors are expected to search for a frame they think has the capacity to become a *strong substantive frame*. We name this choice the Substantive Emphasis Choice. *A* strong frame is a frame that provokes a defensive reaction by the opponents (Koopmans 2004: 374) or that resonates in the media and in the citizen public. In Chong and Druckman's (2007a) experiments, the relative strength of a frame turned out to be the most important dimension of influence, in both one-sided and competitive conditions. This study was, however, concerned with the effects of frames on voters, not on the media. The relative strength of the frame is both issue specific and context specific and difficult to determine in general.

Chong and Druckman (2007b: 100) argue that we have little knowledge about what determines the strength of a frame. They suggest that it depends on two sets of factors: the credibility of its source and its congruence with central cultural themes. As far as the credibility of the source is concerned, the theory of *issue ownership* states that the advantage of certain actors on a given issue arises from the reputations they have developed for effective issue-specific policy making, which is created by the accumulated historical evidence of the actors' activities related to the issues in question. As Scammel (1999: 729) observes: 'Reputation, based on record and credible promises, is the only thing of substance that a party can promote to potential voters'. As far as the congruence with central cultural themes is concerned, Entman (2004: 14) maintains that the most inherently powerful frames are those 'fully congruent with schemas habitually used by most members of society', that ambiguous contested matters are more difficult to frame, and that frames which are incongruent with dominant schemas are blocked from spreading by common culture. Gamson (1992: 135) and Wolfsfeld (1997: 32) make similar points in discussing the concept of 'cultural resonance'. Frames that employ more culturally resonant terms have a greater potential for influence. Snow and Benford (1988: 210) refer to the concept of 'narrative fidelity'. Some frames, they write, 'resonate with cultural narrations, that is, with stories, myths, and folk tales that are part and parcel of one's cultural heritage'. Thus, cultural congruence, cultural resonance, or narrative fidelity increase a frame's appeal by making it appear natural and familiar.

Second, the political actors have to decide how much importance they attach to the opponents' frames compared to their own. This choice is labelled the Oppositional Emphasis Choice. According to a well-known piece of advice, political actors should focus on the issue or issue attributes where they enjoy an advantage. Riker's (1996) 'dominance principle' formulates this type of strategy: 'When one side has an advantage on an issue, the other side ignores it.' Issue-ownership theory (Petrocik 1996) suggests that political parties tend to follow this recipe, which means that they essentially talk past each other in political campaigns.

As a consequence, yes and no campaigners fighting against each other are expected to essentially rely on different frames. However, under some conditions, there are reasons to expect convergence or campaign dialogue (Kaplan, Park and Ridout 2006). *Issue familiarity* is expected to facilitate dialogue because the arguments are already known. This helps the political actors to anticipate the frames their opponents will campaign on, and therefore makes it easier to counterattack them. In contrast, *issue complexity* handicaps dialogue because the topic is more difficult. Political actors might first have to explain what the issue at stake is about and to build frame ownership before they can discuss the issue with each other. Furthermore, according to Kahn and Kenney (1999: 81–86), the *expected closeness* of a vote or an election increases campaign dialogue. They find that candidates involved in close races tackle the opponent's policy agenda and issue position more often than do those in noncompetitive races. Basinger and Lavine (2005) confirm this pattern. They explain the mechanism behind this result as follows: In more competitive campaigns, voters tend to rely on issues or ideological concerns more than on partisan cues in making their voting decisions. This tendency to rely more on issue voting increases the pressure on political actors to discuss the same frames. Neither political actor can allow her opponent to dominate the information flow, and thus will address the frames. In addition, a gap in financial resources between the two camps is expected to decrease campaign dialogue. Kaplan and Kenny (1999: 730) argue that the camps cannot talk about everything they might want to talk about. Having more money helps enables a campaign to address more aspects. Thus, if the difference in financial resources increases, the possibilities of engaging in dialogue become more unequal.

At the frame level, we hypothesize that the *salience* of the frame in the media increases frame dialogue. When a frame receives attention in the media it may become more important to the voters, too, and the political actors may be forced to take position on it. Thus, the political actors are expected to more often use an opponent's frame that becomes salient in the media.

If political actors refer to the frames of their opponents, they can do so either *offensively* or *defensively*. The offensive use of the opponents' frames corresponds to what Sides (2006) has called *'trespassing'*: political actors may use strong images, issues or issue attributes of their opponents in order to appear responsive to the general public. Sides also refers to this strategy as *'riding the wave'*, and shows in his analysis of the 1998 American presidential campaign that it is widely used. Even more widespread, however, may be the defensive use of the opponents' frames. Political actors may feel forced to react to the successful frames of their opponents and to adopt *counter frames* to offer rebuttals, and to counter-attack their adversaries. A full-fledged framing strategy of a political actor should not only mobilize her own constituency and the bystanders, but also try to 'neutralize and discredit the framing efforts of adversaries and rivals, keeping their potential supporters passive' (Gamson 2004: 250). We expect political actors to prefer their own substantive frames, and to rely on defensive strategies only to the extent that their opponents' framing is successful or that they anticipate their opponents framing to be successful.

Concerning the third choice, the political actors have to decide how much importance to attach to the campaign contest compared to the substantive content of the campaign. This is the Contest Emphasis Choice. In this respect, we propose to distinguish between two types of frames – *contest frames* and *substantive frames*.[1] The peculiarity of the former is that they do not address the issue(s) at stake, but focus on the actors involved or on the contest as such – on politics – while the latter focus on the substantive contents of the debate – on policy. Examples of the former include 'strategic frames' (analysing the rationale and strategy underlying the candidate's rhetoric and positions), 'horse race frames' (framing the campaign not as a contest of ideas or policy platforms, but as a race between two teams, each bent on getting more votes than the other), conflict frames (emphasizing conflict between individuals, groups, or institutions), or personalized frames (emphasizing personal characteristics of the actors involved or attacking another person). Contest frames are typically without content. Substantive frames, by contrast, are variable in scope, they can either be issue specific or transcend a single issue (Gamson et al. 1992: 385; Matthes 2007: 58). As is highlighted by Entman's definition, such substantive frames may refer to different aspects of an issue: the problem definition, the attribution of competence and responsibility, the evaluation of the situation, or the formulation of possible solutions.[2] In general, we expect that the political actors would like to get their substantive message across and put a high priority on their chosen substantive frame(s).

In addition, we investigate whether the use of contest frames is dependent on the *power* of the political actor. Numerous empirical studies have shown that the media mostly turn to powerful actors when writing their stories (e.g. Bonfadelli 2000; Gans 1979; Sigal 1973; Tresch 2009). The powerful actors benefit from an 'inherent' news value and get more access to the media. The weak political actors might use more contest frames as an attempt to compensate and attract more news value. They have a valence disadvantage (Groseclose 2001), that is, a disadvantage of non-policy factors such as incumbency, better name recognition, or maybe also as access to the political system. Groseclose examines a situation in which a candidate has a potential valence advantage. He shows that in an attempt to counter the valence advantage, a challenger will take relatively extreme policy positions (e.g. diverge from the median). The challenger does this because it minimizes the salience of the valence advantage (see Groseclose 2001: 864–865). Druckman, Kifer, and Parkin (2009) suggest that the model should be complemented. We support the idea of complementing the model and hypothesize that the weak political actors might emphasize conflicts or personal attacks in order to overcome valence disadvantage. This might especially be the case in direct-democratic campaigns because the choice is binary. The political actors cannot diverge from the median. However, they can resort to the contest frames.

Finally, the *extreme* actors might use more contest frames too. The idea behind this is the following: Extreme actors might pursue a different goal than moderate actors. The latter might pursue influencing the issue at stake or winning the next election. By contrast, extreme actors often do not have enough power to win a direct-democratic campaign or to win an election and must have another reason for their participation. They might aim at maintaining grassroots participation and limiting leadership control. Harmel and Janda called this goal the 'intraparty democracy' goal (1994: 275). We call it the 'grassroots participation' goal. Organizations which pursue this 'grassroots participation' goal seek to continue the activities after a direct-democratic campaign. This is an aim in itself. A direct-democratic campaign can help to reach this goal by strengthen the group identity. One way to strengthen this identity is to distinguish between ingroup and outgroup, and to denounce the others or to point out the conflicts. Thus, the extreme actors are expected to use more contest frames. In addition, members of extreme organizations are found to use a different style of political engagement (McClosky and Chong 1985). They are more likely to attribute personal failings to those who are far from their own political ideals. In other words, they are again expected to use more contest frames. We also control whether the right wing political actors or the governmental coalition use more contest frames.

Data and operationalization

For the present study, we rely on the content analysis of the input for earned media coverage ('input for media': press releases, speeches from media conferences or public statements). We believe that this type of data source is particularly well suited for our investigation because, contrary to biased media reports, they offer an accurate picture of the actors' framing intentions.

Frames constitute the unit of analysis. We operationalize substantive frames with the arguments which the two camps produced to support their own position or to undermine the position of their adversaries. The arguments mainly focus on the aspect of problem definition. While this procedure does not get at all the possible aspects of a frame, it at least deals with the most important one. Subsequently, we use the terms 'argument' and 'substantive frame' interchangeably. In each document – press release, newspaper article, TV news programme and so on – we coded *all* the arguments provided by/reported for each one of the relevant actors (organizations or their individual representatives) in our study in great detail and then summarized them in a limited number of abstract categories (=frames), which we created based on our reading of the controversy. For each side, the main frames are defined based on the relative frequency in the media input. The camp which uses a given frame most frequently is said to own the frame. Note that, for each argument, we introduce two different codes, which allows us to distinguish between the offensive and the defensive use of a frame. The use of a frame owned by the opponent is called 'offensive' if it is used approvingly, 'defensive', if it is rejected.

Let us illustrate the coding with one example, the abuse frame in the asylum case. The pro arguments (in favour of the new law) maintained that 'the abuse of asylum policy must be stopped', that 'there are already too many (bogus) asylum seekers in Switzerland', and that 'Switzerland is too attractive for asylum seekers'. By contrast, the corresponding contra arguments (against the new law) maintained that 'to prevent abuse is impossible', that 'the new law is not needed, since the number of asylum seekers is low/ declining', and that 'tightening the asylum law hits the false/ real refugees'. We summarized these (and additional) related arguments in a single frame, the abuse frame. Since the pro camp used the abuse frame most often in its media input, it is said to have owned this frame, and its use of this frame is defined as offensive use: the pro arguments of the abuse frame are the offensive arguments, while the corresponding contra arguments are the defensive arguments.

Contest frames consist of personal attacks and conflicts. A conflict refers to a dispute without a specific substantive content. For instance, a general statement of the type 'our organization rejects the accusation of our adversaries' is a conflict.

As far as the operationalization of the dialogical character of the campaign is concerned, we rely on two indicators for 'convergence'. On the one hand, we use the formula developed by Sigelmann & Buell (2004) to calculate *campaign-level* convergence (CI 1), which allows to compare frame convergence across campaigns:

$$100 - (\Sigma|P_{pf} - P_{cf}|/ 2),$$

where P_{pf} and P_{cf} refer to the relative frequencies with which the pro and contra camps use a given frame, f. Campaign-level convergence corresponds to the overall convergence summed over all frames. On the other hand, we determine the extent of *convergence at the level of individual frames (CI 2)*, for which we use the following measure proposed by Kaplan et al. (2006), where

P_{pf} and P_{cf} again represent the relative emphasis that the pro and contra camps put on a certain frame f:

$$(1 - |(P_{pf} - P_{cf})/(P_{pf} + P_{cf})|) * 100$$

The determinant factors of framing are operationalized as follows: *Issue familiarity and issue complexity* are based on the consideration of the voters as described in Chapter 2: The asylum law was the most familiar issue, and both the asylum law and the naturalization initiative were not very complex, while the corporate tax issue was very complex. The *expected closeness* of the outcome of the vote is operationalized by the expectations of the key campaigners at the outset of the campaign. In the naturalization campaign, 80 per cent of the campaigners expected a close race, compared to only 60 per cent in the case of the asylum law, and only 40 per cent in the case of the corporate tax. Moreover, also as indicated in Chapter 2, the corporate tax gave rise to the most *imbalanced* campaign; the one for the naturalization initiative also had a one-sided, but less imbalanced, character, while the asylum campaign was quite balanced. Furthermore, the *salience of the media frames* is measured by the relative frequency of a frame in the media output. Finally, we use the reputational measure for *power* that was introduced in the previous chapter, and we also distinguish between *extreme* and moderate actors based on the block-model analysis in the previous chapter: The two centre blocks of the asylum law and the corporate tax reform (the third force, centre-right, and satellite blocks), and the moderate block of the naturalization initiative constitute the moderate actors, while the more extreme blocks (left, populist right, or conservative right) include the extreme actors on the left and on the right. The latter are extreme in relative, not necessarily in absolute, terms.

We will use a rare event logistic regression (relogit) to investigate the determinants of the contest frames in particular. Relogit is used in the case of a binary dependent variable with many more zeros ('non-events', such as substantive frames) than ones ('events', such as contest frames) (King and Zeng 2001).

Results

In each campaign, we find one to two main frames for each camp. On average, the most important frame makes up roughly 40 per cent of the arguments in the case of the contra camp, whereas it accounts for about one-third of the arguments in the case of the pro camp. We also find that the campaigners mainly use their own frames, although there is more dialogue than one would have expected based on the literature.

In the case of the *asylum law*, each side used two main substantive frames. On the contra side, the *humanitarian tradition* frame was most often used.

This frame maintained that the new asylum law violated human dignity and human rights, endangered religious norms, and that it was contrary to the Swiss humanitarian tradition. The second important frame of the no camp can be labelled the *rule-of-law* frame. It maintained that that the provisions of the new law undermined the rule-of-law and violated international law (e.g. the Geneva Convention), that the principle of proportionality was violated by certain provisions of the new law, and that the risk of judicial errors would increase. On the pro side, the *abuse frame* constituted the key substantive frame. It argued that there were too many false asylum-seekers in the country, and that Switzerland needed instruments to fight the abuse of its asylum legislation. The second most important substantive frame on the pro side is a positive one that promises more efficient implementation of the asylum legislation. It does so generally, but also by pointing to specific improvements such as greater flexibility for the Swiss member-states (cantons), especially with respect to returning illegal asylum seekers to their home countries. We call this the *efficiency* frame. Both sides used additional frames, which we summarized under 'other frames' in Table 5.1.

In the case of the *naturalization initiative*, our analysis identifies only one main frame for adversaries. In order to avoid arbitrary decisions, this *rule-of-law* frame asks for fair procedures that comply with basic rights. By contrast, the pro side conceived naturalizations as political acts and not as administrative ones. Therefore, it is not surprising that its key frame is concerned with the claim that people should have the final say (*people-final-say*). Aside from procedural aspects, the proponents adopted a rather xenophobic discourse. They stated that 'mass naturalizations' had to be stopped and also alluded to crimes that occurred during the campaign, especially those committed by recently naturalized persons.

Regarding the *corporate tax reform*, each side again used two main substantive frames. The adversaries of the corporate tax reform mainly focused on matters of *tax equity*. They argued that the tax cuts were an unfair privilege for the well off and went against the principle of fair taxation. They even pretended that the reform was unconstitutional. This line of reasoning mainly applied to a controversial provision that included a reduction in tax rates on dividends for shareholders disposing at least a 10 per cent stake in a corporation. To a lesser extent, the opponents warned that the reform would lead to a shortfall of several hundred million Swiss francs in both direct and indirect taxes. More specifically, a powerful argument was made that the old-age pension scheme would suffer. We decided to label these kinds of arguments as the *tax loss* frame.

The proponents of the new law framed the reform as a necessary promotion of small and medium enterprises (SMEs) which form the backbone of the Swiss economy. The *SME* frame dominated the yes campaign. It stated that these companies needed the benefit of a set of planned measures aimed at reducing financial and administrative burdens. The second most important frame of the pro side turned the public's attention to the reform's overriding

Table 5.1 Substantive and contest frames (percentage shares), and convergence levels of substantive frames: by campaign and camp

Campaign	Asylum law			Naturalization			Corporate tax		
	Con	Pro	C1	Con	Fro	C1	Con	Pro	C1
Substantive frames									
38.8 (Humanitarian tradition) / **49.0** (Rule-of-law) / **48.5** (Tax equity)	**38.8**	24.8	80.1	**49.0**	19.6	61.7	**48.5**	7.7	30.0
21.5 (Rule-of-law) / 21.9 (People-final-say) / 22.3 (Tax loss)	**21.5**	9.3	62.2	21.9	**39.3**	65.8	22.3	8.4	58.9
17.6 (Abuse) / 17.5 (People-final-say) / 5.6 (SME)	17.6	**26.9**	77.0	17.5	20.6	85.6	5.6	**38.4**	23.4
4.0 (Efficacy) / 5.0 (Mass naturalization) / 14.1 (Competitiveness)	4.0	**17.3**	36.1	5.0	7.5	87.9	14.1	27.3	63.6
13.9 (Others) / (Others) / 4.3 (Others)	13.9	16.1					4.3	11.3	
All substantive	95.9	94.3		93.2	87.9		94.8	93.1	
C2			69.9			69.3			41.5
Contest frames									
All contest	4.1	5.7		6.5	13.1		5.2	6.9	
Total	100	100		100	100		100	100	
N	726	335		675	107		462	594	

Frame labels by campaign:
- Asylum law: Humanitarian tradition, Rule-of-law, Abuse, Efficacy, Others
- Naturalization: Rule-of-law, People-final-say, Mass naturalization, Others
- Corporate tax: Tax equity, Tax loss, SME, Competitiveness, Others

Note: C1: Frame-level convergence, C2: campaign-level convergence.

importance for the Swiss economy. The *competitiveness* frame maintained that the new law would boost the economy by encouraging investments and the creation of jobs.

The dialogical character, that is, the degree of convergence, varies from one campaign to the other. The overall convergence levels (C1) are much higher for the immigration ballots (69.9 for the asylum law and 69.3 for the naturalization initiative) than for the campaign on corporate tax (41.5). These results provide strong evidence for our hypothesis: Thus, tax reform was the most complex issue, and it gave rise to a most one-sided campaign. In addition, the tax reform was thought to have the most predictable outcome. All these elements were expected to constrain the dialogical character of a campaign. By contrast, the asylum law was the most familiar issue, whereas the naturalization campaign was expected to be closest. Since the naturalization initiative was easy to understand, familiarity was less important in this case. Accordingly, the high convergence level we found for the naturalization campaign again confirms our expectations.

Turning to convergence (C2) at the frame level, we test for whether media frame salience increases dialogue. In the case of the asylum law, the most important frames of the two camps – the humanitarian-tradition frame and the abuse frame – turned out to be the most salient media frames (see Chapter 9), too. Both are characterized by a high level of frame-specific convergence. In the interviews, the campaigners from the contra camp reported that they felt obliged to counter the abuse frame because it was so prevalent in the public discussion. This provides strong support for our hypothesis. However, salience not always increases frame dialogue. In the naturalization and in the tax reform campaign, the political actors did not converge on the two most salient media frames. These contradictory results do not contribute much to clarify the reasons why campaigners ignore a frame or why they may feel compelled to counter a salient frame. The mechanisms involved might be associated with the familiarity of the issue, with timing or with other yet unknown factors which make a frame a strong frame (Chong and Druckman 2007c).

Table 5.2 provides a rather unequivocal answer to the question of whether the widespread use of the opponents' arguments is a sign of (offensive) trespassing or of (defensive) counter framing. With the exception of the humanitarian-tradition frame, the two camps almost always address the main frames of the contra side defensively. In the case of the asylum law, the pro camp made use of a double-edged argument by endorsing the concern advanced by their adversaries. In a first step, they pointed out that they were strongly in favour of Switzerland's humanitarian tradition. In a second step, they maintained that the revised law would strengthen this claim because it would help fight against abuse, thereby helping those asylum-seekers who really deserved protection. This clever counter-framing strategy found its expression in slogans that combined both aspects: fighting against abuse and maintaining the humanitarian tradition. This kind

Table 5.2 The offensive use of the adversaries' frames (= trespassing): percentage shares of all adversaries' frames used

Asylum law			Naturalization			Corporate tax		
	Con	Pro		Con	Pro		Con	Pro
Humanitarian tradition		18.1	Rule-of-law		0.0	Tax equity		0.0
Rule-of-law		0.0				Tax loss		0.0
Abuse	0.0		People final say	0.0		SME	0.0	
Efficacy	0.0		Mass naturalization	2.5		Competitiveness	0.0	

of message was intended to appeal to moderate voters and cross-pressured voters in order to assure victory.

Next, we look at whether political actors primarily used substantive or contest frames. As expected, contest frames, such as personal attacks and conflicts, are only rarely used by political actors in Swiss direct-democratic campaigns. As shown in Table 5.1, the proportion of the contest frames is somewhat higher in the naturalization and the tax reform campaigns, especially in the case of the pro camp in the naturalization initiative. This might be due to the fact that a former member of the Federal Council from the populist right-wing SVP, Christoph Blocher, was not re-elected but replaced by Eveline Widmer-Schlumpf, from the same party, on 12 December 2007. Since she accepted the vote, she was thrown out of the party, a small minority of Widmer-Schlumpf supporters split off from the party, and the controversy was hot and emotional. The naturalization initiative was the first vote where she was the responsible Federal Council member. We will have a more detailed view on this below. Before, we have a look at the influence factors of contest frames in general.

According to the regression model presented in Table 5.3, our hypothesis with regard to power is confirmed in the first campaign. In the case of the asylum law, the more powerful organizations use fewer contest frames. The opposite is true for the naturalization initiative, whereas in the tax reform the coefficient is not significant. As we already mentioned, the results in the last two campaigns may be influenced by special circumstances. We investigate this aspect later. Moreover, as Table 5.3 also shows, the political actors of the more extreme blocks use more contest frames than the political actors of the moderate blocks. This effect is significant in both immigration-issue campaigns and almost significant in the tax reform. Concerning the controls, no clear pattern can be observed based on the political left–right scale. Actors from the right tended to use more contest frames in the asylum law campaign, whereas in the tax reform they tended to use fewer contest frames. The governmental coalition tended to use more contest frames in

Table 5.3   Rare event logistic regression (relogit) explaining the use of the contest frames

	Asylum law			Naturalization			Tax reform		
	coeff.	Robust s.e.	p	coeff.	Robust s.e.	p	coeff.	Robust s.e.	p
Power	−0.031	0.009	0.001	0.021	0.007	0.006	0.007	0.006	0.287
Extreme	0.988	0.338	0.003	1.647	0.577	0.004	0.744	0.475	0.117
li -re	0.146	0.084	0.081	0.125	0.186	0.500	−0.276	0.157	0.079
Pro	0.159	0.420	0.705				1.408	0.827	0.089
Contra				1.881	1.224	0.124			
Constant	−3.215	0.430	0.000	−6.194	2.158	0.004	−3.067	0.459	0.000
	N = 1061			N = 782			N = 1056		

Table 5.4   Contest frames in the naturalization initiative: percentage shares by camp and actor type

Camp		Con					Pro	
Actor type	Authorities	Ad hoc committees	Parties	Economic interest groups	Citizens' interest groups	Parties	Ad hoc committees
Personal attacks	1.7	4.0	2.0	9.2	6.6	8.1	0.0
Conflicts	5.6	0.0	2.0	4.1	0.5	8.1	0.0
All contest frames	7.2	4.0	4.1	13.3	7.1	16.2	0.0
N	108	25	246	98	198	86	21
Power by actor type (mean)	41.1	18	8.9	8.3	5.0	80.0	18.0

the naturalization and the tax reform campaigns. Further analysis will be needed to show whether this tendency was caused by special circumstances or holds true more generally.

As we saw in Table 5.1, the share of contest frames is comparatively high in the case of the pro camp in the naturalization initiative. Table 5.4 gives a more detailed view on this aspect and shows the use the contest frames by the different actor types. We see that the most powerful actor types, that is, the authorities and the political parties of the pro camp, mainly campaigned with more conflict frames. It seems as if the dispute between Christoph Blocher, the SVP, and Eveline Widmer-Schlumpf caused the *quarrelling* actors to rely more on these frames. The former two actors belonged to the political parties of the pro camp, the latter to the authorities. Whereas the parties of the pro camp used both personal attacks and conflicts, the authorities mainly emphasized the conflict and abstained from attacking personally.

In the tax reform, the political parties of the pro camp also used more contest frames than the other actor types. Since both campaigns took place soon after the non-re-election of Blocher, we presume that the involved actors used more contest frame than otherwise. This might have influenced the effect of power (Table 5.3) in the second and third campaign. However, in general we still can state that in Swiss direct-democratic campaigns, framing is primarily accomplished in substantive terms.

Conclusion

We can summarize our results along the three strategic choices of framing we have outlined in this chapter. With regard to the Substantive Emphasis Choice and the Oppositional Choices, we find that political actors tend to emphasize their own frames, but they do not exclusively revert to this behaviour. In addition, it has been shown that addressing the frames owned by the opponents is largely done defensively rather than offensively, that is, rather by means of counter framing than of trespassing. We have briefly explored a successful way of campaigning on the opposing side. A promising counter-framing strategy consists in endorsing the argument owned by the adversary and in framing it in a way that supports one's own point of view. We have established that convergence levels vary according to familiarity and complexity of the issue and the expected closeness of the run at the campaign level. With regard to the third choice, the Contest Emphasis Choice, we have shown that the political actors mainly focus on substance in direct-democratic campaigns, that is, they mainly rely on substantive framing. We found that actors with more extreme positions use more contest frames and that the dispute between Christoph Blocher, the SVP and Eveline Widmer-Schlumpf caused the quarrelling political actors to significantly rely more on contest frames in the naturalization campaign.

Notes

1. De Vreese (2005) makes a distinction between 'issue-specific' and 'generic' frames. This distinction suffers from the difficulty that it mixes up thematic and contest frames in both the generic and the issue-specific category. In addition, Chong and Druckman (2007c: 107) find it difficult to specify a frame as generic or general. We agree. However, we do not follow these authors when they suggest to call 'script' a 'feature in the communication such as a conflict' (p. 107). Finally, Entman (2004: 5f.) explores two classes of frames, substantive and procedural frames. Our distinction is similar, also in the meaning.
2. Framing devices, as opposed to frames, are condensing symbols that suggest the frame in short hand (Gamson and Modigliani 1989: 3). They include metaphors, illustrative examples (from which lessons are drawn), catch phrases, descriptions, and visual images (icons). What Iyengar (1991) calls 'episodic' frames could be called a framing device.

6
Message Delivery

Laurent Bernhard

Once political actors have selected the content of their campaign messages (see Chapter 5), they have to develop ways of conveying them to the citizens. Indeed, finding the right message does not suffice. It is obvious that voters will not be influenced by messages they have never heard. This chapter considers how political campaigners get their message across by focusing on three choices with respect to 'message delivery': targeting, the use of the appropriate communication channel, and timing. These decisions will be explained as functions of contextual and actor-related characteristics.

Targeting deals with the question of what segments of the population to focus on. As campaign resources are limited, and voters differ in their probability of supporting a given issue position, targeting specific groups is a means of effectively getting messages across. In this chapter, I argue that political actors in direct-democratic campaigns are primarily concerned with their own constituencies. Besides this *mobilizing strategy*, however, focusing on swing voters is of crucial importance, as winning over this category allows for the attainment of the ultimate goal of obtaining a majority of the votes. The decision to revert to this *chasing strategy* is expected to positively depend on the actors' campaign-specific abilities and motivations.

Delivering the campaign messages to citizens also involves the use of the appropriate communication channels. There are four different venues by which messages are transmitted to voters. As far as the media are concerned, *paid media* distinguishes itself from *earned media*. Whereas the former is related to advertising, the latter is linked to the production of newsworthy events. With respect to organizational venues, there is a direct as well as an indirect variant. The *direct organizational channel* involves the activities political actors establish in order to contact the citizens by means of their own channels, such as direct mail. In contrast, when using the *indirect channel*, political organizations rely on activists who serve as middlemen in the communication process. As will be elaborated in the theoretical part of this chapter, the availability of specific campaign resources (money, staff, and volunteers) are expected to predict the use of the various communication channels.

Finally, *timing* will be addressed. Political actors have to decide on when to start with their public-oriented campaign activities and on the points in time they want to intensify them. The second choice will not be considered here, since there is no variance in this regard. Depending on the commune of residence, Swiss citizens receive the voting material between three and five weeks before the vote takes place. Postal voting allows them to cast their votes immediately. Since more than 80 per cent of participating people make use of this option (Swiss Federal Chancellery 2006), most campaigners report that their activities peak about a month in front of the official ballot date. As for the first choice, I argue that the campaign start is structured by institutional aspects. In cases of *optional referenda* (see Chapter 2), I expect that the organizations which take part in the qualification phase will launch their campaign activities at an earlier stage. Among the campaigns under scrutiny, this concerns the opponents of both the asylum law and the corporate tax reform.

The empirical analysis is based on interviews which were conducted with campaign managers who had participated in the three campaigns. The results broadly confirm the theoretical arguments.

Theoretical considerations

Targeting

To make the best use of their limited resources, political actors have to devise an appropriate targeting strategy. Target groups can be defined according to political, socio-economic, or geographical criteria. From the perspective of a given political actor, the population can be classified into three segments: core voters, rival voters, and swing voters. Core voters are predisposed to be in favour of its position, while rival voters tend to be opposed. The issue-specific predispositions of swing voters are either ambiguous or non-existent. I will build on Rohrschneider's (2002) typology, in which focusing on the core supporters is called *mobilizing;* targeting the adversarial camp, *persuading;* and hunting swing voters, *chasing.* Political actors may engage in targeting since the costs of gaining support in these segments of the electorate vary considerably. Obviously, it is much more difficult and requires many more resources to win over swing voters than over the own constituency. In addition to shared beliefs, because of the mechanisms of 'likeability' (Sniderman 2000) and 'credibility' (Druckman 2001), voters of a given constituency are expected to be more receptive to the messages of their preferred organization. By contrast, focusing on rival voters very often turns out to be a waste of time. Worse, persuading strategies even entail the risk that the opponents may benefit from one's own mobilization efforts, since rival voters are likely to support the other side (Cox 1999).

Following this line of reasoning, the model developed by Cox and McCubbins (1986) implies that, in majoritarian campaigns, political actors will primarily allocate their resources to their core voters. However, the counter model of Lindbeck and Weibull (1987)[1] asserts that they will spend most of their time, energy, and money to win over swing voters. In most instances, however, either targeting core voters or swing voters might not suffice to secure victory. In line with Gerber (1999), it can be argued that building a winning coalition consists of both mobilizing and chasing. In other words, campaigners will need to target core voters as well as swing voters.

Therefore, the first hypothesis states that both camps target their respective constituencies, that is, the supporters focus on the pro camp, and the opponents on the contra camp. The second hypothesis is derived from the fact that chasing is more expensive than mobilizing. I expect organizations to be more likely to focus on swing voters when they have the *ability* and the *motivation* to do so. More specifically, political actors should pursue a chasing strategy (a) the more *resources* they invest during the campaign, (b) the more *powerful* they are, and (c) the higher the *salience* they attach to a given ballot proposition.

Communication channel

The study of social movements has proven the usefulness of the action repertoire (Tilly 1978). Analogously, the *communication repertoire* is introduced in order to conceptualize the four channels that are used in campaign contexts (Kriesi et al. 2009). Political actors can reach out to the public via the *media* or their own *organizations*. As shown in Figure 6.1, there is a direct

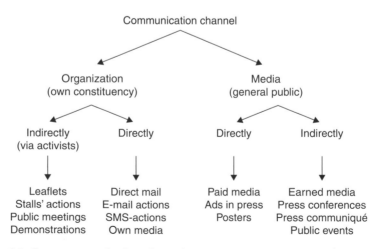

Figure 6.1   Four communication channels

and an indirect possibility in either case. With respect to their own organizational channels, political actors directly communicate with the members of their respective constituencies using direct mail, newsletters, or their own media products. Indirectly, the communication is transmitted to the public by external support, notably of activists (Moe 1980). For this reason, grassroots activities are particularly suited to this form of political communication. Alternatively, the campaigners have the possibility of reaching out to the public via the media. To directly establish contact to the public, they spend their money for ads in the media or for posters in the public sphere (*paid media* coverage). Note that political actors are not allowed to advertise on TV and radio in Switzerland. Indirectly, political actors try to get *earned media* coverage by producing newsworthy events. The organization of press conferences and the editing of news releases are among the most common forms in Swiss direct-democratic campaigns.

Since both camps face similar institutional and issue-specific incentives regarding the communication channel, there should be no contextual differences. Rather, the choice of the communication channels by political actors involved in direct-democratic campaigns is expected to crucially depend on the *type of resources* they rely on. As access to paid media is limited by financial resources, it seems obvious to expect a positive association between the amount of money available to an organization and the use of the direct media channel. Campaigners lacking funds may depend more on their own organizational channels. The choice of the type of organizational channel, in turn, is likely to depend on the kind of personnel an organization has at its disposal. Those organizations that are able to rely on volunteers are likely to privilege indirect organizational channels, enabling them to mobilize at the grassroots. In contrast, organizations that rely more on their own staff members will tend to make use of their direct organizational channels. Finally, earned media is considered a very attractive communication channel in all circumstances, as it entails considerably less cost than paid media. For this reason, all organizations should strive for newsworthiness in order to gain free publicity. As a consequence, I do not expect any systematic relationships between resource types and the use of this communication channel.

Timing

As far as *timing* is concerned, the analysis is restricted to the decision on when to launch the campaign. For *institutional reasons*, the organizations who take part in the qualification phase are expected to start earlier with their campaign activities. This hypothesis only applies to optional referenda, however. Contrary to initiatives, where it takes several years for a proposition to be submitted to the vote, the ballot on optional referenda takes place immediately after the challengers have collected 50,000 valid signatures. As a result, the opponents of the government, who collected the signatures, may choose not to interrupt their mobilization efforts after having qualified the referendum for the ballot, thereby opting for a *first-mover strategy*. I hypothesize that the organizations involved in the qualification stage distinguish themselves by an early campaign start in the cases of the asylum law and the corporate tax reform. This hypothesis stresses that direct-democratic campaigns do not take place in a vacuum. Rather, strategic decisions depend on the institutional setting in which political actors are embedded.

Data, operationalizations, and methods

This section outlines the construction of the indicators and methods used for the analysis. With respect to *targeting*, three separate dichotomous indicators are used. In the ex-ante interview, our research team asked the campaigners whether they intended to target (1) the pro side, (2) the independents, and (3) the contra side. For each item, they could answer with 'yes' or 'no'. The organizations addressing the public at large (threefold no answers) are considered to focus on all three categories.

Concerning the use of the *communication channels*, we submitted a list of activities to the respondents. At the end of the campaign, they were asked to mark all the activities they had used in the course of the campaign. The publication of newspaper ads and billboard posters are assigned to the direct media channel (paid media), while the participation in press conferences and the editing of press releases are activities related to the indirect media channel (earned media). Publishing campaign-related articles in the organization's own newsletters, direct mailings as well as e-mail and SMS activities are considered to belong to the direct organizational channel. Finally, the indirect organizational channel is composed of writing letters to the editor, participating in public assemblies and protest activities, distributing leaflets in the public and canvassing activities. For each of the four different communication channels I use a composite index for the set of activities an organization used in a given campaign context.

With regard to *timing*, our interview partners were asked to indicate the point in time when they started (or would start) with their campaign activities. Based on their answers, I calculated the time interval (in number of days) between the campaign start and the ballot day.

The analysis includes indicators for three types of resources: the number of volunteers, the staff (sum of workload) and the campaign budget (logarithm in Swiss francs). In addition, I account for the salience of the different ballot proposals (on scale of 0 to 3) for the organizations involved as well as for their power. This indicator for power corresponds to the reputational measure introduced in Chapter 4.

To test the hypotheses, a series of multiple regression analyses are performed. Probit models are used for the targeting indicators, ordered probit for the use of the four communication channels, and ordinary least squares (OLS) for the study of the campaign start.

Results

Targeting

According to Table 6.1, both camps targeted mainly their respective constituencies. To a lesser extent, they also tried to influence the swing voters, while largely abstaining from addressing the adversarial side. In other words, mobilizing is more frequent than chasing, which, in turn, is much more prevalent than persuading. This tendency also emerges from qualitative information our research team collected within the framework of the face-to-face interviews. For instance, in the case of the asylum law, Hans Fehr, a veteran campaigner and executive secretary of AUNS (Campaign for an Independent and Neutral Switzerland), an organization belonging to the conservative right, intended to focus on groups ready to be activated: supporters of the revised law and undecided citizens. Approaching 'do-gooders', he observed, is a desperate act. Multivariate analysis (not shown here) confirms that both the supporters and the opponents primarily focused on the part of the population that was well predisposed to their cause.

The most interesting results stem from the targeting of swing voters. The probit models presented in Table 6.2 reveal that there are no differences between the two opposing camps in this regard. Claiming the middle ground is, not surprisingly, the affair of both camps. As expected, the choice to revert to chasing strategies depends on considerations related to the organizations' abilities and motivations. In the case of the asylum law, the amount of the campaign budget exerts a positive effect on the probability of targeting swing voters. This result might be, among other things, a consequence of the opponents' strategy to adopt a so-called complementary strategy. The big and wealthy organizations targeted the public at large,

Table 6.1 The proportion of the interviewed organizations that report to focus on a given target group, by camp affiliation and campaign, in percentages

	Asylum law			Naturalization			Corporate tax		
	Pro	Swing	Con	Pro	Swing	Con	Pro	Swing	Con
Supporters	85.7	64.3	21.4	100.0	62.5	37.5	82.4	64.7	23.5
Opponents	18.8	62.5	81.3	20.0	76.0	100.0	7.7	76.9	76.9

Table 6.2   Probit models explaining the targeting of the swing voters; probit coefficients

	(1) Asylum	(2) Naturalization	(3) Corporate tax
Pro	0.395	−0.027	−0.255
	(0.662)	(1.280)	(1.075)
Budget (log)	0.380*	−0.631	0.073
	(0.166)	(0.462)	(0.168)
Staff	−0.058	6.300	−0.325
	(0.287)	(6.230)	(0.686)
Volunteers	0.000	−0.003	−0.005
	(0.001)	(0.008)	(0.006)
Salience	0.428	4.065*	0.855
	(0.359)	(1.816)	(1.035)
Power	0.034	0.186*	0.107*
	(0.018)	(0.090)	(0.053)
Intercept	−2.749*	−11.30*	−2.627
	(1.306)	(5.478)	(2.249)
N	45	32	30
pseudo R^2	0.316	0.728	0.326

Note: Standard errors in parentheses; * p<0.05.

while various minor organizations were encouraged to mobilize their own constituencies. With respect to the naturalization campaign, swing voters were more likely to be targeted the more powerful the organizations and the higher the perceived salience of this proposition. Finally, in the case of the corporate tax reform power also is positively associated with the probability of chasing strategies.

Communication channels

Next, I turn to the results pertaining to the communication channels. Because space here is limited, I do not show the regression tables. Consistent with the theoretical expectations, the ordered probit estimation for the use of the *direct media channel* (i.e. newspaper and billboard ads) is decisively shaped by monetary resources. The campaign budget has a significant positive effect on the choice of this channel throughout all the campaigns. In a nutshell, the campaign budget dictates whether funds can be spent on paid media. Furthermore, the number of volunteers exerts a negative effect on the use of the direct media channel in the case of the corporate tax reform. This result points to a trade-off between capital- and labour-intensive modes of campaigning. With respect to the use of the *indirect media channel* (earned media), the findings are unequivocal and in line with the hypothesis. None of the variables included in the three models is able to explain the efforts in getting free media attention. This lends support to the view according to which earned media attention is equally important to all collective actors.

Regarding the use of the *direct organizational channel*, the hypothesis that postulates a positive relationship between personnel in terms of staff members and the use of this channel is only confirmed for the campaign on the corporate tax reform. In the other two cases, the corresponding coefficients are not distinct from zero. This result might be attributable to the fact that the corporate tax reform concerns an economic issue, which means that economic interest groups have played a large role in this campaign. Economic interest groups, who are largely absent from campaigns on cultural issues, not only have more staff members than citizens' interest groups, but they also rely more heavily on direct organizational channels. The hypothesis that the number of volunteers has a positive impact on the use of the *indirect organizational channel* is only confirmed in the case of the vote on naturalizations. This finding is not surprising given that most organizations were short of funds in this campaign. To make up for this handicap, those political actors who were able to revert to volunteers mainly relied on the activities related to the indirect organizational channel. Additional factors are found to have significant effects on the use of such channels in the other two campaigns. In the asylum law campaign, indirect organizational channels have been used more frequently by organizations with larger budgets, and in the corporate tax campaign, the opponents and the organizations for which this vote was very salient used this kind of channel more frequently.

Timing

Table 6.3 shows, for supporters and opponents in each campaign, the average daily difference between their campaign start and the ballot date. In line with my institutional argument, opponents launched their campaigns much earlier than supporters in the contexts of the two optional referenda. Indeed, the differences are 60 days in the case of the asylum law and 40 days in the case of the corporate tax reform. As expected, the corresponding gaps increase when participation in the collection of signatures among opponents is taken into account. In the case of the naturalization initiative, we do not observe such a pattern, which is again in line with my hypothesis. The supporters even seem to have opted for a first-mover strategy. However, in this case, the difference between the two opposing sides is just 18 days. In the pro camp, the distance between the actors who took part in the 2004 qualification phase and those who did not is only one week. This contrasts

Table 6.3 Daily distance between the campaign start and the ballot date, by camp and participation to the qualification phase

	(1) Asylum	(2) Naturalization	(3) Corporate tax
Campaign type	Optional ref.	Initiative	Optional ref.
Supporters	102	74	95
Opponents	166	56	136
- Collection of signatures*	186	79	153
- No collection of signatures*	136	72	67
All organizations	146	60	113

Note: *Among opponents for optional referenda and among supporters for initiatives.

Table 6.4 Ordinary least squares (OLS) regression models explaining campaign start; unstandardized coefficients

	(1) Asylum	(2) Naturalization	(3) Corporate tax
Pro	−54.17 (28.40)		−0.80 (52.03)
Con		−15.28 (7.81)	
Signatures	62.24* (25.55)	5.38 (12.63)	17.53 (45.94)
Budget (log)	−1.49 (6.12)	1.87 (1.48)	−2.97 (6.36)
Staff	−0.03 (0.11)	−0.08 (0.11)	−0.21 (0.17)
Volunteers	−0.011 (0.014)	0.003 (0.046)	0.09 (0.18)
Salience	−31.57* (15.22)	−1.57 (4.75)	33.05 (32.02)
Power	−0.14 (0.63)	0.09 (0.30)	2.48* (1.18)
Global justice movements			346.30*** (49.31)
Intercept	223.5*** (43.31)	71.11*** (15.34)	−9.71 (73.02)
N	45	32	30
pseudo R^2	0.322	0.341	0.766

Note: Standard errors in parentheses; * $p < 0.05$, ** $p < 0.01$, *** $p < 0.001$.

with the two referendum campaigns where the within-camp differences are 50 and 85 days, respectively. Finally, the self-reported starting dates confirm that the campaign on naturalizations was much shorter than the other two. This was undoubtedly a result of the hype that surrounded the exclusion procedure of Eveline Widmer-Schlumpf from the Swiss Peoples' Party (see Chapter 2). On average, political actors started 60 days in front of the vote, while the corresponding points in time are 146 days for the asylum law, and 113 days for the corporate tax reform.

The regression models presented in Table 6.4 confirm the hypothesis with respect to timing for the two immigration campaigns: In the case of the asylum law, the organizations that participated in the collection of signatures started significantly earlier with their campaign activities than the supporters and the remaining opponents. In the case of the naturalization initiative, there are, as expected, no differences between the three actor types. The same result is found regarding the corporate tax reform, which contradicts the impression of the descriptive statistics. The surprising result is due to two outliers, Attac and the Berne Declaration. In order to provoke a debate on their core concern, international tax justice from a north–south perspective, these two organizations of the global justice movements decided to launch the campaign at a very early stage. Indeed, Attac reports to have begun 419 days before the vote took place; and the Berne Declaration, 360 days before.

Conclusion

This chapter focused on decisions related to 'message delivery'. I formulated a set of hypotheses of the various choices with respect to targeting, the use of the communication channel and timing. As far as targeting is concerned, it has been shown that campaigners of both sides primarily address their own public. In addition, they tend to focus on swing voters when they are able and willing to do so. With respect to the communication channels, the analysis rather lends support to the general hypothesis that specific types of resources affect the venue through which messages get aired. Money clearly favours the use of paid media. The number of volunteers and the availability of staff members were found to enhance the use of the direct and the indirect organizational channel in one out of three cases, respectively. Finally, the results regarding timing were consistent overall with our expectations in two out of three campaigns. The exception concerned the corporate tax reform. In contradiction to my hypothesis regarding optional referenda, the opponents did not launch their campaign significantly earlier than the supporters. Taken together, these results suggest that analysing strategic decisions requires taking into account both actor-related and contextual factors.

Note

1. Although these models were formulated in the context of election campaigns in a two-party system, their implications apply equally well to direct-democratic contests for the simple reason that they also follow a majoritarian logic.

7
Media Organizations in Direct-Democratic Campaigns

Patrick Rademacher, Matthias A. Gerth, and Gabriele Siegert

Media are a crucial actor in direct-democratic societies. In the political communication process, as we saw in Chapter 1 (see also Buchanan 2001), media basically transport political messages from political actors to citizens. Media thus serve democracy as an important and indispensable instrument. However, commercialization of the media, a shift from the dominance of journalistic values to the dominance of financial considerations, and a shift from citizen orientation to consumer orientation, puts in danger the democratic functions of the media.

In this chapter we want to examine whether market orientation – being conceived as one element of commercialization – can be examined for Swiss media organizations in the context of political campaigns. In a first step we discuss the democratic functions of the media, before we introduce in a second step market orientation as a challenge to these democratic principles. In a third step we focus on media organizations, and we develop indicators how market orientation could be observed and measured at this level. We then confront these indicators with data from our expert interviews with chief editors and business managers. In a fourth step a conclusion summarizes our findings and puts them into a larger context.

Democratic functions of the media

The media make an important contribution to the functioning of modern democratic societies. They convey political information, create publicity, criticize, and control (Gurevitch and Blumler 1990). Political actors need the media to communicate their messages and standing. From a normative point of view, media should offer this opportunity to as many different actors as possible to include all different arguments, positions, parties and candidates. Only this way of reporting political news allows citizens to make enlightened decisions and allows political actors to articulate their positions and to be accountable to citizens. Political knowledge and participation is 'the currency on which democracy operates' (Delli Carpini and Keeter

1994). Curran (2005: 120) summarizes the function of the media in a democratic society as follows: '[...] the media should keep people informed about public affairs so that individuals are adequately briefed when they take part in the process of self-government. The media should be fearless watchdogs, vigilantly examining the exercise of power and protecting the public from wrongdoing. The media should also provide a platform of open debate that facilitates the formation of public opinion. In addition, the media should be the voice of the people, representing to authority the citizenry's views and expressing the agreed aims of society. In short, the primary democratic tasks of the media are to inform, scrutinize, debate, and represent.'

These functions of the media correspond to theories on deliberative democracy (Chambers 2001; Cook 2005; Picard 2005). The quality of the formation of societal decision is closely related to the quality of public deliberation and thus to the quality of information provided by the media. We could thus speak of 'mediated deliberation' (Page 1996). However, we should not speak of 'the media' in general. Different media types and different formats can make different kinds of contribution to the functioning of democracy (Curran 2007). Citizens use different kinds of media outlets[1] to get political information, even if the news are combined with entertaining elements (what is often called infotainment). Hence, not only traditional ways of reporting can be referred to as good journalism; we need to include all kinds of political news formats (Curran 2007: 42).

Market orientation as a challenge to the democratic functions of the media

Traditional media pursue two central objectives: '(1) reporting on important events, people, and issues, particularly those involving governmental institutions and actors, in ways that are accurate and balanced, and (2) generating sufficient advertising and circulation revenue to make a profit regarded by the stock market or private owners as acceptable' (Entman 2005: 58). It is no question that only financially successful media organizations have sufficient resources to produce qualitatively appealing journalistic content. Challenges which could pose a problem for the media to fulfil their functions to serve democracy are derived from debates on the commercialization of the media. Commercialization means the dominance of economic principles in the media system and especially a strong influence by the advertising industry, in short: an increasing market orientation. The main causes of this development, are processes like deregulation, globalization, intense competition, media concentration, and convergence of media and information technology (Meier and Jarren 2001; Hamilton 2005; Picard 1998). This has obvious consequences for media production, employees, communication processes and the audience, and, more generally speaking, influences the cultural, economic and political environment (Saxer 1998). The consequences for public political communication are clearly demonstrated through positive media economics theories, in particular through those of goods systems and market failure (Kiefer 2005; Doyle 2002; Heinrich 2001; Picard 1998). The coverage about political campaigns is obviously affected by the fact that most media are market-driven organizations. If 'news that sells' (Hamilton 2004) or 'market-driven-journalism' (McManus 1994) is becoming the most important premise of journalistic production, the quality of coverage of political campaigns produced is different than if the primary concern is informing citizens.

Within a media organization, both the editorial side and the management side are equally important for defining the company-specific logic of news production, and in our particular case the way political campaigns are dealt with. Journalists represent the editorial positioning of a media outlet, whereas the management is mainly responsible for the resources of a media company. Both areas of responsibility of news production are in a multifaceted, recursive field of interaction with each other as well as with various external actors from advertising and PR (see further below) and the audience (McManus 1995). The relationship between editorial department and media management is in a constant area of conflict between journalistic professional standards and economic pursuit of profit (McManus 1994; Underwood 2001; Hamilton 2004; Zaller 1999). The effects of market orientation can be observed in analysing this relationship in detail. If the economic side becomes dominant, then journalistic values can get much less important. In case the management, due to economic calculations, decides to constrain the editorial budget, this could mean either to cut back the overall coverage or to cut back the investigation on every single story. As a consequence the appealing character of a story gets more important than its relevance. Like that one could explain the 'horse-race' style of covering election campaigns or the personalization and emotionalizing tendencies in covering political issues in general (e.g. Iyengar, Norpoth, and Hahn 2004). Thus, the function of the media to provide the audience with the information it needs to make enlightened voting decisions is put into question.

The consequences of an increasing market orientation as it can be observed from an outside and rather overall perspective can be summarized as (1) the media addressing the audience as consumers and not as citizens; (2) advertising-friendly production and high product affinity, that is, a tendency towards more consumer friendly and less critical editorial environments; and (3) dominance of cost competition over quality competition and the resulting media production under cost optimization conditions. These three consequences of commercialization are regarded as negative as they are in clear contradiction with the democratic society's expectations of the political function of the media as described above.

Market orientation in media organizations: an empirical examination

Editorial decisions are made with respect to the organizational structure of a media organization in general, the editorial department, and basic journalistic values. It is obvious that these values (see Bonfadelli et al. 2003; Entman 2005) differ between media types, political, and cultural contexts (cf. Weaver et al. 2007; Weischenberg, Scholl, and Malik 2006; Marr, Wyss, Blum, and Bonfadelli 2001). Electronic media, for example, have other constraints than printed media (space/time availability, regulation, dependence on a single or various revenue sources).

The dominance of economic principles within a media organization does not necessarily have negative consequences for its editorial department. The introduction of a controlling system for example could be seen, one the one hand, as a means to put the editorial department under pressure. On the other hand, such a system could be considered as a means of professionalizing the organization, which would have a positive effect on journalistic quality and output in the long run. Consequently, all indicators of market orientation should be first described neutrally and then be evaluated for its consequences. Perhaps some consequences of market orientation turn out to even foster the contribution of the media to the functioning of modern democratic societies. In the following we try to elaborate a sample of relevant indicators of market orientation that could be observed within media organizations:

- *Editorial positioning:* Media organizations try to attract as many consumers as possible for economic reasons. A media organization would, therefore, avoid displeasing users by taking a clear stand on political issues. Moreover, in order to avoid expensive journalistic investigations, it would closely model its news coverage on the coverage of competitors.
- *Audience:* Media organizations depend on the users of their media outlets in economic terms. They would, therefore, adjust their news coverage with regard to the expectations and wishes of their audience.
- *Financial resources:* First, covering a political campaign with its own journalistic investigation implies high costs for a media organization. A media organization would, therefore, try to keep these costs low. Second, as a large part of the financial resources available to a media organization stems from advertising, its editorial departments would provide advertising-friendly editorial environments.
- *Handling of Public Relations:* In a media organization, the chief editor and business managers are under great pressure to reduce costs. Thus, they would look for lower-cost content which for example is made available by PR.

In the following we will discuss these indicators in more detail and present corresponding results from our empirical study.[2]

Editorial positioning: taking a stand

The editorial positioning is done by the editorial department, following corporate guidelines. Thus, it is the editorial department where content decisions about how to cover a political campaign are made. The position of a media outlet on a political issue depends on many different influences. In addition to the corporate and editorial guidelines, the political orientation of each journalist covering an issue can play a role (Donsbach and Patterson 2004). Of course, taking a political stand does not mean completely partial coverage. One of the basic journalistic values is to clearly separate commenting and reporting. To report on a political campaign means to include the different positions in a neutral way and to give a voice to political actors from the yes camp and the no camp. The political position of a media outlet can be observed in the commenting line.

However, taking a stand can also have negative effects for a media organization. Media organizations need to attract as many users as possible for two reasons. First, if the media product has to be paid for, having more users means more direct revenue. Second, more users means higher advertising revenues. Taking a clear stand on a political issue implies the risk that a considerable number of users do not agree with the stand and thus dislike the coverage. A possible consequence would be that those users cease to use this media. Here, the size of the media market plays a decisive role for the behaviour of a media organization. In a large media market like the United States, a media outlet could take a clear stand and still find a considerable number of users who are in line with this stand (Bennett and Iyengar 2008: 723; Gentzkow and Shapiro 2006). In a rather small media market like Switzerland, clear political positioning could have the effect that a media outlet does not reach the critical mass of users to be economically successful. Consequently, a Swiss media outlet trying to maximize the number of its users tends not to take a stand on a political issue. Of course, this economic reason holds particularly true for privately owned media organizations. Another reason for not taking a stand is a rather legal one: Due to their mission, Public Service media seek to be neutral and balanced in covering political campaigns.

We wanted to know whether media outlets take a stand in political campaigns or not. We first asked chief editors (N=23) whether or not they usually take a stand in direct-democratic campaigns. The results show that slightly less than half of the chief editors always take a stand, about a fourth do so depending on the campaign issue, and another fourth never do. Free newspapers and the Public Service TV news never take a stand. We further asked the media professionals for each campaign whether they took a stand

and *how* they published it. Each time, the majority of the media professionals confirmed that they had taken a stand. But they differed with respect to
how they published their decisions: For each campaign, the most prominent
way was by writing comments/editorials about the campaign issues. These
comments are separated from the regular coverage. Less frequently, the
coverage was weighted according to the media's preference, or, the media
explicitly gave a voting recommendation.

We also asked those chief editors who had confirmed that they take a
stand at least sometimes (N=16), who was responsible for the decision (using
a five-point scale, 1 = no influence, 5 = high influence). They see themselves as the most influential actor in this respect (Means: 4.9), followed by
the editor of the section which is most relevant for the specific campaign
issue (M=4.1). The actors in charge of the business and financial questions,
such as the executive board (M=1.0) and the financial head (M=1.0), but
also the publisher (M=2.0), do not have a significant influence on the
decision.[3]

To conclude, a clear majority of media outlets take a stand in political
campaigns. Only free newspapers and the Public Service TV media do not
take a stand at all. Public Service media have to be neutral and balanced in
their coverage and should not favour certain positions in political campaigns
because of their mission. In contrast, free newspapers unanimously chose
not to take a stand – a decision that could be due to economic reasons. The
media that take a stand generally separate their comments from the reports.
And apparently the managers in charge of business and financial questions
do not have any influence on the direction of the stand. Thus, apart from
free newspapers, we have no evidence of commercialized media organizations so far.

Editorial positioning: competitors

An important point of orientation for media organizations are competitors.
A journalist carefully follows the news selection and the way of reporting
of competing media outlets. Now, the Internet allows doing so throughout
the day, as most traditional media outlets have a website. Weekly newspapers (including Sunday newspapers) in particular have the possibility
to invest in extended investigations throughout at least one week and are,
therefore, often able to present scoop-stories which are then picked up by
other media outlets. Depending on the campaign issue, one or the other
media outlet is perceived as opinion leader not only by the audience, but
also by the journalists. We can distinguish here between opinion leaders,
followers and laggards (Jarren and Donges 2006: 187). As a consequence,
media organizations or news rooms as a whole, but also individual political
journalists mutually influence one another. In the literature this influence
has been discussed as 'inter-media-agenda-setting' (Weaver, McCombs, and
Shaw 2004).

This influence also has an economic dimension: Covering a political campaign, with journalists conducting their own investigation, implies investing costly resources for a media organization. In order to avoid expensive investigations, media organizations have two options: first they could base their coverage on information stemming from news agencies or from political PR. Second they could orient their news coverage on the coverage of competitors. Both options make a clear and independent editorial positioning impossible. We concentrate on competitors in this section.

We asked media professionals directly whether they orient their news coverage about the direct-democratic campaigns on other media (using a five-point scale, 1 = not at all, 5 = very strong). For the naturalization and the corporate tax campaigns (see Table 7.1), the media professionals unanimously seem to be convinced that their orientation towards other media was very low.

This result is not really surprising, as it would be embarrassing for a chief editor to admit that his editorial department took its cues from other media outlets. However, to get an answer to our question we chose an indirect approach: As discussed above, we assume that market-driven media organizations avoid doing their own journalistic investigations and instead orient their news coverage to the coverage of competitors in order to keep costs low. As a result, the news coverage of such market-driven media organizations should not have much of an impact on other media organizations. The opposite should also be true: Media organizations that invest considerable resources into the coverage of political campaigns can be considered as having an influence on other media organizations.

We asked all media professionals to rate the influence of the 50 most important media in Switzerland (print, TV and radio) using a six-point scale (1 = no influence, 6 = very strong influence). As it turns out, we did not find

Table 7.1 Orientation towards other media

	Corporate tax reform (n=21–22)		Naturalization initiative (n=20–21)	
	Means	SD	Means	SD
Pick up actors cited by other media	2.0	1.0	2.0	0.9
Pick up issues introduced by other media	1.7	0.7	2.0	0.9
Pick up journalist style used by other media	1.4	0.7	1.4	0.7
Adaptation of amount of coverage to other media	1.3	0.7	1.2	0.4

Note: 1 = not at all, 5 = very strong.

Table 7.2   Ten most influential media on other media

	Corporate tax reform (n=34–37)			Naturalization initiative (n=20–27)		
	Rank	Means	SD	Rank	Means	SD
Neue Zürcher Zeitung	1	5.6	0.8	2	4.4	1.1
Sonntagszeitung	2	5.5	0.8	10	4.0	1.1
NZZ am Sonntag	3	5.4	0.9	5	4.2	1.1
Tages-Anzeiger	4	5.3	0.9	4	4.2	1.0
Le Temps	5	5.3	0.9	3	4.4	0.9
Arena	6	5.0	1.0	1	4.9	1.2
10vor10	7	5.0	1.0	7	4.1	1.1
Weltwoche	8	4.9	1.0	9	4.0	1.0
Blick	9	4.9	1.0	8	4.1	1.2
SonntagsBlick	10	4.9	1.1			

Note: 1 = no influence, 6 = very strong influence.

any differences between the two campaigns (see Table 7.2). For both campaigns the media professionals saw the same media as most influential: the four dominant elite media (*Neue Zürcher Zeitung, NZZ am Sonntag, Le Temps, Sonntagszeitung*), the biggest German speaking regional newspaper with national radiation (*Tages-Anzeiger*), the biggest German language tabloid (*Blick*), the most important German language news magazine (*Weltwoche*), the late prime time German language Public Service TV news (*10vor10*), and the German language Public Service TV discussion show (*Arena*). At the other end of the scale, the media professionals unanimously rated all free newspapers as the media having the least influence on other media for both campaigns.[4]

In other words, some media from different media types (mainly elite newspapers, Public Service TV, and news magazines, but also tabloid newspapers) do influence other media with their coverage of political campaigns. This could be due to the fact that these media invest important resources in their news coverage, thus making them interesting as a point of reference for other media. By contrast, free newspapers do not have this influence. Their coverage of political campaigns apparently contains nothing of particular interest to other media. This does not automatically mean that free newspapers orient their coverage on competitors, but it provides further evidence that free newspapers are more market-driven than media outlets from the other media types.

The audience

As discussed above, media organizations try to attract as many users as possible because having more users leads to higher direct revenues and/or higher advertising revenues. In order to maximize the number of its users, a media organization is thus expected to adjust its news coverage with regard to the expectations and wishes of its audience.

As Bonfadelli and Marr (2007) show, the audience's taste is an important determinant of the work of journalists. Equally, it is one important determinant of the work of media managers. The audience is addressed in at least two different roles: as consumers and as citizens. As consumers, the audience is addressed either directly, as consumers of the media, or indirectly, as consumers of goods and services, aimed at by advertising messages. In the latter case, the media act as an advertising vehicle and attempt to address the relevant consumer values and attitudes of the audience. As citizens, the audience is addressed to be informed so as to be able to participate in democratic processes. In this case, the political value system and the political attitude of the audience are addressed. Moreover, the media either aim at a mass audience or at a specific, segmented target group. Segmentation is particularly important because the audience cannot be seen as one single homogeneous actor. The audience of the mass media is a heterogeneous group of individuals without an organizational structure and without elaborated goals or the same specific interests. This means that as many readers, listeners, users, or viewers as possible should be reached, or at least consumers who together can be seen as target groups in terms of advertising relevance.

We wanted to find out whether the audience, advertising customers, and the general editorial positioning have an influence for media organizations in taking a stand on the issue of a direct-democratic campaign (using a five-point scale, 1 = no orientation, 5 = strong orientation). This question, too, we could only ask those chief editors who had confirmed that they take a stand at least sometimes (N=16). Not surprisingly, the general editorial positioning serves as a very strong point of orientation (Means: 4.4). By contrast, advertising customers do not play any role in this context (M=1.3). Even tabloid newspapers (N=3) do not orient themselves towards advertising customers in this regard (M=1.7). The audience lies somewhere in between with a moderate average value (M=2.4). Taking a closer look at the different types of media, we find that the audience orientation of the news coverage heavily differs between the different types of media: The media professionals from the tabloids see the audience as very influential (M=4.0), whereas the media professionals from the other types (elite, regional, news magazines) do not share this point of view.

We also asked all media professionals (N=37) how media organizations learn about the expectations and wishes of the general audience (using a five-point scale, 1 = not at all important, 5 = very important). Their answers indicate that 'own occasional audience surveys' (M=3.9) are the most prominent method through which media organizations learn about their audience's expectations, followed by 'continuous audience surveys by an extern company' (M=3.7). 'Systematic analysis of letters or e-mails to the editor' (M=3.2), and 'one-to-one interviews with important readers' (M=3.1) are less important. When we have a closer look at how the professionals from the different types of media evaluate the different tools and methods, we find clear differences: Both free and tabloid newspapers make heavy use of surveys to get to know the audience better: Media professionals from free newspapers (N=7) and tabloids (N=5) have higher rates for 'continuous audience surveys by an extern company' (both M=4.6) and 'own occasional audience surveys' (both M=4.4) than the other media types.

To conclude, tabloid and free newspapers, especially, are eager to learn about the expectations of their audiences, and apparently are willing to spend a lot of money to get this information, as continuous audience surveys in particular are a rather costly tool. Once they know about their audience's expectations, they are also willing to use these as a point of orientation when covering political campaigns. These results give further evidence that free newspapers and also tabloid newspapers can be seen as the most market-driven media organizations.

Financial resources: resources invested in political campaigns

After establishing a certain budget for the editorial department, the media management has to decide to which issues it wants to attribute financial and human resources. This also includes the decisions about how political campaigns will be covered. A market-driven media organization is expected to avoid costly ways of covering a campaign.

We asked the editors-in-chief whether they had organized special events on the occasion of the direct-democratic campaigns. For the corporate tax campaign about one-third (N=22) confirm having conducted a survey about the campaign issue, and more than one-third have organized special debates (open or not to the public). For the naturalization campaign the editorial departments were a bit more active: More than half of the media (N=22) conducted surveys via the Internet or in the streets, some of which were representative surveys. And about half of them have also organized special debates (open or not to the public). This means, however, that even for the naturalization campaign the other half of the media professionals did not invest in any special campaign event. They did not invest many additional resources in the coverage of the campaigns either, as is shown by Table 7.3, apart from the fact that on the Sunday of the vote more journalists worked in the newsroom than on Sundays without a vote (using a five-point scale 1 = not at all, 5 = on a big scale).

Do these results mean that Swiss media organizations do not invest any resources in covering political campaigns, and is this because they are all market-driven? We do not think so. To understand the backdrop of these

Table 7.3 Resources invested in the coverage

	Corporate tax reform (n=21)		Naturalization initiative (n=19–22)	
	Means	SD	Means	SD
Journalists working Sunday of the vote	3.7	1.8	3.6	1.8
Called in journalists of other sections	2.5	1.4	2.1	1.5
Journalists made overtime	1.7	1.1	2.1	1.3
Engaged additional freelancers	1.1	0.2	1.2	0.8
Engaged additional journalists	1.1	0.2	1.0	0.0

Note: 1 = not at all, 5 = on a big scale.

findings, we have to look at the broader context, that is, the importance of political news coverage for Swiss media organizations in general. We asked the media professionals to evaluate how important the different news departments were in the overall editorial department budget (N=22) (using a five-point scale: 1 = not at all important, 5 = very important). The results show that 'domestic news' is by far the most important news department for Swiss media organizations (M=4.0), followed by 'sports' (M=3.6) and 'economy' (M=3.5). As domestic news also includes the coverage of political campaigns, political news coverage thus is very important for Swiss media organizations, and they spend important resources for it.

Our interpretation is that for Swiss media organizations, direct-democratic campaigns are no extraordinary events requiring specific resources, but are rather routine business. However, we can more find differences when we have a closer look at how the different media types evaluate the importance of 'domestic news': Both free newspapers and tabloid newspapers invest far fewer resources for this particular news department: Media professionals from free newspapers (M=3.6) and tabloid newspapers (M=3.5) have lower rates for 'domestic news' than the other media types. Once more, our findings give further evidence that both free newspapers and tabloid newspapers seem to be more market-driven than media outlets from the other media types.

Financial resources: advertising revenues

A large part of the financial resources available to media organizations derive from advertising. Another way to analyse how important direct-democratic campaigns are to media management in terms of financial resources is, therefore, to look at the amount of advertising made possible by political campaigns. The question is whether political campaigns are a source of advertising revenues for media organizations.

We have already noted that the media organizations do not really orient their news coverage and positioning towards advertising clients. In addition, we asked the financial heads about the share of the annual advertising revenues that was made up by general political advertising. Nearly all (N=10) answered that political advertising was responsible for a maximum of 10 per cent of revenues. We then asked specifically about the two campaigns.[5] The results are once more very clear: For both campaigns, almost all the financial heads indicated that political advertisement concerning the referendum campaign made up less than 10 per cent of all advertising revenues during the two months preceding the ballot. The potential of direct-democratic campaigns to generate revenues thus seems to be fairly limited, which supports the assumption that direct-democratic campaigns are not exceptional events, but matters of everyday routine to the media in Switzerland. Since the revenues that media organizations can realize in this context seem to be rather negligible, even for market-driven media organizations, the incentive to provide an advertising-friendly editorial environment is very low.

The relation between politicians and the media

To conclude, we would like to turn to the more general relationship between politicians and the media, and how the media see their role in covering political campaigns. On the one hand, it is assumed that this relationship has come down to an adaptation of political actions to the needs of the media, that is, that it has come to a 'mediatization of politics' (Kepplinger 2002; Mazzoleni and Schulz 1999). On the other hand, the media's dependence on political actors is evident. According to Bennett (2009, 1990), government and representatives of political institutions are crucially important for the media. Accordingly, market orientation thus leads to an extensive use of institutional sources instead of investment in careful and independent reporting. Market orientation, in this context, means a shrinking number of professional journalists and editors, and an expanding number of PR professionals producing ready-to-print (or broadcast) messages for the media. As Russ-Mohl (1994: 317) has put it: With high competitive pressure in a commercialized media system, there will always be the temptation for media managers to cut back on reporting and editing services, as the system of public relations continues to provide more and more free material prepared to suit the media.

The literature provides different designs for the relationship between political actors and the media. Some authors see PR as more or less dominating the media (Baerns 1979; McNair 2003); some see a mutual cooperation (Russ-Mohl 1994), and others do not see any domination of PR at all (Saffarnia 1993). Following the majority of current studies, we assume a pattern of reciprocal adaptation (Bentele, Liebert, and Seeling 1997; Kepplinger 2007; Cook 1998). If the relationship between editorial positioning and public relations is reciprocal, it does not necessarily have to be balanced. The extent to which the relationship is balanced depends on the campaign issue, on the editorial positioning of the respective media organization, on the media type, the journalism style, and the level of professionalism of the PR (Blumler and Gurevitch 2001). Finally, it also depends on the expectations of political actors and the way journalists deal with sources of political information. Every political journalist needs sources or facilitators for his or her investigations. Political actors not only deliver information, but also provide access to important places of action and prominent interview partners (Patterson 1998).

To analyse the interdependent relationship between politicians and political PR on the one hand, and the media on the other, we asked media actors in the context of both campaigns whether they have editorial guidelines describing how to deal with political PR, and if this was the case, what these guidelines said. We tried to trigger spontaneous reactions by asking an open question. We found clear evidence that most media organizations do have principles in their dealings with politicians and political PR, but that, in most cases, these principles are not codified in editorial manuals or journalistic codices. Most media actors described their relationship with politicians and political PR actors as 'interdependent'. Political actors are providers of exclusive information, and the media distribute this information to citizens. A business manager of one free newspaper comments: '[...] a news room, to a certain extent, plays the role of a goalkeeper. These PR people want to score goals, and journalists need to catch the balls. In the end, some are better in scoring, others are better in catching'. Only one single business manager spontaneously reacts completely negatively with respect to political PR: 'Yes, we have very strong guidelines [...]. This [PR] just doesn't take place [...].'

Most media actors spontaneously use the same words to describe the role of the media in covering political news: independence, balance, transparency, and critical distance. Not surprisingly, it is the representatives from Public Service TV who strongly underline that political news coverage needs to be balanced. One editor-in-chief comments: 'It is our formula for success to always include both sides, or sometimes even three or four different voices, in each and every political campaign.' Representatives from elite newspapers emphasize the importance of independence, the verification of information, and the use of not just a single source, but different sources. Representatives of tabloid newspapers focus on the interdependence of the relationship. One editor-in-chief describes it as a 'reciprocal business deal'.

Weekly print news magazines emphasize the importance of getting scooped stories from political actors. For representatives of regional and free newspapers, we cannot identify a homogeneous and media-type specific line of argumentation. However, they support the general picture drawn here.

Conclusion

In this chapter we argued that media are a crucial actor in democratic societies, and we introduced market orientation as a challenge to the democratic functions of the media. In the context of political campaigns we analysed the extent to which a market orientation exists among Swiss media organizations. Overall, our results show little evidence that Swiss media organizations are exclusively market-driven – market orientation does not prevail over journalistic values. Swiss media organizations spend important resources on the coverage of political news, and journalistic values seem to play an important role. Eventually, our results should be seen in connection with those from the content analysis to be presented in the next chapter, but the findings in this chapter already suggest that there is reason to be optimistic about the quality of the debate in Swiss direct-democratic campaigns. This conclusion is also supported by the fact that we did not find any significant differences between the two campaigns we examined here. Direct-democratic campaigns are a routine business for Swiss media organizations, dealt with on a high-quality level.

However, tabloid and free newspapers are significantly more market-driven than other types of media outlets. This result is important, because the free press especially has gained considerable importance in Switzerland recently. Our data do not allow predicting the future success of the different types of media, but we have no reason to believe that free newspapers will become the only source of information for most Swiss citizens in the long run and that quality papers may become the exception.

Notes

1. We use the term 'media outlet' as distinct from 'media organization'. One and the same media organization can produce various media outlets.
2. We conducted expert interviews with the chief editors and the financial heads of the most important media organizations for each campaign. Whereas the guideline-based expert interviews for the asylum law campaign were conducted as an explorative study, the structured surveys for both the naturalization and the corporate tax campaign were partly standardized. For more information see Chapter 3, 'Design of the Study'.
3. Of course, we have to keep in mind that the media professionals answering the question are themselves chief editors. Moreover, it is possible that the chief editor of a media outlet has been selected for his 'stands' and that he anticipates the reactions of the media managers in the stands he takes.

4. The contrast between the answers to the two questions above (media having influence on other media in general and influence of other media on their own media) shows that there could be something like a 'third media effect' among the media professionals, that is, the presumption that there are several powerful media having an influence on other media, but that the own media is immune to this influence.

5. This question was not asked to media professionals from Public Service TV as political advertising on TV is not allowed in Switzerland.

8

Coverage of the Campaigns in the Media

Matthias A. Gerth, Urs Dahinden, and Gabriele Siegert

Mass-media coverage is important for both citizens and political actors: Citizens use the media as their main source of information for opinion formation. 'Some minimal level of information facilitates the exercise of citizenship' (Bennett and Iyengar 2008: 717). Political actors aim at influencing the judgement and voting decisions of citizens, but most of them have very limited resources (e.g. financial resources) to get into contact with their target audience by their own organizational channels (e.g. party newsletters, etc.) or by paid media (e.g. political advertising). Thus, getting access to the editorial content of mass media by means of political public relations messages (earned media) is a crucial strategy to convey campaign messages to the citizens. The success of this strategy heavily depends on the way the media treat political public relations messages, and on the degree of professionalization of PR in political organizations.

The results presented in this chapter stem from our content analysis of the Swiss media during the three campaigns. We will present different types of results: those based on the articles in our sample of media outlets and campaign weeks, on the relevant campaign actors presented in the articles, and finally, on the number of arguments presented by the relevant actors. We compare or summarize the three campaigns. If possible, we include TV and printed media outlets in our presentation. However, for some analysis we concentrate on newspapers only.

We begin with a presentation of the intensity and the development of the three campaigns in the media, and then discuss the style of coverage and the actors covered by the media; we conclude with a short discussion of the arguments in the media coverage.

Intensity of the campaigns and their development in the news

The mass media still have their own logic of covering political processes (Altheide and Snow 1979; Meyer 2002) and do not just follow the strategies of political actors and public relations professionals (Mazzoleni 1987; Meyer 2002; Strömbäck 2008). From a normative and legal point of view, the media are institutionalized as organizations that are independent of political actors. Moreover, according to given journalistic norms, the media should provide citizens with diverse, non-manipulative information that helps them to form their own opinions (Graber 2001). But, as we discussed in the previous chapter, the media are also market-driven organizations with specific strategies and business models (e.g. free, tabloid, regional and elite press, and public TV). The market orientation challenges resource-intensive ways of covering politics. Formats like comments/editorials or extensive reportages may be replaced by emotionalized, personalized and provocative horse-race coverage, or by simple reprints of press releases of political-campaign actors. The process of increasing professionalization of political PR is often referred to as the 'Americanization' of political-campaign coverage in Europe (Hallin and Mancini 2004; Jarren and Donges 2006). To the extent that the media are market driven, we would expect them to cover familiar, emotional, and uncomplex campaign issues more prominently than unfamiliar and complex issues. Our data allow us at least a partial test of this hypothesis.

To get an idea of the intensity of the three campaigns in the media, we can simply compare the number of articles published during the campaigns. The asylum law and the naturalization campaigns were covered with similar intensity. Both campaign issues were familiar and controversial (see Chapter 2). They focused on the role of migrants and their integration into the Swiss society. By contrast, significantly fewer articles have been published in the context of the corporate tax campaign. As we already know, the corporate tax reform issue was rather unfamiliar and complex compared to the asylum topic. This result supports our hypothesis, and as we will see, it is also supported by various indicators about style of the coverage and, even more strikingly, by the types of actors presented in the campaign coverage. Still, the amount of coverage for the corporate tax campaign is relatively high and does not fall far short of the coverage of the two campaigns related to migration. We did not expect this complex issue to have such resonance in the media. Regional newspapers largely dominate the coverage, accounting for more than two-thirds of the overall coverage. In the case of the corporation tax, their domination was even more pronounced, with 74.3 per cent of all articles. This particularly strong attention to the corporation tax by the regional press may be explained by the fact that the corporate tax reform was a crucial issue for many small and medium-size companies, which are the most important employers in local and regional areas. This interpretation is supported by the fact, that even though the corporate tax was a national vote, regional newspapers published 20 per cent of all articles in their regional/local sections, that is, with a focus on the regional context and consequences of the vote (see Table 8.1), which is not more than in the asylum campaign (22 per cent), but more than in the naturalization

Table 8.1 Articles per section, context and focus of the coverage

Media type	Print elite			Print regional			Print tabloid			Print free			Print newsmagazine		
Campaign	AL	NI	CT	AL	NI	CT	AL	NI	CT	AL	NI	CT	AL	NI	CT
Politics National	66.2	57.7	43.7	34.4	35.2	26.0	47.1	71.4	38.5	0.0	88.1	85.7	–	42.9	00
Economy	0.0	0.0	12.6	0.0	0.0	1.3	2.0	0.0	15.4	0.0	0.0	7.1	–	0.0	80.0
Regional/Local	5.3	6.7	7.6	22.4	12.9	18.2	0.0	0.0	0.0	100.0**	4.8	0.0	–	0.0	0.0
Others*	28.5	35.7	36.1	43.3	51.9	54.5	51.0	28.6	46.2	0.0	7.2	7.1	–	57.1	20.0
N	207	119	193	646	550	642	51	39	49	63	14	42	–	5	7

Notes: AL = asylum law; NI = naturalization initiative; CT = corporate tax reform; * mainly letters to the editor and articles not published in an identifiable section; ** the sections are not easy to identify in free newspapers; therefore, we further detailed our codebook for the naturalization and the corporate tax campaign, but we can't compare the results here.

campaign (13 per cent). For the asylum law, we have to take into account that asylum seekers are accommodated in several 'centres' which are embedded in local communities. This is sometimes a very controversial and emotional situation, associated with fear, xenophobia, and strong reservations in local communities. For a regional newspaper, the asylum issue is a lot about the individual destinies of members of the local community, on the one hand, and asylum seekers, on the other hand.

To get a more accurate and comparable picture of the intensity of the campaigns, we need to take into account the variable number of issues of newspapers published and of the number of TV-news programmes broadcast during the different campaigns. This is important, because the campaigns took place at different times during the year, which means that we need to take into account general holidays and Christmas. We calculated the number of articles/programmes per issue/per TV news and shows for all different types of media (see Table 8.2). Again, we can see that the asylum law and the naturalization campaign triggered a significantly higher amount of coverage than the corporate tax campaign. In particular, both tables indicate that the tabloids and the free newspapers published significantly fewer articles for all three campaigns than the elite and regional press. This confirms that they are strongly market driven.

Figure 8.1 shows the development of the intensity of the campaign based on the number of arguments, aggregated for campaign weeks. In general, we get a coherent picture for all three campaigns, with only a few small differences. First, the campaigns – after being covered on a very low level for some weeks – really started only seven weeks (for the corporate tax) or six weeks (for the asylum law and the naturalization campaign) before the day of the vote. Second, we see that they reach their climax in the fourth and the third week before the vote. Finally, we see that the coverage of the debate in all three cases significantly drops to lower levels in the two weeks before the vote. This result corresponds with what has been found in previous research

Table 8.2 Average number of articles/reports per issue/programme

	Asylum law	Naturalization initiative	Corporate tax reform
Print elite	0.91	1.10	0.67
Print regional	0.74	0.91	0.80
Print tabloid	0.24	0.28	0.22
Print free	0.39	0.17	0.06
Print Newsmagazine	–	0.27	0.19
TV News	0.18	0.11	0.12
TV Show*	–	–	–

Note: *Normally there is only one TV-show per campaign topic; therefore, we don't include TV shows here.

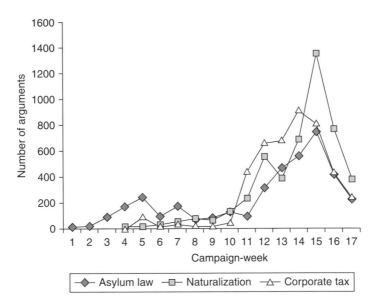

Figure 8.1   Intensity of the campaign coverage in the media

about referendum campaigns (e.g. De Vreese and Semetko 2004). In the Swiss case, the way the votes are organized is likely to reinforce the coverage pattern: thus, the majority of the citizens who cast their ballot vote by mail, that is, they send in a letter with their ballot some weeks before the official voting day.

There are two exceptions to this general picture. First, the media coverage of the asylum law campaign started three weeks before the naturalization and the corporate tax campaign. As described in Chapter 2, this is due to some political actors who presented their arguments 17 or 16 weeks before the day of the vote. Second, we see a small decline in the campaign intensity for the corporate tax campaign in week 13, but a striking climax, with 30 per cent of all arguments in only one week (week 15).

Style of the coverage

Primarily market-driven media are not expected to invest in commenting or in extensive factual reporting of direct-democratic campaigns. To save money, they can be expected to heavily rely on news agencies as sources for their coverage. Market orientation not only challenges resource-intensive ways of covering politics, but also jeopardizes balanced and objective coverage. Following recent literature on media-bias theory (Bennett and Iyengar 2008; Gentzkow and Shapiro 2006), we assume that market-oriented media rationally decide to provide content that is biased. If we think of the US television network FOX or the Swiss weekly news magazine *Weltwoche*, we see that in practice some media use politically biased journalistic profiles as a unique selling proposition and a means of distinguishing themselves from competitors (Bennett 2009; Bennett and Iyengar 2008; McNair 2003), while other media outlets need to address a very heterogeneous audience and therefore are expected to produce a more balanced coverage.

A first indicator of the journalistic style of the campaign coverage is the format of the coverage (see also De Vreese and Semetko 2004: 75). Our data (see Table 8.3) endorse some obvious characteristics of the different types of media. First, three formats dominate the coverage of direct-democratic campaigns – articles, letters to the editor, and short notices. The market-driven character of the free newspapers is revealed by the predominance of short notices in their coverage. It is, for example, no surprise that the amount of short notices is generally higher in free newspapers than in all other types. Weekly newsmagazines, in turn, do not cover political campaigns with short notices but with extended articles, editorials, interviews, and comments.

Second, comparing the three campaigns (details not shown here), we find that media generally dedicated more editorial space to the asylum law campaign than to the naturalization and the corporate tax campaigns. This supports our idea that familiar and uncomplex issues are more intensely covered. By contrast, the amount of letters to the editor, a content-format which is not produced but only edited by the newspapers, is much higher

Table 8.3 Journalistic formats for covering the campaigns (aggregated for all campaigns in % of articles)

	Print elite	Print regional	Print tabloid	Print free	Print news-magazine*	TV News	All media
Short notice	18.3	20.7	17.9	52.9	0.0	0.0	21.1
Article	35.2	25.9	31.6	33.3	41.6	71.4	29.1
Interview	10.2	6.0	18.7	5.1	16.6	7.1	7.5
Reportage	1.9	1.4	2.1	1.7	0.0	16.6	1.8
Comment, editorial	11.9	9.2	7.9	2.5	41.6	2.3	9.4
Letter to the editor	18.1	33.0	15.1	0.0	0.0	0.0	27.1
Voting recommendation	0.5	0.2	0.0	0.0	0.0	0.0	0.2
Others	3.6	3.3	6.4	4.2	0.0	2.3	3.6
N (articles)	519	1838	139	117	12	42	2667

Note: *Newsmagazines were only included in the naturalization and corporate tax campaign.

for the naturalization and the corporate tax campaigns. This result is most striking for regional newspapers, where 41.8 per cent of all articles in the unfamiliar and complex corporate tax campaign were letters to the editor, whereas in the asylum law campaign, the figure was only 24.5 per cent. Deviating from the general pattern, tabloid newspapers produced a high amount of comments/editorials in the corporate tax campaign (17.9 per cent of all articles).

For the naturalization and corporate tax campaign, we added a new format category – explicit voting recommendations. Some of the elite and regional newspapers explicitly told voters how they should vote, but tabloid and free newspapers as well as newsmagazines abstained from doing so. As we pointed out in Chapter 7, they usually do not take a stand. Whereas taking a political stand through commentaries, editorials, and voting recommendations is routine business for elite and regional newspapers, this does not belong to the repertoire of tabloid and free newspapers. The frequency of voting recommendations among the quality papers indicates that, despite the quasi-disappearance of the partisan press, we can still find a certain amount of press–party parallelism or partisan bias in Switzerland (Tresch 2009; Van Kempen 2007). The fact that tabloids and the free press do not provide recommendations, by contrast, is again in line with their market-driven character. Taking a stand and giving voting recommendations can, however, not only be seen as a transparent and consistent form of commentary, it can also be viewed as a violation of the journalistic principle of political independence (Curran 2005). From the point of view of democratic theory, it seems more important that, throughout the campaign, both the pro side and the contra side have access to the coverage.

Transparency about the sources of the coverage is another criterion for democratically desirable journalism. In our data, we can see a coherent picture throughout the three campaigns (see Table 8.4). Elite and regional

Table 8.4   Sources of coverage (print only; aggregated for all campaigns)

	Print elite	Print regional	Print tabloid	Print free	Print news-magazine*	All print media
Editorial contribution (journalist as a source)	81.5	84.6	84.9	29.4	100.0	81.6
News agency	11.6	10.9	0.0	33.6	0.0	11.5
No source	6.9	4.5	15.1	37.0	0.0	7.0
N (articles)	519	1838	139	119	12	2627

Note: *Newsmagazines were only included in the naturalization and corporate tax campaign.

newspapers almost always explicitly named the source of their articles, whether a journalist or a news agency. By contrast, the amount of articles with no explicit reference to the source is higher for tabloid (15.1 per cent) and free press (37.0 per cent).

To further assess the style of the campaign coverage for different types of media, we analysed the placement of the articles. The asylum law campaign created more front-page stories than the naturalization and corporate tax campaign, especially for elite and regional newspapers. Elite newspapers covered the asylum law campaign more prominently than the naturalization and corporate tax campaign. In this specific type of media, 40 per cent of all articles on the asylum law campaign were leading stories, either on the front page or another page, whereas this rate was significantly less for the naturalization (29.1 per cent) and corporate tax (24.4 per cent) campaign. For regional newspapers, the differences are a bit smaller. For the asylum law campaign, 30 per cent of the articles were lead stories; for the naturalization campaign, 20.9 per cent, and for the corporate tax, 21.8 per cent. We only found one front-page story in a free newspaper (naturalization campaign); all other articles were placed either as lead stories or regular articles inside the newspapers. As for newspapers, and in TV, too, the asylum law campaign was reported more prominently than the naturalization and corporate tax campaign. A total of 38.1 per cent of the reports in the asylum law campaign were headline stories, compared to only 30 per cent for naturalization; and 18.2 per cent for the corporate tax campaign.

It is no surprise at all that national political campaigns are mainly covered as an issue of national politics for all three campaigns and all types of media (see Table 8.1). Only the corporate tax campaign was partly covered as a specific economic issue, as the corresponding articles were published in the business section instead of the national-politics section of the newspapers (see Table 8.1). As we discussed earlier and as is shown by Table 8.1, regional newspapers cover regional aspects of the three national campaign topics, and 'break down' the national issue to the regional and local level.

Actors in the media coverage

We now turn to the presence of political actors (individuals, organizations, and parties) in the coverage of the three campaigns (for details on the political actors, see Chapter 2). Following many authors in the field, we can expect that high-level government representatives are the main source for political news coverage (Bennett 1990; Gans 1980; Tresch 2009). They have 'a bonus in the distribution of media attention' (Van Aelst, Maddens, Noppe, and Fiers 2008: 198). This also applies to Switzerland, where, as stated by Tresch (2009: 85), 'Swiss media mostly [...] largely reproduce existing hierarchies and structures of influence.' This reflects the media logic of selecting sources, what Bennett (1990) called 'indexing', which is nothing but 'a weighting system for what gets into the news' (Bennett,

Lawrence, and Livingston, 2007: 49). We, therefore, expect members of the government to be covered more prominently than other types of political actors.

Before analysing actors on an individual and aggregate level, we need to note that many articles did not contain arguments explicitly associated with individual or group actors. So the level of personalization was generally not very high. Thus, more than half of the arguments provided during the campaign were not associated with a particular member of the political elite, but were provided either by letter-to-the-editor writers or journalists. In the case of the asylum law, the share of arguments not directly associated with an individual political actor was as high as 72 per cent; for the other two campaigns, it was still above 50 per cent (55 and 54 per cent, respectively, for the naturalization and the corporate tax campaigns).

Table 8.4 gives an overview of the ten most cited individuals for each of the three campaigns. For all the three campaigns we can identify one dominant individual actor who, in every case, was the member of the national government in charge of the campaign issue: Christoph Blocher (Minister of Justice at the time of the asylum law campaign), Hans-Rudolf Merz (Minister of Finance), and Eveline Widmer-Schlumpf (Minister of Justice since 2008). Blocher's dominance is particularly important in the asylum case because he was not only the Minister in charge of the asylum policy but was at the same time a very charismatic and polarizing representative of the right-wing Swiss People's Party, which was the dominant party representing the pro camp during the campaign.

Representatives of the political establishment – members of government and of the Federal Parliament – generally dominate over representatives of the civil society. An exception in this respect is Markus Rauh, the main representative of the centre-right committee against the asylum law, an ad-hoc coalition opposing the asylum law, and former Federal Councillor Ruth Dreifuss (Social Democrats) also was a member of this coalition. Of all coded arguments, 5.5 per cent were associated with either Dreifuss or Rauh, which still falls far short of Blocher's share, who alone claimed 8.9 per cent of all arguments in the news coverage on the asylum law.

As the results of the naturalization campaign indicate, Blocher's charisma and polarizing speeches alone were not sufficient to make him the leading speaker of the entire campaign. He also relied on his position as the minister in the charge of the campaign. The naturalization issue was again important for the Swiss People's Party and its then vice-president Blocher. The party was by far the most prominent collective actor during this campaign (see Table 8.5). But Blocher was no longer a member of the government and, therefore, did not reach the same level of dominance as he had in the asylum law campaign.

What is true for the individual level of actors is also supported by the results at the aggregate level, as presented in Table 8.6. We have regrouped

Table 8.5 Most important individual actors of the campaigns (relative number of arguments raised by an individual actor) (in % of arguments)

	Asylum law*		Naturalization*		Corporate tax*	
1	Christoph Blocher (Federal Councillor and Minister of Justice at that time, Swiss People's Party)	8.9	Eveline Widmer-Schlumpf (Federal Councillor, new Minister of Justice, Swiss People's Party)	5.8	Hans-Rudolf Merz (Federal Councillor and Minister of Finance, Liberal Democrat)	6.8
2	Ruth Dreifuss (former Federal Councillor)	3.5	Christoph Blocher (Swiss People's Party, and former Minister of Justice)	4.4	Susanne Leutenegger-Oberholzer (National Councillor, Social Democrats, Basel-Land)	2.3
3	Markus Rauh (centre-right-committee against the asylum law)	2.0	Toni Brunner (National Councillor, and President of the Swiss People's Party, St. Gallen)	2.3	Robert Waldburger (expert, University of St. Gallen)	1.7
4	Karin Keller-Sutter (Cantonal Government Councillor, St. Gallen)	1.4	Kurt Fluri (National Councillor, Liberal Democrats Solothurn)	0.9	Gerold Bührer president economiesuisse)	1.5
5	Claude Ruey (National Councillor, Liberal Party, Vaud)	1.3	Giusep Nay (former chairman of the Swiss Federal Court SFC)	0.8	Peter Spuhler (National Councillor, Swiss People's Party, Thurgau)	1.3
6	Ueli Maurer (National Councillor, Swiss People's Party, Zurich)	1.2	Daniel Jositsch (National Councillor, Social Democrats, Zurich)	0.7	Simonetta Sommaruga (Councillor of States, Social Democrats, Bern)	1.3
7	Hans-Jürg Fehr (National Councillor, Social Democrats, Schaffhausen)	1.2	Christian Wasserfallen (National Councillor, Liberal Democrats, Bern)	0.7	Alain Berset (Councillor of States, Social Democrats, Fribourg)	1.2
8	Urs Hadorn (ex Federal Office for Refugees)	1.2	Adrian Amstutz (National Councillor, Swiss People's Party, Bern)	0.7	Christian Keuschnigg (expert, University of St. Gallen)	0.9

Continued

Table 8.5   Continued

	Asylum law*		Naturalization*		Corporate tax*	
9	Jürg Krummenacher (Caritas)	1.0	Guy Parmelin (National Councillor, Swiss People's Party, Vaud)	0.7	Hans-Jürg Fehr (National Councillor, president of the Social Democrats, Schaffhausen)	0.9
10	Eduard Gnesa (Federal Office for Migration)	0.9	Thomas Pfisterer (former Councillor of States, Liberal Democrats, Aargau)	0.6	Maximilian Reimann (Councillor of States, Swiss People's Party, Aargau)	0.9
	10 most important actors of the campaign in total (N = 3906 arguments)	22.5	10 most important actors of the campaign in total (N = 4774 arguments)	17.6	10 most important actors of the campaign in total (N = 4468 arguments)	18.8

Notes: *More than half of the arguments are either not associated with an individual actor, have been raised by writers of a letter to the editor, or by the journalists (asylum law: 71.99%; naturalization: 55.82%; corporate tax: 54.01%); in case a campaign actor was named but not quoted with an argument, he was counted once.

Table 8.6   Most important collective actors (excluding parties) (in % of arguments)

	Asylum law		Naturalization		Corporate tax	
1	National Council	11.9	National Council	12.7	National Council	9.7
2	Federal Council	10.3	Federal Council	8.6	Experts	6.6
3	Cantonal councils	6.5	Cantonal councils	1.8	Federal Council	5.7
4	Centre-right-committee (asylum)	3.9	Federal Dept of Justice and Police	1.7	Members of cantonal councils	4.4
5	Local Parliaments	2.7	Swiss Federal Court (SFC)	1.7	Council of States	4.1
6	Federal Dept. of Justice and Police	2.1	Council of States	1.7	Federal Department of Finance	3.5

Continued

Table 8.6 Continued

	Asylum law		Naturalization		Corporate tax	
7	Council of States	1.8	Local governments/ parliaments	1.1	Economiesuisse	2.5
8	Federal Office of Migration	1.5	Cantonal government councils	0.5	Local governments and parliaments	2.4
9	Centre-left committee (asylum)	1.5	Swiss Fed. of Trade Unions	0.5	Federation of small businesses/trades	2.2
10	Swiss Red Cross	1.4	Federal Office of Migration	0.4	Cantonal government councils	2.2
	10 most important collective actors (without parties) in total: 43.6 (arguments not associated with a specific collective actor: 41.14) (N = 3906 arguments)		**10 most important collective actors (without parties) in total: 30.7** (arguments not associated with a specific collective actor: 41.10) (N = 4774 arguments)		**10 most important collective actors (without parties) in total: 43.3** (arguments not associated with a specific collective actor: 22.81) (N = 4468 arguments)	

the individual actors by their institutional origin, irrespective of any party membership. In a second version, we aggregated the individual representatives by party membership (see Table 8.7). For all the three campaigns, the institution whose members are most frequently cited is the National Council. The Federal Council comes in a close second in the asylum and naturalization campaigns, and is in third place in the corporate tax campaign. In the latter campaign, experts come in second place. All other institutions, including the Second Chamber of the Federal Parliament – the Council of States – are less prominently represented in the campaigns.

The important presence of experts in the case of the corporate tax confirms the results found above and in Chapter 7: In the case of very complex and unfamiliar issues, experts apparently are important. The result further supports the assumption of De Vreese and Semetko (2004) that lower prominence of key representatives of the political elite goes hand in hand with a lower visibility of the campaign in the media.

Civil society actors did not get the same amount of attention in the media coverage as the members of the key political institutions did in any of the

Table 8.7   Ten most important collective actors of the campaigns (in % of arguments)

	Asylum law*		Naturalization*		Corporate tax*	
1	Social Democrats	8.4	Swiss People's Party	28.8	Social Democrats	16.7
2	Swiss People's Party	7.8	Liberal Democrats	7.6	Liberal Democrats	9.1
3	Federal Council (as a body)	7.7	Social Democrats	5.0	Christian Democrats	7.2
4	Liberal Democrats	6.8	Christian Democrats	4.7	Experts, Professors etc.	5.1
5	Christian Democrats	5.7	Federal Council (as a body)	3.6	Swiss People's Party	5.0
6	Centre-right-committee (asylum)	3.4	Green Party	2.5	Federal Council (as a body)	3.8
7	Cantonal parliaments/ governments	2.4	Liberal Party	2.0	Federal Department of Finance	2.4
8	Green Party	2.2	Swiss Federal Court	1.7	economiesuisse	1.9
9	Federal Dep. of Justice and Police	1.8	Evangelical Party	0.9	Green Party	1.8
10	Liberal Party	1.7	Green Liberals	0.7	Fed. of small businesses/trades	1.3
	10 most important collective actors in total: 47.8 (arguments not associated with a specific collective actor: 29.70) (N = 3906 arguments)		**10 most important collective actors in total: 57.3** (arguments not associated with a specific collective actor: 22.35) (N = 4774 argument)		**10 most important collective actors in total: 54.3** (arguments not associated with a specific collective actor: 13.47) (N = 4468 arguments)	

Note: *If an actor was quoted as a member of a political party and other collective actors (such as member of a Parliament chamber) at the same time, it was counted only once as a party-member.

campaigns. Apart from the experts in the corporate tax campaign, the only prominent actors composed of civil society actors is one of the ad-hoc committees in the asylum law campaign (the centre-right committee against the asylum law).

For all the campaigns, the four biggest political parties constituted the most prominent collective actors in the campaign, together with the Federal Council (as a body), and the experts (in the case of the corporate tax campaign) (Table 8.7). In two campaigns, the key opponents of the government – the Social Democrats in the case of the corporate tax, and, even more explicitly, the Swiss People's Party in the case of the naturalization initiative – achieved the greatest prominence. This confirms an earlier finding by Höglinger (2008), who showed that political parties are reinforced during direct-democratic campaigns in Switzerland. In the case of the asylum campaign, the attention to the four big parties was more equilibrated.

Arguments in the media coverage

Media-bias theory predicts that we should find a bias in the coverage of the arguments of the two opposing camps. But, based on Tresch's (2009) empirical findings that the direction of bias in the Swiss media varies – 'there is hardly any evidence that media decisions are biased toward parliamentarians of a particular partisan color' – we do not expect to find the media always favouring the same political camp.

Figure 8.2 and Table 8.8 allow for testing these arguments. Figure 8.2 shows that pro and contra arguments develop in a similar way across the three campaigns. Hence, in general, when the number of pro arguments increases, the number of contra arguments increases as well, and vice versa. However, asymmetries between the pro arguments and the contra arguments are found in all three cases. For the asylum and the naturalization campaign, the two more familiar and less complex campaign issues, the contra arguments got much more attention in the media than the pro arguments did. In both cases, the contra arguments were the

Table 8.8 Distribution of pro arguments and contra arguments* (in % of arguments)

Campaign	Asylum			Naturalization			Corporate tax		
Camp	Pro	Contra	n	Pro	Contra	n	Pro	Contra	n
Print elite	33.0	50.2	799	26.7	44.4	1029	41.3	36.1	670
Print regional	28.6	57.7	1898	27.5	45.2	2934	44.7	37.8	3156
Tabloid	20.5	58.9	120	22.3	33.7	193	44.2	43.2	197
Free	29.9	48.2	175	18.5	37.0	162	29.0	55.3	76
News magazine	–	–	–	14.7	61.8	34	39.1	41.3	46
TV news	20.2	41.1	76	26	46.9	96	43.6	41.0	39
TV show	38.7	60.5	246	52.2	45.7	326	45.5	46.9	222
Total	29.8	55.0	3906	28.4	44.5	4774	43.9	36.6	4406

Note: *Arguments that were either coded as neutral or could not be identified are not included in the table.

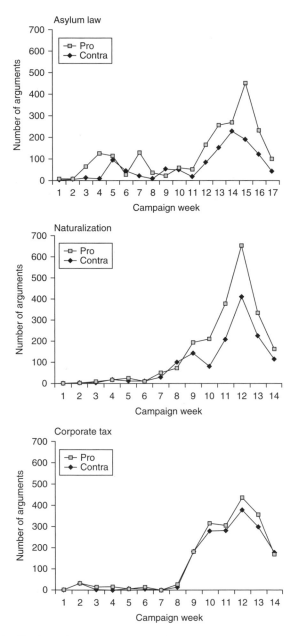

Figure 8.2   Distribution of pro arguments and contra arguments

arguments of the left. By contrast, in the corporate tax campaign, the asymmetry was less pronounced, and in this case, the pro side, that is, the centre-right coalition made up of the two components of the right, predominated. Even the findings for public TV news and shows confirm this result. It is normatively expected from public service media to deliver balanced and unbiased news, but this expectation does not seem to be fulfilled here.

Conclusion

We found consistent results for the timing of the coverage of the three campaigns. All three campaigns followed the same pattern with the climax of the media coverage occurring two to five weeks prior to the vote. The different character of the three campaign issues did not change this at all. So, with some reservation – we only analysed three campaigns – we can conclude that campaign coverage is a routine and ritualized business for the media. We found some evidence to support this conclusion in Chapter 7. The two familiar and uncomplex campaign issues were covered significantly more intensively than the complex and unfamiliar corporate tax. What also slightly differed was the style of coverage. In general, direct-democratic campaigns seem to be objects of national political news coverage. However, the corporate tax reform was also partly reported as an economic issue, and regional newspapers apparently tried to 'regionalize' the national campaigns by covering them in their regional and local sections. As shown in Chapter 7, the special role of tabloids and free newspapers is confirmed here as well. Free newspapers, in particular, but to some extent the tabloids as well, do not really invest in the coverage of direct-democratic campaigns, even though they offer some coverage.

Even though the campaigns did not seem to be highly personalized, there are some dominant individual and collective actors for each one of the campaigns and for all types of media. Media do give a platform to government representatives and to members of the Federal Parliament. In each case, the most important individual actor is the member of the federal government who is in charge of the campaign issue. By far the most important collective actors in the media coverage are still the four big political parties.

What the results presented in this chapter show is the rather high intensity, diversity and prominence of coverage, which produced a debate among media users, documented, for example, by the large number of letters to the editor that were published. We conclude that direct-democratic campaigns are important events for the Swiss media to cover. There was a bias in the presence of the pro camp and contra camp, which we shall analyse in more detail in the next chapter. Adding the results of the present chapter to the ones of Chapter 7, we conclude on a quite optimistic note about the quantity and variety of news coverage of direct-democratic campaigns. The media are still able to offer a respectable contribution to public debates in a direct democracy.

9
Key Factors in Frame Building
Regula Hänggli

In this chapter, we focus on the relationship between political actors and the mass media. We use media frames as dependent variables and investigate the processes that influence the creation or changes of frames applied by journalists (the frames in 'news media'). This has come to be known as 'frame building' (Scheufele 1999). These mechanisms have been largely neglected so far. This chapter first explores the ability of political actors to use their media input to influence media frames, and investigates whether the relationship between political actors and journalists is reciprocal or unidirectional. Based on the assumption that media input by political actors influences news media frames, the chapter then looks at the factors in more detail, with particular emphasis on the influence of power, the salience of frames in media input, and the multiplication effect of the minister (i.e. the Federal Councillor).

Who is the driving force?

As noted in Chapter 1, our general approach for conceptualizing the relationship between political actors and the mass media is an actor-oriented political process model as introduced by Wolfsfeld (1997). The relationship between the campaigners in the public debate and the mass media is one of mutual dependence, but significantly, as Gans (1979) stressed, this relationship is likely to be an asymmetrical one: 'Although it takes two to tango, either sources or journalists can lead, but more often than not, sources do the leading'. Wolfsfeld's key hypothesis (p. 3) makes the same point: The political process is likely to be the driving force in this relationship. The reasons he provides for this hypothesis are numerous, but, most importantly, he suggests that the mass media are much more likely to react to political events than to initiate them. Thus, *political actors* are expected to take the lead in the frame-building process. By framing the issue strategically, we argue (Hänggli and Kriesi 2010, Chapter 5) that political actors face at least three strategic choices. First, the strategic actors search for a strong substantive frame ('Substantive Emphasis Choice'). A strong frame is a frame that provokes a *defensive reaction by the opponents* (Koopmans 2004: 374) or that resonates in the media and in the citizen public. Second, political actors decide about how much attention they want to pay to the opponents' substantive frame(s) and if they use their opponents' frame(s) whether they want to trespass or counter-frame ('Oppositional Emphasis Choice'). Third, political actors decide about the amount of attention they want to give to the campaign contest ('Contest Emphasis Choice'). Journalists contribute to the debate by clarifying the opposing positions (which Bennett et al. 2004 call 'recognition') and by eliciting mutual reactions from the opposing political actors (which they call 'responsiveness'). With regard to the first choice (Substantive Emphasis Choice), we generally expect journalists to respect the lead taken by the political actors. With regard to the second and third choices involved in frame building (Oppositional Emphasis Choice and Contest Emphasis Choice) we expect that moderate market competition slightly increases the journalists' preferences for the offensive strategy and for contest frames.

Power of the political actor, salience of frames in media input, and the role of the minister

The impact of a promoted frame depends on the *power* of the political actors involved. Numerous studies have shown that media attention is biased toward more powerful actors (e.g., Gans 1979; Bennett 1990; Wolfsfeld 1997; Entman 2007). The reliance on powerful actors is expected not only to influence the attention an actor can garner, but to be also essential in the frame-building process too: More powerful political actors should have more influence in frame building. We call this the *power-bias* hypothesis. Swiss direct-democratic procedures have been shown to increase the media standing of actors who are notoriously weak, such as social movement organizations or the Swiss political parties (Höglinger 2008). However, while outsiders might gain more attention in the media because of direct-democratic instruments, we expect that their influence on frame building is still restricted.

Next, the *salience* of the frame(s) in the media input is crucial. This is in line with studies of agenda building which have confirmed that the salience of issues in the media input is positively related to the salience of issues in news media (Kiousis et al. 2006). The salience of the frames in the media input can be measured by the frequency with which they are mentioned in the media input of the political actor. The theoretical idea behind this factor is that journalists follow the political actors based on the professional norms in journalism. In Western democracies, neutral-informational professional journalism is dominant (Hallin and Mancini 2004). Based on this neutral-informational journalistic norm, the media should give an accurate account of important events, actors, and messages within the institutionalized arenas of the political system, and make the political process transparent for the citizen public. Journalists are expected to disseminate information as neutral chroniclers and impartial observers. This norm is in line with the mirror approach. The mirror approach conceives of the media as a mirror of political reality (e.g. Schulz 1976; McQuail 1992). Thus, the media are assumed to report the frames proportionally to the degree to which they are promoted. This can be measured by the frequency with which a frame is mentioned in the media input of the political actor. We call this the *salience* hypothesis.

In line with this argument, the messages of the *ministers*, or in general, of the most prominent institutional speaker of the debate, are expected to be met with higher response by the media than the messages of the other actors. We call this expectation the *multiplication* hypothesis. We refer to the members of the Federal Council as ministers. The Federal Council is the Swiss government, which has seven members. Federal Councillors are confronted with a double task: They are a member of the governing college, and they direct one of the seven federal ministries (Kriesi and Trechsel 2008). Based on the news values theory, the minister responsible for the proposition being submitted to a vote is expected to garner more media attention. Both, the prominence and prestige of a given actor are expected to increase the news value of a frame promoted by this actor (Galtung and Ruge 1965; Schulz 1976; Price and Tewksbury 1997).

As introduced in Chapter 2, there are two different direct-democratic instruments in Switzerland: initiatives and referendums. Both confront the voters with a binary choice – a choice either in favour (pro) or against (con) the issue-specific proposition at stake. However, we can distinguish the instruments according to the *source* of the proposition. Since, in the case of a referendum, the legislative act is worked out (sometimes over several years) and proposed by the government and its administration, the minister is expected to be more important in referendum campaigns than in initiative campaigns.

Before turning to the context, let me summarize the hypotheses. First, we expect that the political actors take the lead in the frame-building process. Second, the power-bias hypothesis states that powerful actors get easier access to the media with their frames than weak actors. Third, the salience of the frames in the media input is crucial for its frequency in the media output (salience hypothesis). Fourth, the minister's frames are multiplied most by the media, especially in the referendum campaigns (multiplication hypothesis).

Context: issue characteristics and external events

Concerning the issue characteristics, we expect *familiarity* and *complexity* to be crucial. When it comes to familiar issues, frame building may be less restricted to powerful actors because more political actors are familiar with the issues and have developed a clear stance. Possibly, the access is more open in the case of familiar issues. By contrast, the role of the minister is expected to be more important in complex issues. In complex issues, fewer actors are experts and have access to information, and it is more difficult to become an expert. The issue characteristic also influences the strength of a frame. In more complex issues, the frames are expected to become less strong. Complexity hinders the debate. In addition, the larger the number of main frames in a given camp, the lower the average strength of its frames is expected to be, because each individual frame has to compete for attention with the other frames of the same camp.

External events taking place during the campaign can be relevant with regard to frame building as well. Lawrence (2000) argues that high-profile media coverage of unplanned events provide a special opportunity for reframing. The same has been shown by Baumgartner et al. (2008), where unexpected and scandalous events in and around the death penalty debate in the United States have triggered a shift in the existing debate towards the innocence frame. Also, banalities such as summer or Christmas holidays structure the debate.

Data and operationalization

For the present analysis, we rely on the content analysis of all the campaign material produced by political actors for communication with the media – input for earned media coverage ('media input': press releases, speeches from media conferences, or public statements), as well as on a content analysis of the media's news reporting ('news media'). This material was coded with the same codebook on a daily basis. We also call the frames in the media input the 'promoted frames'.

As introduced in Chapter 5, we operationalize the substantive frames with the arguments the two camps have produced to support their own position or to undermine the position of their adversaries. For each side, the main frames are defined based on the relative frequency in the media input. The camp which uses a given frame most frequently is said to 'own the frame'. For each argument, we introduced two different codes, which allowed us to distinguish between the offensive and the defensive use of a frame. The use of a frame owned by the opponent is called 'offensive', if it is used approvingly; 'defensive', if it is rejected. *Contest frames* consist of personal attacks and conflicts. A conflict refers to a dispute without a specific substantive content. For instance, a general statement of the type 'our organisation rejects the accusation of our adversaries' is a conflict.

The strength of the frames is operationalized by the opponents' defensive reactions with respect to a given frame, that is, by the shares of the opponents' counterarguments, averaged over the promoted frames and the media frames. This means that trespassing (= offensive use of substantive frames) is not part of our measure of strength. We believe that trespassing is an attempt to 'steal' the opponent's frame by using the same argument and taking the same position. We consider that a frame which can be stolen is not a strong frame. Let us give an example of the calculations involved: In the asylum campaign, the pro camp counter-framed the humanitarian tradition frame of the contra camp with a share of 20.3 per cent of its media input, and attained a news media share of 12.6 per cent with its defensive use of this frame. The average of the two shares is 16.5 percent ((20.3 + 16.5)/2 = 16.5), which corresponds to our measure for the strength of this frame (see Tables 9.1 and 9.2).

We operationalize *power* by a reputational measure, as described in Chapter 4. The sum of daily power corresponds to the total amount of power of the actors' who promote a given camp on a certain day. For example, two actors of the pro camp hold a media conference together, while no other actor of their camp is active on this day. Actor A is a powerful actor who scores 86 on the power measure, whereas actor B reaches only a score of 18. Together, they arrive at 104 points, the sum of daily power of the pro camp. Alternatively, one could have used the mean or median of the power of the actors involved. The results hardly change, if we use these alternative operationalizations.

For the data analysis, we pursue a double strategy, and treat the campaign agenda both as an aggregate and a daily phenomenon. The purpose of such a double strategy is to find mutually reinforcing results. In the analysis of daily effects, we shall use a zero-inflated negative binominal regression model. Given that we are dealing with count data, the Poisson model is appropriate; but, given the over-dispersion found in our data, we use the negative binomial – a special version of the Poisson model that is adapted to this particular type of data.[1] When interpreting zero-inflated models, it is easy to be confused by the meaning of the effect parameters (the incidence-rate ratios). Such models have two parts – an inflation model and a count model. The inflation model estimates the effects (incidence-rate ratios) on the possibility that an argument does not make it into the media, that is, on the possibility of its absence from the media, whereas the count model estimates the effects (incidence-rate ratios) on the frequency of an argument's presence in the media. When the same independent variables are included in the equation for both models, the effects from the two models often point in opposite directions, that is, the one is smaller, the other larger, than one. This makes substantive sense: In the inflation model, a ratio smaller than one implies a high probability that the argument does make it into the media; correspondingly, in the count model, a ratio larger than one implies a strong presence in the media. In other words, the two models allow distinguishing between frame presence in the media, on the one hand, and frame frequency in the media, on the other hand. Accordingly, frame building can be conceived of as being composed of two processes – the daily frame *presence* (=non-absence) and the daily frame *frequency*. In a similar way, Tresch (2009) defines two dimensions of standing: presence and prominence. Since both, presence and frequency, are measured on a daily basis, we refer in this context to the daily frame presence and the daily frame frequency.

For the estimation of the model (Table 9.3), we use a stacked file, with five (four in the naturalization campaign) cases for each day, one for each of the main frame categories, plus one for the residual category. We shall introduce a dummy variable for each one of the main frames, in order to control for their variable salience. To control for contemporaneous correlations, we cluster the standard errors over time (=robust s.e.).[2] We also lag the dependent variable by one day to control for the autoregressive effect. Zero-inflated models may be very sensitive to the specification of the inflation model. It is therefore important to perform a sensitivity analysis. Most importantly, we will include the lagged effects of power, of the counts in the media input, and of the minister variable.

Results

The lead of the political actors

Figure 9.1 compares the percentage shares of the frames in the media input with the shares of the frames in the media's news reporting. There are two graphs for each campaign – one with the shares of the contra camp (on the left) and one with the shares of the pro camp (on the right). The overall impression is that, in general, the *news media* rather faithfully reproduce the framing by the two camps. Thus, the percentage shares of the frames in the news media are generally similar to the shares found in the media input. This result is strongly supported by more detailed analyses (not shown here; see Hänggli 2010): The framing by the political actors from both camps on the previous day significantly influences the framing by the news media in all three campaigns. The reverse does not apply: The framing by the media on the previous day has a decreasing or no effect on the framing by political actors on the following day. Thus, we feel comfortable in considering the political actors and their frames in the media input to be the driving force in the frame-building process. There are two instances (the abuse frame of the pro camp in the asylum campaign and the mass-naturalization frame of the pro camp in the naturalization campaign), where the news media

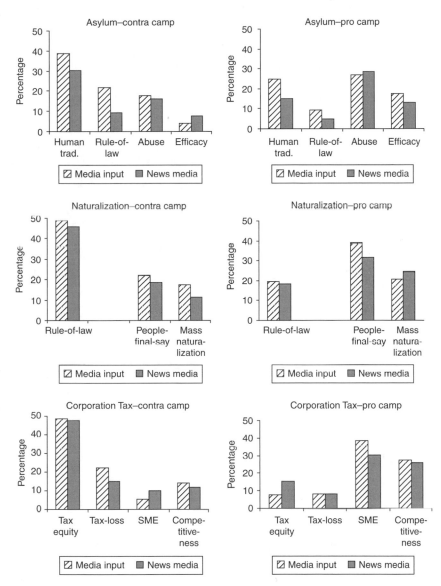

Figure 9.1 Comparison between the percentage shares of the frames in the media input and in the news media

increased the share of the *main* frames compared to the media input. This finding is probably due to the advertisements: In both cases, the pro camp was very active with advertisements and focused on the respective frames in the ads. Moreover, compared to media input, the media doubled the share

Table 9.1 Substantive (offensive and defensive use) and contest frames of the two camps in the media input and the news media, percentages

Asylum

Substantive	Frame	Media input Con	Media input Pro	News media Con	News media Pro
Offensive	Humanitarian traditional	38.7	4.5	30.2	2.5
	Rule-of-law	21.5	0.0	9.3	0.3
	Abuse	0.0	26.9	0.0	27.8
	Efficacy	0.0	17.3	0.0	12.8
	Others	13.9	16.1	23.8	22.1
	All offensive	74.1	64.8	63.4	65.6
Defensive	Humanitarian traditional	0.1	20.3	0.0	12.6
	Rule-of-law	0.4	9.3	0.0	4.5
	Abuse	17.6	0.0	16.2	0.5
	Efficacy	4.0	0.0	7.5	0.1
	Others	0.0	0.0	0.0	0.5
	All defensive	22.2	29.6	23.8	18.3
Contest		4.1	5.7	12.8	16.2
		100%	100%	100%	100%
n		726	335	1528	927

Naturalization

Substantive	Frame	Media input Con	Media input Pro	News media Con	News media Pro
Offensive	Rule-of-law	48.9	0.0	46.0	0.0
	People-final-say	0.0	39.3	0.1	31.5
	Mass naturalization	0.4	20.6	0.1	24.8
	Others	4.9	7.5	7.2	5.8
	All offensive	52.6	65.5	53.3	62.1
Defensive	Rule-of-law	0.2	19.6	0.0	18.5
	People-final-say	21.9	0.0	18.5	0.0
	Mass naturalization	17.0	0.0	11.1	0.0
	Others	0.2	0.0	0.0	0.0
	All defensive	40.6	19.6	29.6	18.5
Contest		6.5	13.1	17.0	19.0
		100%	100%	100%	100%
n		675	107	1176	733

Corporation Tax

Substantive	Frame	Media input Con	Media input Pro	News media Con	News media Pro
Offensive	Tax equity	48.5	0.0	47.8	0.3
	Tax loss	22.3	0.0	15.2	0.2
	SME	0.0	38.4	0.3	30.2
	Competitiveness	0.0	27.3	0.0	25.9
	Others	4.3	11.3	2.5	4.5
	All offensive	75.1	76.9	65.8	61.0
Defensive	Tax equity	0.0	7.7	0.0	15.0
	Tax loss	0.0	8.4	0.0	8.2
	SME	5.6	0.0	9.7	0.2
	Competitiveness	14.1	0.0	11.8	0.2
	Others	0.0	0.0	0.0	0.0
	All defensive	19.7	16.2	21.6	23.5
Contest		5.2	6.9	12.7	15.5
		100%	100%	100%	100%
n		462	594	943	1123

of the pro camp's tax equity counter-frame and also increased the share of the contra camps' efficacy and SME counter-frames. This finding reflects the media logic which favours dialogue.

Table 9.1 gives a more detailed overview of the frames in the media input and in the news media of the three campaigns. Compared to Figure 9.1, it adds the distinction between the offensive and defensive use of the frames, and also reports the residual category ('others') and the 'contest' frames. Compared to the media input, there are few additional differences in the media's news reporting. First, in the case of the asylum law the media framing is more diverse than the political actors' input, since the 'other' thematic frames account for roughly one-fourth of the media frames on either side, while they make up only one-seventh (contra camp) or one-fifth (pro camp) of the input material produced for the media. The use of this residual type of frame can be interpreted as a sign for of newspaper's independence from the government's position, since the most important quality paper of Switzerland – the Neue Zürcher Zeitung (NZZ) – contributed substantively to this category. In the other two campaigns the media made no special effort with their own or other frames. Thus, the media do not show more frame-building power in the case of the unfamiliar issue, the corporate tax reform. Second, as one might also have expected based on the American and British experience, the media, in their news reporting, more heavily rely on contest frames. But even in their case, substantive frames largely predominate. Thus, we can state that, in Swiss direct-democratic campaigns, framing is primarily done in substantive terms. Third, there is not much trespassing (i.e. offensive use of the opponent's frame) in the media, either. If opponents' frames are used, they are used defensively, which makes for the dialogical character of the campaigns, which we have observed in Chapter 5.

The strength of the frames is presented in Table 9.2. As this measure shows, in the asylum law campaign the main frame of the pro camp – the abuse frame – turns out to have been slightly stronger than the humanitarian tradition frame – the most important frame of the contra camp. The other frames of the two camps, that is, rule-of-law and efficacy, still provoked a defensive reaction in the opponent's camp, but to a much more limited extent. In the naturalization campaign, the rule-of-law frame proved to be slightly stronger than the people-final-say frame, which was the main frame of the pro camp. In this case it is also important to note that the core frame of the pro camp was stronger than its second main frame. This is an important finding because it indicates that the pro camp's strategic framing change was unsuccessful: As a matter of fact, in political advertisements, the pro camp changed its framing strategy (not shown). Instead of the 'people-final-say' frame, it increasingly relied on the 'mass naturalization' frame towards the end of the campaign, because the campaigners had received feedback from their activists indicating that the 'people final say' frame was not convincing. In addition, the pro camp had more funds available

Table 9.2 Strength of the frames

Asylum	Strength	Naturalization	Strength	Corporation Tax	Strength
Humanitarian tradition	16.5	Rule-of-law	19.1	Tax equity	11.4
Rule-of-law	6.9			Tax loss	8.3
Abuse	16.9	People-final-say	20.2	SME	7.7
Efficacy	5.8	Mass naturalization	14.1	Competitiveness	13.0

than its operators had originally planned. This allowed them to publish a significant number of political advertisements in the last three weeks of the campaign. They tested different arguments and decided to primarily promote the 'mass naturalization' frame. In the corporate tax reform, the competitiveness frame was the strongest frame despite that it was only the second most important frame of the pro camp. Surprisingly, the main frame of the pro camp, the SME frame, is found to be the weakest frame of the whole campaign. This may be because it remained without controversy during the debate. The second strongest frame was the core frame of the contra camp (tax equity), which more often came under attack in the media. Comparing the three cases, we generally see that the frames in the naturalization campaign were strongest, whereas the frames in the corporation tax reform campaign were weakest. This is in line with our hypotheses that both the number of frames used in a campaign and the complexity of the issue at stake reduce the strength of a frame.

Having established the predominance of substantive framing and shown the limited use of trespassing, we now focus exclusively on the substantive frames, that is, on the arguments, and combine the offensive and defensive use of the substantive frames.

Even though political actors take the lead in the frame-building process, the media also report on the campaign independently of explicit input from the two camps. The media have *established their own routines* for how to deal with direct-democratic campaigns. As is shown by the panels in Figure 9.2, which present the daily development of the media coverage of the two camps – without letters to the editor and only for the two main frames on each side, these routines imply a 'critical period' of press coverage towards the end of the campaign, when the citizens have received their voting material and do their voting (mainly by mail). For the asylum law and, to a lesser extent also for the tax reform, there is also a first, hot phase at the beginning when the Swiss media presents the basic issues of the campaign and the contrasting positions of the two camps. Furthermore, *external events* structure the debate, too. In the asylum law campaign, summer holidays brought a reduction of media coverage in the middle of the campaign (weeks 9–6). In the naturalization initiative, the first 100 days

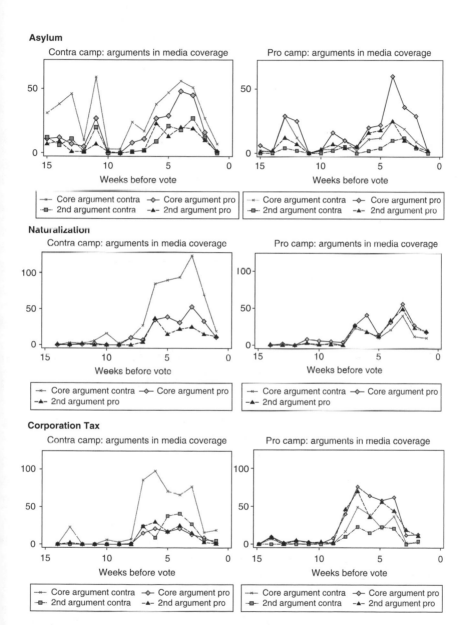

Figure 9.2 The development of the campaign on a weekly basis – by camp and campaign: absolute counts of substantive frames

of Eveline Widmer-Schlumpf's term in office as a minister clearly structured the campaign. Only when these first 100 days had past, in the eighth week before the vote, the campaign and media coverage about this issue really got started. In the case of the corporate tax reform, the campaign did not start until after Christmas break.

Power of the political actor, salience of the frames in the media input, and the role of the minister

Table 9.3 presents the regression results for the three campaigns. The media's framing constitutes the dependent variable. We use the daily power of the two sides for the explanation of their presence in the media in the inflation model (but not for frame frequency in the count model). In the count model, we use the numbers of arguments promoted in the media input and a dummy indicator for the presence of the minister for the explanation of frame frequency (for a discussion of model specification, see Hänggli 2011). As mentioned, a dummy variable for each one of the main frames controls for the variable salience. In both the count and the inflation models the lagged dependent variable (media (t-1)) controls for serial correlation. The corresponding ratios in the inflation model (presence) are consistently smaller than one, which means that the presence of a frame in the news media reduces the probability that it will be absent in the media on the following day. In other words, the media also report on the campaign independently of explicit input from the two camps. This confirms what is shown in Figure 9.2. All power ratios are smaller than one. This means that power reduces the probability that a frame is absent in the news media. In other words, the more power the actors presenting a given camp's arguments on a given day have, the higher the chance that the argument will be covered in the media on the next day. However, the corresponding ratios are not always significant. Thus, in the asylum law campaign, power has no significant impact on frame presence in the media. This result meets our expectation that, in familiar issues, access to the public debate is not as restricted to powerful actors as it is in less familiar cases. In the naturalization initiative, the power of the contra camp is highly relevant, while the power of the pro camp is not. There are two reasons for this difference: First of all, only two actors were involved on the pro side. One of them produced 75 per cent of all frames, which means that there is almost no variation in the power variable. In addition, the pro camp did promote only few arguments, i.e. 94 percent of the counts are zero counts because, for most of the days, no frame was promoted. The small number of cases reduces the significance. In the corporate tax reform, the effects of power are also somewhat limited: Powerful actors of the pro camp could not significantly increase the presence of their frames whereas, for the contra camp, power was significant at the.10-level only.

Table 9.3 Zero-inflated negative binomial regression on media framing; ratios, robust standard errors, and p-levels

| | Asylum | | | | Naturalization | | | | Corporation Tax | | |
	Ratio	Robust S.E.	p		Ratio	Robust S.E.	p		Ratio	Robust S.E.	p
Count model (frequency)				*Count model (frequency)*				*Count model (frequency)*			
Media (t-1)	1.019	0.018	0.294	Media (t-1)	1.008	0.013	0.528	Media (t-1)	1.007	0.008	0.380
Contra (t-1)	1.033	0.014	0.015	Contra (t-1)	1.032	0.006	0.000	Contra (t-1)	1.082	0.017	0.000
Pro (t-1)	1.010	0.097	0.916	Pro (t-1)	1.059	0.038	0.074	Pro (t-1)	1.059	0.025	0.015
Minister (t-1)	2.043	1.062	0.169	Minister (t-1)	3.038	0.747	0.005	Minister (t-1)	4.290	1.345	0.000
Humanitarian tradition	0.956	0.129	0.737	Rule-of-law	3.572	0.690	0.000	Tax equity	5.102	1.017	0.000
Rule-of-law	0.401	0.066	0.000	People-final-say	2.928	0.496	0.000	Tax oss	2.802	0.561	0.000
Abuse	0.931	0.114	0.563	Mass naturalization	2.421	0.412	0.000	SME	3.780	0.641	0.000
Efficacy	0.477	0.065	0.000					Competitiveness	3.875	0.596	0.000
Inflation model (presence)				*Inflation model (presence)*				*Inflation model (presence)*			
Media (t-1)	0.308	0.905	0.193	Media (t-1)	0.106	1.075	0.042	Media (t-1)	0.183	0.614	0.006
Power contra (t-1)	0.851	0.235	0.490	Power contra (t-1)	0.000	0.832	0.004	Power contra (t-1)	0.863	0.087	0.092
Power pro (t-1)	0.953	0.161	0.763	Power pro (t-1)	0.944	0.015	0.118	Power pro (t-1)	0.980	0.013	0.120
Constant	0.749	0.356	0.035	Constant	1.971	0.335	0.000	Constant	0.980	0.310	0.000

n total: 560, n zero obs.: 262
Vuong: z = 5.70, Pr > z = 0.000

n total: 364, n zero obs.: 203
Vuong: z = 6.14, Pr > z = 0.000

n total: 445, n zero obs.: 246
Vuong: z = 6.49, Pr > z = 0.000

It is surprising that the power of the actors of the pro camp was not more significant in this particular campaign, because the most powerful and resource-rich interest group, Economiesuisse, was the leading house of the pro committee and was heavily involved in this campaign. There are three reasons which may explain this unexpected finding. First, in this campaign, Economiesuisse was evaluated as the most powerful actor, the one that provided the money, pulled the strings, and led the campaign. Nevertheless, it preferred to stay in the background and turn the spotlight on the political parties with whom it had formed a coalition. Its influence on the media is, therefore, underestimated because it was mainly an indirect one, via its political-party allies. The model, however, does not account for indirect effects. If we re-estimate the model and try to take this indirect influence into account by assigning the power value of Economiesuisse to the allied political parties or by lumping Economiesuisse and its party allies together to form one single actor, the corresponding effect become significant at the 0.10 level. Second, Economiesuisse and the ad hoc pro committee were no longer proactive with press releases and press conferences during the last six weeks of the campaign. In this last phase, they had planned to concentrate on political advertisements. Moreover, with its three reactions to the press conferences of the Social Democrats, the ad hoc committee could not garner any attention.

Third, and maybe most importantly, the arguments of the Social Democrats – who were in charge of the contra committee during the campaign – resonated well with external events happening at the same time. The Social Democrats mainly argued that tax cuts were an unfair privilege for the well off and went against the principle of fair taxation (tax equity). They even pretended that the reform was unconstitutional. This line of reasoning mainly applied to a controversial provision that included a reduction in tax rates on dividends for shareholders with a stake in a corporation of at least 10 per cent. In the last phase, the Social Democrats presented the portraits of individuals who would profit from the reform in the press. By that time, the subprime crisis of the UBS had become a political issue: On 10 December 2007, UBS had already unveiled 11 billion Swiss francs of subprime write-downs and announced that it had obtained an emergency injection of capital from the Singapore sovereign fund and an unnamed Middle East investor. On 30 January 2008, in the middle of the campaign for the corporate tax reform, UBS announced it would write down another 4.4 billion Swiss francs in bad investments for the year 2007, and it would report a net loss of 12.5 billion Swiss francs in the fourth quarter of 2007. On 14 February 2008, UBS confirmed a net loss of 4.4 billion Swiss francs in 2007.[3] For many people, these losses at one of the two major Swiss banks were a strong contradiction to the very high bonuses some managers were compensated with. However, only towards the end of the campaign, on 14 February, did the Social Democrats make the explicit link to the UBS and its president of the board, Marcel Ospel, by claiming that very rich managers such as Mr. Ospel would primarily benefit from the corporate tax reform. These events possibly gave support to the tax equity frame and, at the end, may have convinced undecided voters and may help to explain why the vote unexpectedly (see Chapter 2) became so close.

Next, let us look at the upper part of Table 9.3, the count model (frequency). Overall, the lagged number of promoted frames and the lagged minister dummy significantly increase the daily frequency of the frame in the news media. The results are quite robust (not shown here). There is variation with regard to the specific campaigns. In the asylum law, the contra camp significantly influenced the daily frequency of the news media frames. The pro camp remained without influence. This makes sense for several reasons. First, the economic interest groups remained more or less uninvolved. Second, the centre parties, which belonged to the pro camp, led a half-hearted campaign and preferred to stay invisible, whereas the right-wing party was more active with political advertisements. Third, the pro camp was active indirectly through the responsible minister, who had been a member of the right-wing party. The minister officially wanted to keep a low-profile campaign. He refused, for instance, to participate in the most important TV debate on Swiss German television. The influence of the minister is probably underestimated in this campaign because he was very active unofficially. He gave several speeches at public meetings of the right-wing party. In the *naturalization* initiative, the number of frames promoted by the contra camp was important, whereas the promoted frames of the pro camp was significant at the .10-level only. The pro camp invested a lot of money in political advertisements and was less active with media input. Finally, the minister dummy is also significant. In the corporate tax reform, the number of promoted frames of both camps and the minister dummy significantly increase the frequency of the news media frames on the next day. The regression results support the salience hypothesis and the multi-plication hypothesis, which state that the number of promoted frames is crucial, and that the input by the minister is amplified by the news media. The results indicate that the minister plays a particularly important role in complex issues.

Conclusion

The direct-democratic campaigns in Switzerland are a contest of thematic framing, a clash of arguments which, in the final analysis, allows the voters to evaluate the merits of alternative ways of framing an issue. Just as is argued by Sniderman and Theriault (2004: 158), in real life politics, 'opposing camps campaign on behalf of competing ways of understanding what is at issue'. Our analysis confirms that the input of the political actors' plays a decisive role in Swiss direct-democratic campaigns. It is the political actors who introduce the most important frames into the public discourse.

With regard to the Substantive Emphasis Choice, we find that the political actors tended to emphasize their own frames and that their framing input was decisive for the media output. The media tended to respect frame ownership and reported accordingly. With regard to the Oppositional Emphasis Choice, we can summarize that while the political actors, indeed, predominantly focused on their own frames, they did not exclusively do so, but referred to their adversaries' frames as well. They did so mainly in a defensive way, however, relying more on counter-framing than on trespassing. The journalists reported on both camps, referring to their adversaries' frames too, and they attributed a slightly more offensive stance to both camps. Overall, the results clearly suggest that the main frames on either side were strong frames, since they both could not be ignored, but both elicited strong defensive reactions from the opponent's side in the media input and the news media. However, in two cases the framing strategies of the political actors were not fully successful. In the corporate tax reform, the core frame of the pro camp (SME) remained the weakest of all the main frames because it was without controversy during the debate. In addition, the pro camps' strategic change from the 'people-final-say' to the 'mass naturalization' frame in the naturalization initiative occurred too late to have an impact. With regard to the Contest Emphasis Choice, we observe that political actors mainly focus on substance, that is, they mainly rely on substantive framing. Substantive frames also dominated in the media. However, the journalists put more emphasis on conflicts than the political actors.

The results also support the salience, power-bias, and multiplication hypotheses. With regard to the daily frame *presence* (inflation model), the campaign-specific power of a political actor is important, whereas the number of promoted frames and the minister play an influential role for the daily frame *frequency* (count model). It can be shown that power was not important in the case of the familiar issue (asylum law), but further research is needed to determine the relative importance of power in complex issues. The minister's influence is highest in the case of the complex issue (corporate tax). Finally, external events can moderate the influence of frame building.

The question is what the results imply for the quality of direct-democratic debates and for the question of the manipulability of the outcome of direct-democratic votes. We find that the minister (=Federal Councillor) plays an important role. The Swiss political elites are somewhat uneasy with the authorities having this important role in direct-democratic campaigns (Kriesi 2009): According to an informal, traditional conception, the minister is expected to exercise his or her campaigning role with a certain restraint. Although the authorities are entitled to provide the voters with a balanced diet of information, they should leave opinion formation in the general public primarily to civil society, the social and political forces of the country. This low-key government approach is not confirmed in the present study. We find that the minister is very influential in the frame-building process in direct-democratic campaigns. The view that the government's task is to govern would be more adequate. In a direct-democratic campaign, this means that the government is responsible for the quality of the debate. The best way to guarantee the quality of direct-democratic campaigns is not to prevent the government from defending its position, but to guarantee that the competition of frames is not suppressed by the preponderance of any one actor during the campaign – be it the government or some actor from civil society.

The results give rise to optimism with regard to the question of the manipulability of the outcome. Even though the power of the political actors helps to be present with a frame, it does not help to dominate the framing of an issue. In addition, political actors supply three or four rival main frames with the respective counter frames, and all of them find their way into the media in all three campaigns. Thus, the voters can evaluate the merits of three or four alternative ways of framing an issue and there is no single dominant perspective. Finally, even though, in terms of financial resources, corporate tax reform campaign was the most one-sidedly dominated campaign of all the campaigns since the beginning of the 1980s, Economiesuisse (the leading house of the pro side in this campaign) was not able to dominate with its frame in the public debate, in spite of all its money.

Notes

1. Over-dispersion implies the presence of greater variability (statistical dispersion) in the predicted counts for a given value of the independent variable than would be expected based on the Poisson regression model. Stata provides a likelihood-ratio test for over-dispersion. In addition, because of the excess zeros in the data, also called zero inflation, a zero-inflated count model is necessary. Greene (2008) has proposed the Vuong (1989) test for non-nested models in order to decide whether a zero-inflated model is necessary. Zero-inflated count models assume that there are two latent (i.e. unobserved) groups: An Always Zero and a Not Always Zero group, and that zero counts are generated by two independently operating processes. In the first process (inflation model), the zeros belonging to the Always Zero group are generated. This process is binary, it generates zeros or ones. An argument in the zero group has an outcome of zero with a probability of one. If the first process results in a one, the second process is assumed to come into play: a negative binominal regression process (count model) which generates the probabilities for

the Not Always Zero group. An argument in this group might have a zero count, but there is a nonzero probability that it has a positive count.

2. This correction was designed for linear models, and it is not totally clear whether it works as well for this kind of model. However, the results are also robust without the clustering.

3. <http://www.drs4news.ch/www/de/drs4/themen/news/wirtschaft/die-ubs-im-strudel-der-finanzkrise/72270.64530.chronologie-der-ubs-finanzkrise.html>, 16.03.2009.

10
The Role of Predispositions

Hanspeter Kriesi

As pointed out in the introduction to this volume, Lazarsfeld, Berelson and Gaudet's (1968 [1944]: 74) *The People's Choice* has already pointed to significant campaign effects in that 'political campaigns are important primarily because they *activate* latent predispositions'. More recently, the idea that campaigns help voters make decisions that are in line with their pre-existing predispositions has been picked up by other scholars, who provide considerable evidence that activation effects actually do occur during the course of campaigns. According to the activation model, during the campaign the citizens' attention becomes more generally focused on politics and on the specific political issues highlighted, and the citizens learn a lot about the choices they have to make. How the context of the voters' choice influences the activation process is, however, still a very open question.

In addition, little attention has so far been paid to the question of how the activation process works in the presence of inconsistent predispositions. Policy choices are usually determined by many different predispositions, including values, other core beliefs, and affect towards the groups targeted by the policies. When these predispositions pull a voter in different directions, it creates ambivalence (Steenbergen and Brewer 2004: 95f.). In this case, the voter has some grounds to favour the policy and other grounds to oppose it. The relatively benign view of possible campaign effects implied by the activation model depends, among other things, on its neglect of the possibility that campaign operators might exploit the voters' ambivalence about policies.

In this chapter, we shall analyse the extent to which the three direct-democratic campaigns have activated pre-existing political predispositions, and how the activation process varies from one campaign to the other. In particular, we shall analyse the role of a very specific set of predispositions – the combination of partisan orientation, that is, of the voters' general ideological predisposition, with a basic issue-specific orientation, that is, with a predisposition linked to the substantive content of the specific choice at hand. In the case of direct-democratic campaigns, where voters decide on policy-specific propositions, not parties or candidates, the relationship between partisan orientations and voting choices does not carry the flavour of tautology that is potentially inherent in parliamentary and presidential elections. The direct-democratic campaigns are likely to activate the partisan predispositions and connect them to the available choice options. But campaigns as information-rich events are also likely to activate fundamental issue-specific predispositions which, for specific types of voters, may not necessarily coincide with their partisan orientations.

Theoretical considerations

Definition of campaign effects

Lazarsfeld et al. (1968 [1944]) had originally distinguished between three possible campaign effects – reinforcement, activation, and conversion, which we should clearly keep separate. The three effects can be defined on the basis of the inter-relationships of initial predispositions, initial vote intentions, and eventual vote choices. Assuming that there are three original vote intentions in a direct-democratic vote – pro, con, and undecided – and two final choices – pro and con, we can distinguish between six possible combinations. As displayed in Table 10.1, there are two versions for each one of Lazarsfeld et al.'s effects. We speak of *reinforcement* when the final vote corresponds to the original intention, irrespective of whether the original intention was consistent with the voter's predispositions. We speak of *conversion* when the final vote is inconsistent with the voter's predispositions, and the original intention was either consistent with the predispositions or the voter was still undecided. Conversely, *activation* consists in bringing about a vote that is consistent with the voter's predispositions, starting out either with an inconsistent or an undecided

Table 10.1 Definition of overall campaign effects

	Predisposition/	
Effect	Intention	Vote
Reinforcement	Consistent	Consistent
	Inconsistent	Inconsistent
Activation	Inconsistent	Consistent
	Undecided	Consistent
Conversion	Consistent	Inconsistent
	Undecided	Inconsistent

vote intention.[1] Note that activation has sometimes also meant to refer to other types of effects (Bartels 2006).

Context effects

The context characteristics we consider in this chapter are *issue familiarity* and *issue complexity.* In the case of familiar propositions, voters know by experience how the issues at stake are related to their – partisan or substantive – issue-specific predispositions. In such a case, where the connection with the choice at hand already exists at the outset of the campaign, its effects are likely to be comparatively weak and to take the form of reinforcing pre-existing predispositions. By contrast, in the case of unfamiliar propositions, voters may have a hard time connecting their underlying policy orientations to the specific proposals submitted to them in the campaign. The campaign then serves to establish a link between pre-existing predispositions and the choice at hand, that is, the campaign is likely to have strong activation and/or conversion effects. Which of these two effects predominates will depend above all on *issue complexity.* If an issue is only unfamiliar, but not complex, the original uncertainty about how to link predispositions to the choice at hand will be easy to overcome in the course of the campaign, and activation is likely to be the dominant effect. If, however, an issue is not only unfamiliar, but also complex, linking predispositions to the choice will be more difficult and many voters will end up making choices which are inconsistent with their predispositions. In other words, conversion is likely to be most important.

What does this mean in terms of our three cases? Table 10.2 formulates the corresponding expectations based on their familiarity and complexity. As discussed in Chapter 2 (Table 2.3), we operationalize familiarity with the share of undecided voters at the beginning of a campaign (the larger

Table 10.2   Expectations about overall campaign effects for the three campaigns

Criterion/strong effect	Asylum	Naturalization	Corporate tax
Criterion			
Familiarity	High	Low	Low
Undecided	14.3%	35.7%	28.7%
Complexity	Low	Low	High
With difficulties	38.0%	27.0%	61.1%
Relatively strong effect			
Reinforcement	x		
Activation		x	
Conversion			x

the share of undecided voters, the more unfamiliar the proposal submitted to the vote), and complexity with the share of voters who have had difficulties in making up their minds in the course of the campaign. Based on these criteria, we expect comparatively strong reinforcement effects for the asylum law, rather strong activation effects for the naturalization initiative, and relatively strong conversion effects for the corporate tax reform. The conversion effects in the case of the corporate tax reform are likely to be further reinforced by the imbalance of the campaign, which has been very much in favour of the pro camp in this particular case (see Chapter 2).

Predisposition-specific effects

In his analysis of the activation of *partisan orientations* in American presidential elections, Bartels (2006) finds 'remarkably little evidence of partisan activation in recent general election campaigns'. In Swiss direct-democratic campaigns, we expect to find stronger activation effects for partisan orientations. On the one hand, direct democracy puts considerable information demands on voters. On the other hand, as argued in Chapter 2, in the Swiss version of direct democracy, parties play a key role in providing information to the voters. This information comes both in the form of heuristic cues (voting recommendations) and in the form of substantive arguments for systematic, argument-based decision-making. Parties are relatively weak actors in the Swiss polity, but, as we pointed out in Chapter 2, their standing in the media is considerably enhanced during direct-democratic campaigns. During such campaigns, they get access to a public audience that far exceeds their usual reach. Accordingly, knowledge about partisan cues is likely to increase in the course of the campaign and this partisan knowledge will help the voters to connect their partisan orientations to the choice at hand. The activation of partisan orientations may come about not only because the adherents of the different parties blindly follow the recommendations of their respective parties, but also because they subscribe to the arguments favoured by the parties to whom they feel close. Given that most Swiss campaign committees hide behind anonymous acronyms, it is even possible that some voters are persuaded by certain arguments of the parties to whom they feel close without knowing by whom the arguments have been made (Kriesi 2005: 171). We expect partisan activation to operate across the board in all three campaigns, since partisan attachments provide a general ideological orientation, independently of the specific characteristics of the policy proposition submitted to the vote.

Additional guidance is provided by the set of relevant *issue-specific values and attitudes*. During a direct-democratic campaign, the voters are not only finding out about how the proposition at stake relates to their general ideological orientations, but they are also likely to learn more about how it relates to these substantive issue-specific values and attitudes (their policy-core beliefs), and about the choice that best serves to do them justice. We expect this kind of learning to be generally less widespread than partisan learning, and to depend more heavily on the issue characteristics. Partisan cues are more easily linked to the choice at hand than are issue-specific arguments, which are numerous and contradictory. This is especially the case for more unfamiliar and complex issues, such as the corporate tax reform, for which we expect issue-specific activation to be less prevalent than for the familiar and more straightforward immigration issues.

Undecided voters and political interest

In terms of *individual characteristics*, we generally expect greater activation and conversion effects for the originally *undecided* voters. This is partly a tautological expectation, since, by definition, the undecided cannot exhibit a reinforcement effect (see Table 10.1). However, when we control for this tautological effect, some of the undecided voters are also likely to have a relatively high 'sufficiency threshold', that is, they are likely to be relatively accuracy and validity minded (Eagly and Chaiken 1993), and to have a higher demand for information than the voters who already have a vote intention at the beginning of the campaign. This contributes to activation effects in particular.

In addition, the individuals' *political interest* (their political sophistication or awareness) is likely to play a key role for determining the campaign effects. As far as partisan cues are concerned, the use of party voting recommendations makes few demands on the individual's information-processing capacity, but using such recommendations is nevertheless a non-trivial task that presupposes contextual knowledge (e.g. about where to find such cues), as well as a minimum of motivation to make the effort of learning about the issue-specific positioning of the party to which one is attached. Accordingly, we expect politically very interested voters to be more likely than politically (rather) uninterested voters to make use of such information and to align their vote with their partisan orientations. Linking issue-specific orientations to the choice at hand implies the acquisition of some knowledge about the details of the proposed legislation, which is likely to involve an even greater effort on the part of the voters than identifying their preferred party's voting recommendation. Accordingly, we expect politically very interested voters to be more capable and motivated than uninterested voters of using such information and to align their vote choices with their issue-specific orientations. Summing up, we expect *reinforcement to be much more important for the politically very interested voters,* whereas we expect *the uninterested voters to be more exposed to activation and conversion effects.*

Ambivalence

In the minds of the members of the political elite, partisan predispositions and issue-specific predispositions typically tend to be consistently aligned. For the average voters, however, for whom politics is usually only of secondary importance, this is less likely to be the case. Usually, average voters are unlikely to care about such inconsistencies. Campaigns as information-rich events are likely to draw their attention to such conflicting predispositions. To the extent that voters, indeed, observe a mismatch between their partisan and issue-specific predispositions, and to the extent that they experience a conflict between the two, they are likely to be *cross-pressured* or *ambivalent* with respect to their vote choice. The political consequences of such a state of ambivalence are contested in the literature. Ambivalent attitudes have been shown to be widespread and to offer less reliable decision cues, to increase response variability in policy choices, attitude instability, volatility in partisan opinions, and moderation of candidate evaluations and related attitudes (Alvarez and Brehm 1995, 2002; Basinger and Lavine 2005; Huckfeldt and Sprague 2000; Keele and Wolak 2006; Meffert et al. 2004; Rudolph 2005). In sharp contrast to these and other studies, however, Steenbergen and Brewer (2004) find only mild levels of ambivalence and few effects on Americans' attitudes on four different policy issues (abortion, affirmative action, gay rights and social welfare). Based on their assessment of the political consequences of ambivalence, these authors maintain that ambivalence does not have to breed volatility. They conclude that, 'indeed, in the face of conflicting orientations, people seem to do a remarkable job in piecing together consistent opinions' (p. 121).

Ambivalence may, of course, also be *context dependent* (Keele and Wolak 2008). In an attempt to reconcile these contradictory findings, Saris and Sniderman (2004: 6–7) argue that the differences may have a lot to do with the objects of ambivalence and the different tasks involved. Studies finding important effects of ambivalence usually deal with the electoral choices of candidates or parties, which get a lot of attention, so even people with little political interest get a lot of information on the objects involved. This may lead to widespread ambivalence, with substantial consequences. By contrast, under normal circumstances, most people collect little information on public policy issues and, accordingly, are not aware of any inconsistencies in their corresponding attitudes. Now, direct-democratic campaigns are rather like electoral campaigns with respect to the level of information on the objects involved, which means that specific policy issues become the object of political interest and information. Under such circumstances we may expect policy-specific ambivalence to become widespread with substantial political consequences, just as for ambivalence with respect to candidates and parties in electoral campaigns.

For the case of the asylum law, we indeed have been able to show that ambivalence increases voters' uncertainty about how to vote (Selb et al.

2009). In the present context, the key question is how the voters will resolve their ambivalence in a direct-democratic vote. Do they follow their partisan orientation and remain loyal to the party line, or do they follow the issue-specific orientation and stick to their specific principles and interests? Reviewing a considerable amount of literature, Sniderman and Levendusky (2007: 451) suggest that the way they resolve ambivalence will, more often than not, be guided by party loyalty.

In our view, this conclusion should be qualified by the task at hand, which, in the present case, is a direct-democratic vote on a specific issue. Whether or not, when cross-pressured, voters remain loyal to the party line is likely to *depend on the issue in question*. Not all issues may be equally critical for the loyalty of a given party's electorate. Contrary to elections, the direct-democratic context allows voters to selectively abandon their own party line without giving up their overall political identity. Even members of the Swiss political elites practise such *selective disloyalty*. The average voters, whose ideological coherence is generally less developed, are even more likely to do so. There are two sets of factors involved here – one linked to party, and another linked to individual predispositions. On the one hand, there are issues which touch the core of a party's ideological position and issues which are rather secondary for a party's overall ideological orientation. We suggest that it is easier for ambivalent voters to abandon the party line for issues which are secondary for their parties' ideology. On the other hand, there are issues which touch the core of the voters' specific predispositions and issues which are only loosely connected to them. A voter's incentive to abandon her party line is obviously stronger for the former than for the latter. Combining the two sets of factors, the strongest pull away from the party line is likely to exist for propositions which are secondary from the point of view of the voter's party ideology, but closely linked to the individual's specific predispositions; conversely, the weakest pull for party disloyalty is likely to exist for key partisan issues that are weakly linked to the individual's specific predispositions. In intermediary combinations, the party perspective is likely to predominate. Table 10.3 summarizes the four possible cases.

Table 10.3 Expectations about disloyalty incentives

Issue's link to voter's issue-specific predispositions	Issue's importance for party's ideological position	
	Ownership	Secondary
Close	Party loyalty	Strong incentive to abandon party line
Loose	Strong incentive for party loyalty	Party loyalty

In terms of our three campaigns, the relevant issue-specific values and attitudes include xenophobia (for asylum and naturalization), and ideological commitments to the market economy (for the corporate tax). There are certainly other values and attitudes involved here, too, but we shall look only at these issue-specific predispositions. Both asylum and naturalization concern issues belonging to the core of the programme of the conservative/ populist right, which arguably enjoys issue ownership of both issues. Not only in Switzerland, but all over Western Europe, immigration constitutes a key issue for mobilization by parties belonging to this party family, who has acquired a reputation for credibly representing large parts of public opinion on such issues. For a long time, both the moderate right and the left largely ignored immigration issues, and to the extent that they have come to deal with them, their positions have remained mainly reactive and lacking in a long-term perspective. This is why we consider them secondary for these two-party families. By contrast, the issue of the corporation tax belongs to the core of economic policy, which, in turn, has always belonged to the core of the programmatic positions of both the left and the moderate right, but not of the conservative/populist right.

Of the two immigration issues, asylum law is more closely linked to xenophobic predispositions than is the naturalization initiative. The initiative addressed the issue of immigration more obliquely, since it was dealing much more with procedural questions relating to the integration of foreigners who had been long-term residents in Switzerland. As for the corporation tax, it was difficult to link to the underlying predispositions, given its highly technical nature – especially for the voters with low stakes in the economy. Accordingly, we expect the strongest incentive for partisan disloyalty among ambivalent voters on the left in the case of the asylum law. Conversely, the incentives to become disloyal should have been particularly weak for ambivalent (non-xenophobic) voters on the conservative/populist right for the asylum law.

There is another, complementary explanation of the voting behaviour of ambivalent voters, which refers to their cues taking. It may be possible that cross-pressured voters abandon their own party's position because they also take their cues from other parties (see Gilens and Murakawa 2002: 26f.). In the setting of a Swiss direct-democratic vote, the cues of the moderate right, which takes a pivotal position, may be of particular importance for voters both from the left and the conservative right. Thus, in the case of the asylum law, cross-pressured voters on the left may have been less hesitant to abandon their party because, not only the conservative, but also the moderate right was opting for the tough new law. In the case of the naturalization initiative, voters on the left may have been rather more hesitant to abandon their party's position, because the moderate right was siding with their parties, and not with the populist right. Conversely, the cross-pressured voters from the conservative right may have been more hesitant to abandon their party in the asylum case because the moderate right was siding with their parties, and less hesitant in the naturalization case, where the moderate right had joined forces with the left. If issue ownership is not at stake and issue linkage is less than straightforward, cues from the pivotal parties may become particularly important.

Operationalizations and methods

The variables

In this section we present both the variables and the statistical models. This very parsimonious model for estimating the different types of effects on vote intentions/vote choices makes full use of the panel structure of the data. It estimates vote intentions/vote choices on the basis of the two key individual predispositions. The variable to be explained always corresponds to the vote intention, except for the measurement at the end of the campaign, where we use the vote choice for those who have participated in the vote. This variable distinguishes the supporters of the propositions (coded as 1) from both their opponents and the (remaining) undecided voters (coded as 0). For the group of the originally undecided voters, we introduce a dummy variable that takes care of the previously mentioned tautological effects attributable to this group. It takes the value of 1 for those who were undecided at the beginning of the campaign, and 0 otherwise.

There are only three explanatory variables in the model – one each for the two key predispositions and one for ambivalence. It is important to note that the two predispositions have been measured just once, at the beginning of the campaign. What we would like to find out is how the predispositions measured at the outset of the campaign determine vote intentions and the eventual vote.

Following Tillie (1995) and van der Eijk et al. (2006), we have chosen to operationalize the *partisan predispositions* on the basis of propensity scores, that is, a set of questions asking respondents to indicate how likely it is that they will ever vote for each one of the four major Swiss parties – SPS, CVP, the Liberals (FDP or LPS), SVP, as well as for the Green party (GPS). The responses range from 'will never vote for this party' (score 0) to 'will certainly vote for this party at some time in the future' (score 10). Based on this information, we have mapped both parties and voters onto a single latent continuum using a non-parametric multiple unidimensional unfolding technique (see Coombs 1964; Van Schuur 1993). Using voters' preference orderings among parties, non-parametric unfolding models rank order both parties and voters on a latent dimension.[2] Subsequently, the achieved party ordering can be tested against the null-hypothesis that the parties are not represented along the la*tent scale in terms of their rank in the unfoldable order. As is shown by the first row of* Table 10.4, the unfolding model unveils a rank

Table 10.4 Characteristics of partisans of the five major Swiss parties

Characteristics	Party				
	GPS	SPS	CVP	FDP-Liberals	SVP
Preference scores[a]					
Mean partisan score	–1.42	–0.95	–0.03	0.66	1.35
Mean xenophobia	–0.53	–0.47	0.07	0.12	0.62
Mean stakes	–0.49	–0.34	0.15	0.10	0.22
Ambivalence[b]					
Share of xenophobes	**14.7**	**16.3**	**32.0**	**34.6**	58.7
Share of non-xenophobes	61.2	58.2	**31.1**	**29.8**	13.3
Share of high stakes	**18.3**	**23.1**	26.8	37.4	40.3
Share of low stakes	55.4	43.8	**21.3**	27.6	**26.1**

Notes: [a] All three scales have been standardized: mean = 0, S.D. = 1; [b] Shares indicated refer to score values > .5 (high) and < – .5 (low); ambivalent groups are indicated in bold.

ordering of the five parties from left to right that matches conventional wisdom (GPS, SPS, CVP, FDP, SVP) and that corresponds to the assumption of unidimensionality for all three campaigns.

The measure for the issue-specific predisposition depends on the type of proposition. *Xenophobia*, the issue-specific predisposition for the asylum and naturalization campaigns, is measured by a set of questions about the perception of threats caused by foreigners. The respondents were asked how much they 'strongly agree' or 'disagree' with a series of five statements about threat perception (see Sniderman et al. 2004). Using factor analysis, we have extracted a single factor from the five items with an Eigenvalue of 3.3/3.3 and factor loadings of .78/.77 or higher for the asylum law and the naturalization initiative, respectively. The resulting factor-scores range from non-xenophobic predispositions (negative values) to xenophobic (positive values) ones. For the corporation tax, the issue-specific predisposition score is intended to measure the individual's stakes in the market economy. These stakes are measured by three items referring to economic values and beliefs. The three items were also factor-analysed and provide one factor with an Eigenvalue of 1.3 and factor loadings of .77, .72, and .43, respectively. The resulting factor-scores range from low stakes (negative values) to high stakes (positive values). Table 10.4 also presents the mean scores for the two issue-specific predisposition scales for the partisans of each major party. As this table shows, on average, both issue-specific preference scales are closely correlated with the partisan scale, but the partisan scale turns out to be much more polarized than the other two scales.

Our *ambivalence* measure is simply the product of a respondent's score on the partisan predisposition-scale and the negatively signed issue-specific predisposition-scale.[3] For xenophobia, this implies that ambivalent voters, that is, xenophobic voters on the left and non-xenophobic voters on the right, receive high scores, while voters with congruent predispositions receive low scores on this measure. Similarly, voters from the left with high stakes in the economy and voters from the right with low stakes in the economy receive high scores on the ambivalence measure for the corporation tax. The second part of Table 10.4 gives an idea of the order of magnitude of ambivalence among Swiss voters. As expected, it turns out to be rather widespread. With respect to xenophobia, the partisans of the moderate right are the most ambivalent. Whether their parties join the left or the conservative right, about a third of them will be ambivalent. The critical group of the xenopobic partisans of the left, by contrast, is relatively small – roughly one-sixth of the voters on the left. Similarly, the non-xenophobic voters of the conservative right are also rather few. Concerning the stakes in the market economy, between a little less than one-fifth and a bit more than one-fourth of the voters on both sides of the left–right divide are ambivalent.

The model

Our model is a random intercept probit model, which takes the following form:

$$\text{vote}_{it} = (\alpha + u_i) + \beta_1 ip_i + \beta_2 pp_i + \beta_3 amb_i + \Sigma_j (\alpha_j + \beta_{4j} ip_i + \beta_{5j} pp_i + \beta_{6j} amb_i)$$
$$+ \beta_7 un_i + \Sigma_j un_i{}^*(\beta_{8j} ip_i + \beta_{9j} pp_i + \beta_{10j} amb_i) + v_i,$$

where 'vote' is a dichotomous indicator, either the vote intention or vote at time t as previously described, 'ip' is the respondent's issue-specific predisposition, 'pp' her partisan predisposition, 'amb' stands for ambivalence, and 'un' for undecided. The index j refers to later time points in the campaign – the midpoint (only in the case of the asylum law) and the end of the campaign, and the index i refers to respondent i. In this model, the intercept ($\alpha + \alpha_j + u_i$) varies from one time point to the other ($\alpha + \alpha_j$) and from one individual to the other (u_i). It stands for variations in vote (intentions) during the campaign that are not accounted for by factors related to the two individual predispositions. The period effect is α_j; and u_i the individual effect. The coefficients β_1 to β_3 measure the effects of the two predispositions and their interaction, independently of the time point of the campaign. They show the 'constant' effect of predispositions on the vote intention/vote. In other words, these coefficients provide an indication of the reinforcement effect: β_1 and β_2 are expected to be highly significant and positive in all three cases: The larger they are, the more important will be the reinforcement effect. According to our hypotheses, both the size and the sign of β_3 will depend on the issue in question. The effect is expected to be largest for the asylum law. The coefficients β_{4j} to β_{6j} measure the effects of the predispositions at later points in time. These coefficients measure the combination of activation and conversion effects. The larger and the more positive they are, the stronger activation is compared to conversion. Small coefficients indicate that either both effects are weak or both are strong and compensate each other. Negative effects occur, when the campaign weakens the impact of the predisposition in question, that is, when conversion predominates activation. The coefficient β_7 accounts for the tautological effects of undecided voters and is of no further interest. The coefficients β_{8j} to β_{10j}, however, measure how the activation and conversion effects for undecided voters differ from those of voters who had already held a more or less clear vote intention at the beginning of the campaign. The stronger and the more significant these coefficients are, the stronger the activation effects for the originally undecided voters as compared to the other voters will be.

Results

We have estimated this model separately for each campaign, using stata.[4] Table 10.5 reports the results. For the asylum law, it presents the model without the coefficients for the originally undecided voters, since in this particular case, all the substantive effects for the undecided turned out to be insignificant. The upper part of the table contains the fixed effects, which are most important for our interpretation. In the lower part of the table the reader finds the information related to the random effects.[5] At first sight, the pattern of effects largely corresponds to the theoretical expectations we have formulated. But given the presence of interactions, and given the fact that some coefficients indicate a combination of activation and conversion effects, we need some additional clarification for the interpretation of these results.

Overall effects

Let us first consider the *overall effects* of the three campaigns. Based on the results shown in Table 10.5, we can calculate the predicted vote (intentions) for each respondent at the beginning and at the end of the campaigns. These predicted estimates correspond to the vote (intentions) we expect on the basis of a voter's specific set of predispositions. We can compare these estimates with the final vote as indicated by the raw data. As is demonstrated in the first part of Table 10.6, the estimates based on our model allow us to reproduce the results based on the raw data quite faithfully.

Table 10.5 Estimates from the random intercept probit models of the vote choice/ vote intentions for the three campaigns, unstandardized regression coefficients, standard errors and levels of significance[a]

	Asylum			Naturalization			Corporate tax		
	Coef.	Std. Err.	P>z	Coef.	Std. Err.	P>z	Coef.	Std. Err.	P>z
Fixed part									
Issue pref	0.69	0.07	***	0.52	0.07	***	0.22	0.07	**
Partisan pref	0.59	0.07	***	0.28	0.07	***	0.33	0.07	***
Ambivalence	0.41	0.07	***	0.14	0.06	**	0.08	0.07	ns
t2	0.15	0.08	*						
Issue pref t2	0.21	0.09	**						
Partisan pref t2	0.46	0.09	***						
Ambivalence t2	−0.04	0.09	ns						
t3	0.49	0.09	***	−0.63	0.10	***	0.41	0.08	***
Issue pref t3	0.17	0.10	ns	0.06	0.10	ns	0.18	0.10	ns
Partisan pref t3	0.48	0.10	***	0.47	0.11	***	0.24	0.10	**
Ambivalence t3	0.06	0.10	ns	−0.11	0.10	ns	0.28	0.09	**
Undecided				−1.56	0.17	***	−1.22	0.13	***
un_issue pref t2				0.78	0.22	***	−0.16	0.15	ns
un_party pref t2				1.13	0.22	***	−0.10	0.14	ns
un_ambivalence t2				0.66	0.21	***	−0.56	0.14	***
Constant	0.48	0.07	***	−0.25	0.07	***	0.25	0.08	***
Random part									
/lnsig2u	0.42	0.14		−0.63	0.32		−0.27	0.22	
sigma_u	1.23	0.09		0.73	0.12		0.87	0.10	
rho	0.60	0.03		0.35	0.07		0.43	0.06	
Chibar2	259.23	P=	.000	19.08	P=	.000	50.30	P=	.000
rho-Null-model	0.78	0.02		0.51	0.04		0.56	0.04	

Notes: ***p < .001, **p < .01, *p < .05; [a]Asylum: n observations = 3262, respondents = 1323; Naturalization: n observations = 1859, respondents = 997; Corporate tax: n observations = 1669, respondents = 853.

Next, we can compare the predicted vote (intentions) with the combination of the individuals' original vote intentions and their final votes to arrive at the empirical equivalent of Table 10.1, which is presented in the second part of Table 10.6. Our comparison considers the overall consistency of the

Table 10.6   Overall campaign effects: percentage distributions

a) Comparison between raw data and estimated effects

% No change of voters with	Asylum		Naturalization		Corporate tax	
	Raw data	Estimated	Raw data	Estimated	Raw data	Estimated
Pro intention	80.5	84.3	48.0	51.7	76.0	76.3
Con intention	73.7	69.2	90.0	86.0	79.0	77.8
% Final vote of undecided						
Pro	47.7	52.1	21.3	20.2	51.6	54.7
Con	48.4	44.7	73.9	76.5	48.3	45.2
n	919	847	860	862	952	816

b) Estimated shares of reinforcement, activation and conversion

Predisposition		Projects		
Intention	Vote	Asylum	Naturalization	Corporate tax
Reinforcement		**68.7**	**47.3**	**56.8**
Consistent	Consistent	61.0	42.5	42.5
Inconsistent	Inconsistent	7.7	4.8	14.3
Activation		**21.5**	**42.1**	**23.5**
Inconsistent	Consistent	11.8	13.9	9.3
Undecided	Consistent	9.7	28.2	14.2
Conversion		**9.9**	**10.7**	**19.6**
Consistent	Inconsistent	6.9	5.5	7.8
Undecided	Inconsistent	3.0	5.2	11.8
Total		100.0	100.0	100.0
n		847	729	816

c) Estimated shares of activation and conversion, by camp

	Originally con, final vote pro	Originally pro, final vote con	Undecided, vote pro	Undecided, vote con	Total
Asylum					
Activation	21.0	9.1	**41.5**	30.9	21.5
Conversion	9.8	6.7	10.6	13.8	9.8
n	276	464		107	847
Naturalization					
Activation	12.2	32.0	9.9	**71.9**	42.1
Conversion	1.9	16.2	10.3	4.6	10.7
n	321	253		288	862
Corporate tax					
Activation	12.1	17.0	16.0	**38.7**	23.5
Conversion	**14.1**	11.5	**39.2**	6.1	19.6
n	216	388		212	816

individuals' *combinations* of predispositions with their original intentions and final votes. As is shown in the second part of Table 10.6, all three campaigns have very strong reinforcement effects. By contrast, conversion is the weakest of the three effects in all three campaigns. In comparative terms, however, our expectations are largely confirmed by the data: Reinforcement is strongest for the most familiar and least complex issue (asylum); activation is by far strongest for the originally unfamiliar, but straightforward issue (naturalization); and conversion is strongest for the unfamiliar/complex issue (corporate tax).

In addition, the model introduced here allows for an overall assessment of the campaigns of the two camps in terms of their activation and conversion effects. The corresponding results are presented in the part (c) of Table 10.6. As in the first part of this table, we distinguish here between voters who originally had an opinion and subsequently changed it, and voters who were originally undecided and subsequently formed an opinion. In addition, we now also distinguish between the types of change – activation or conversion. As it turns out, in the asylum case, the pro campaign was more successful, because it activated more voters in both categories – those who originally had an opinion and those who were originally undecided. In the case of the naturalization initiative, the contra campaign was much more successful in terms of activation: it succeeded in activating most of the originally undecided voters, and it also activated a larger share of the voters who originally had an opinion. Finally, in the case of the corporate tax, both camps were approximately evenly successful overall, but the pro camp was more successful in terms of conversion, while the contra camp was more successful in terms of activation, especially among the undecided. Remember that, in this particular case, the pro camp had massively outspent its adversaries. While money does not seem to have had any impact in the other two cases, it is likely to have contributed to the conversion effects among the originally undecided in the corporate tax case.

Partisan effects

Turning to the effects of *partisan orientations*, we rely on a graphical presentation to better understand, what the results tell us. For these illustrations, we have calculated the predicted vote (intentions) for different combinations of the two types of predispositions. Figure 10.1 presents the partisan effects, controlling for issue orientations. For each campaign, the figure includes two graphs, one each for negative- and positive-issue predispositions. We find strong partisan activation across the board, in all three campaigns and at all levels of issue predispositions. This is illustrated by the fact that the curves linking partisan orientation to the probability of a 'yes' vote get consistently steeper as we move from the beginning to the end of the campaign. As expected, campaigns serve to link partisan orientations to the choices on offer, and they do so irrespective of other aspects

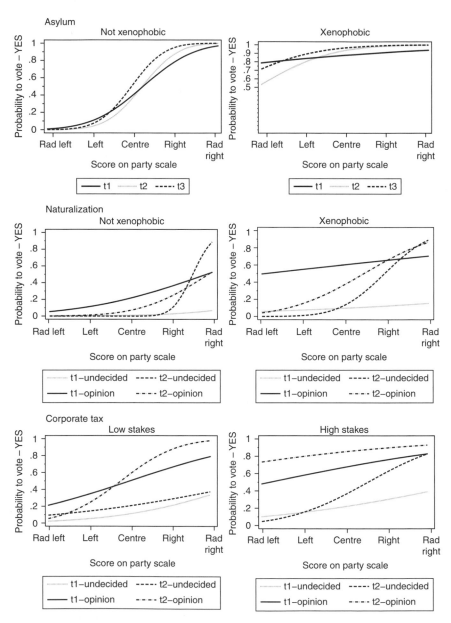

Figure 10.1 Impact of party predispositions, controlling for issue predispositions (at −1 /+1 s.d.): all three campaigns

of the campaigns. The three time measurements of the asylum case reveal that this activation takes place progressively throughout the campaign. As the campaign proceeds, voters increasingly align their vote intentions with their party orientations.

Having noted the pervasive activation effects of partisan orientations, we should, however, insist on some remarkable differences. In the *asylum* case, we find the expected *ambivalence effect* among voters on the left: The more xenophobic they are, the less such voters are loyal to their parties in the vote on the asylum law. The effect is extraordinarily strong. As more detailed analyses (not shown here) indicate, we cannot explain this effect with the socio-demographic composition of the xenophobic minority on the left (e.g. with a low level of education or an above average age), nor with their lack of political knowledge or the importance they attach to the asylum or immigration policy in particular. By contrast, as predicted, ambivalent voters on the conservative right, follow their party line in this particular case.

For the *naturalization* case, we expected a weaker ambivalence effect for the xenophobic left, given the more tenuous link of this initiative with the underlying xenophobic predispositions. At the beginning of the campaign, the ambivalence effect turns out to be significant and of the expected sign, but as expected, weaker than in the asylum case. By the end of the campaign, the effect tends to disappear, and it ends up being particularly weak among the originally undecided voters from the left (and the moderate right). This means that partisan activation eventually dominated on the left and the moderate right. By contrast, in this case, it is the non-xenophobic voters on the right who, with the exception of the originally undecided voters from the conservative right, do not tend to follow their party line. Taken together, these results suggest that the campaigners of the conservative/populist right did not succeed in establishing a link with xenophobic predispositions. Combining the ambivalence effects in the two cases also provides support for our alternative hypothesis, which suggests that the voters of the polar camps tend to take their cues not only from their own parties, but from the moderate right parties as well: In the asylum case, where the moderate right took a tough stance, xenophobic voters of the left largely abandoned the party line, while they did not do so in the naturalization case, where the moderate right was allied with the left.

Partisan activation operates in the *corporate tax* case, too, especially among the voters with low stakes who originally had an opinion, and among the originally undecided voters with high stakes. However, for the voters with high stakes and an original opinion, we find a situation resembling the asylum case. Among these voters, the partisan effect is small and ambivalent voters on the left end up voting in favour of the law, in spite of the fact that this issue was all but secondary for their parties. While this result does not correspond to our first ambivalence hypothesis, it lends support to the partisan cues hypothesis, which suggests that ambivalent voters on the left also took their cues from the parties on the moderate right. Finally, in the corporate tax case, the originally undecided voters with low stakes from the right did not follow their party line either and voted massively against the law. Just as the voters with high stakes on the left, they resolved their ambivalence in favour of their issue-specific opinions. However, their behaviour is incompatible with either one of our two hypotheses concerning the factors determining ambivalence. Given their low stakes in the reform, they might just as well have followed their party line, especially since the moderate right also provided cues in favour of the reform. Possibly, their disloyalty is linked to the particularly technical nature of this issue, but it may also be related to the external events associated with the involvement of the UBS in the subprime crises, which intervened towards the end of the campaign (see Chapter 9) and which may have had an influence on this disoriented group of voters in particular.

Issue-specific predispositions

We can look at the same results from the perspective of the issue-specific predispositions. For the two immigration issues, this alternative perspective hardly offers any new insights. For the corporate tax case, however, it provides some additional information (Figure 10.2), which allows us to clarify our previous results. In this particular case, voters from the left behave rather differently from voters on the right. While the former follow their issue-specific predispositions to a considerable extent – the originally

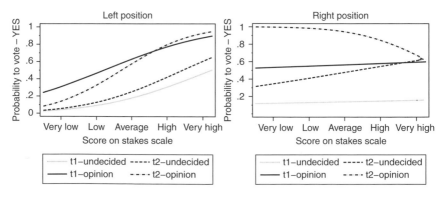

Figure 10.2 Impact of issue predispositions, controlling for party predispositions (at –1 s.d./0/+1 s.d.): corporate tax campaign

undecided somewhat less than those who already had an opinion at the beginning of the campaign, the voters on the right display a behaviour which, from the point of view of their issue-specific predispositions, is partly counter-intuitive. On the one hand, the bulk of the voters on the right who originally had a negative opinion on the reform are eventually activated to support it, as are some parts of their originally undecided colleagues. The massive pro campaign apparently ended up bringing lots of voters from the moderate and conservative right with low stakes in the market economy over to the pro side. For many of these voters, the issue may just not have been important enough to bother with much, which is why they ended up accepting the pro position by default, even if it was not in line with their predispositions – typical examples of the widespread conversion effects in this particular case. On the other hand, however, part of precisely those voters on the right who had the highest stakes in the market economy proved to be most difficult to be persuaded of the reform's advantages. How to explain this unexpected result? Possibly, for this particular group, the reform was not so attractive after all. From their point of view, it may not have gone far enough. As we have pointed out in Chapter 2, the reform constituted a compromise forged in Parliament – a compromise that may have been rejected by the staunch adherents of the market creed. Thus, some voters on the right with high stakes in the economy thought that tax reduction should have benefited all shareholders, and not only the larges ones. Among this group, only 33.3 per cent supported the law, compared to 78.3 per cent among those voters on the right with high stakes in the economy who did not share this particular line of critique of the new law.[6]

Political interest

Finally, we turn to the impact of political interest on the campaign effects of partisan and issue-specific predispositions. We ran our model separately for the politically 'very interested' and the '(rather) not interested'. We do not present detailed results, but provide summary information in Table 10.7, which replicates the part (b) of Table 10.6 for the politically very interested and the (rather) not interested. As is immediately apparent from this table, our expectations are largely confirmed: Compared to politically uninterested voters, the reinforcement effect is always stronger in the politically very interested group. While the differences are relatively small for the highly familiar asylum campaign, the reinforcement effect is almost twice as large among the very interested voters in the more unfamiliar and complex cases. Conversely, both activation and conversion effects are more widespread among the little interested voters. In particular, activation effects are much stronger in the naturalization

Table 10.7 Campaign effects for the very interested and the (rather) uninterested: percentage distributions

Predisposition		Asylum		Naturalization		Corporate tax	
Intention	Vote	Interested	Not interested	Interested	Not interested	Interested	Not interested
Reinforcement		71.4	65.8	63.9	32.1	64.3	34.3
Consistent	Consistent	67.1	56.3	60.0	29.8	53.0	28.4
Inconsistent	Inconsistent	4.3	9.5	3.9	2.3	11.3	5.9
Activation		20.0	21.5	30.3	50.4	21.6	31.4
Inconsistent	Consistent	11.9	11.4	10.9	18.3	10.6	15.7
Undecided	Consistent	8.1	10.1	19.4	32.1	11.0	15.7
Conversion		8.6	12.6	8.9	17.6	14.0	34.3
Consistent	Inconsistent	6.7	6.3	5.4	9.2	8.7	14.7
Undecided	Inconsistent	1.9	6.3	3.5	8.4	5.3	19.6
Total		100.0	100.0	100.0	100.0	100.0	100.0
Ratio activation/conversion		2.3	1.7	3.4	2.9	1.5	.9
n		210	158	258	131	264	102

case (30.3 vs. 50.4 per cent activated), and conversion effects are much stronger in the corporate tax case (14.0 vs. 34.3 per cent converted). This adds another, more serious, twist to the interpretation of the corporate tax case. It turns out that it was above all the politically uninterested voters from the centre and the right, who were probably swayed by the massive campaign of the pro side despite their issue-specific predispositions, which actually provided them with an incentive to vote against the reform.

As predicted, partisan and issue-specific predispositions always have stronger effects among the politically very interested. The difference is particularly large for the corporate tax reform, where predispositions are hardly at all reinforced among the uninterested. Even in this case, however, we find some partisan activation among the uninterested voters.

Figure 10.3 illustrates the differential effects in the two groups for the asylum and the naturalization campaign from the perspective of the

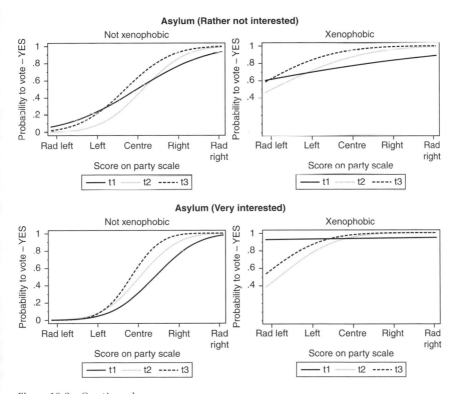

Figure 10.3 Continued

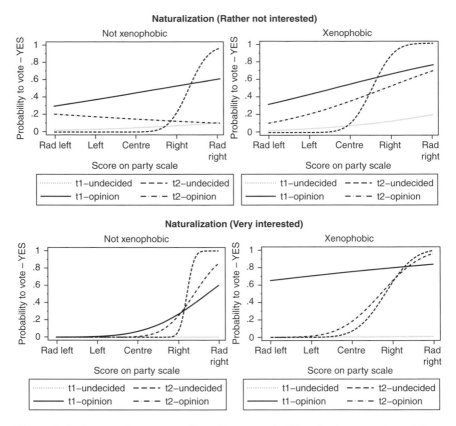

Figure 10.3 Impact of party predispositions, controlling for issue predispositions (at –1/+1 s.d.) and level of political interest: immigration campaigns

partisan orientations. For the asylum law, differences between the two groups are relatively small – an illustration of what happens when the proposition is familiar and of low complexity. By contrast, the graphs for the more unfamiliar naturalization initiative shows much more important differences, which mainly apply for the group of voters who initially had an opinion, while they turn out to be relatively small for the initially undecided voters. Among the politically very interested voters who originally had an opinion, the partisan orientation is strongly activated in the course of the campaign, while this is much less the case among the politically uninterested voters. Especially the non-interested and non-xenophobic voters hardly followed their party line. They virtually all voted against the initiative.

Conclusion

In this chapter, we have studied the activation of partisan and issue-specific orientations by direct-democratic campaigns. The overall thrust of the results is in line with our expectations. We have found that all three campaigns had massive effects. They all reinforced and activated previously held predispositions. Reinforcement was paramount in the referendum on the asylum law – our most familiar and least complex case. Activation was most prominent in the vote on the naturalization initiative – an unfamiliar, but not a complex proposal. Conversion turned out to be very important in the referendum on the corporate tax reform – a reform that was both unfamiliar and complex, and subject to an intense and extremely one-sided campaign.

We have found strong evidence for both partisan and issue-specific activation. While partisan activation tends to be stronger than issue-specific activation, the specific mix of the two effects depends on the issue at stake. As expected, ambivalence is quite widespread (varying between 14.7 and 34.6 per cent of the relevant groups of voters), and ambivalence works out differently, depending on the issue-specific circumstances. Thus, ambivalent voters behaved quite differently in the two immigration cases: On the left, they followed their issue-specific preferences in the asylum case but adopted their party line in the naturalization case. On the right, they behaved in the exact opposite way. The combined result is in line with our hypothesis about partisan cues taking, which posits that the voters on both ends of the left–right spectrum take their cues not only from their own parties, but also from pivotal parties of the moderate right. The behaviour of the ambivalent voters in the corporate tax case also tends to support this hypothesis: Both the ambivalent voters on the right (with low stakes) and the ambivalent voters on the left (with high stakes) are won over to support the reform. Both may have taken their cues from the moderate right who supported the tax. In this particular case, however, the situation is complicated by the fact that there are actually two kinds of ambivalent voters on the right: in addition to the classical type, there are those, for whom the reform did not go far enough. As we have seen, many in this small, but very convinced minority voted their issue-specific preferences against the recommendations of their parties.

We have postulated that, because of their higher sufficiency threshold, undecided voters should experience greater activation and conversion effects. This hypothesis was not confirmed in the asylum case, where we found no significant effect for the undecided voters. However, in the naturalization case, the originally undecided experienced a significantly greater activation effect than the rest of the voters, and we also found a particularly strong ambivalence effect for them in the corporate tax case (caused above all by the undecided voters on the right, who did not follow their party line). We could also confirm that the reinforcement effects tend to be much stronger among the politically interested voters.

Taken together, the two immigration-related campaigns provide comfort for the 'enlightenment model' of campaigning, although they give rise to quite different effects. In both cases, most voters ended up voting in line with their original predispositions – 90 per cent in the asylum case, and 85 per cent in the naturalization case. In the corporation tax case, however, only roughly two-thirds of the voters eventually voted in line with their predispositions. Even if we keep in mind that some of the voters whom we counted as voting inconsistently may have been voting in line with their predispositions – for example, the special case of the voters on the right for whom the reform did not go far enough, we still found a large share of voters with low stakes in the proposition and/or politically uninterested voters, who were converted to vote in favour of the reform, although this was not in line with their predispositions. The outcome in this particular case comes closest to a manipulative success of the pro camp and suggests that all is not well with the way direct-democratic campaigns work in Switzerland.

In this chapter, we have only presented an overall assessment of the impact of the campaign on voters' choices. We have shown that the campaigns contribute to the establishment of links between voters' predispositions and their eventual choices, but we have not documented the mechanisms establishing these links in detail. This will be the object of the next chapters.

Notes

1. With some modifications, this definition follows the lead of Finkel (1993: 15). Contrary to Finkel's definition, ours makes the consistency between predispositions and the final vote the defining criterion, to distinguish between activation and conversion.
2. We have used MUDFOLD 4.0 for our analysis (see van Schuur and Post 1998).
3. The most common measures used for ambivalence are the multiplicative measure used here (see Keele and Wolak 2006: 680), and Griffin's ambivalence index (or a modified version of this index) (see Steenbergen and Brewer 2004: 103–4).
4. The procedure we used is xtprobit. For this estimation, we have created a stacked file including all the respondents with valid data points at each panel wave.
5. Sigma_u is the variance of the individual error component. The chibar2-values at the bottom of the table refer to a particular likelihood-ratio test that checks whether rho (the proportion of variance attributable to differences between respondents) is zero or not, which is equivalent to the hypothesis that $u_i=0$. Since the P-values for these tests are large, the null-hypothesis has to be rejected in each case.

6. The groups involved are quite sizeable: n=54 for the voters with high stakes on the right who share this critique, that is, who both support the argument that the reduction should benefit all shareholders and who reject the argument that it should benefit the large shareholders, and n=248 for those who do not. The result is statistically highly significant at the.000 level, and the bivariate correlation coefficient is impressive (gamma=–.76).

11
Learning and Knowledge in Political Campaigns

Heinz Bonfadelli and Thomas N. Friemel

This chapter focuses on the role of media use and voter learning during referendum campaigns. The basic question is twofold: First, what kind of media do citizens use in the context of referendum campaigns and how much attention do they pay to these various sources of information? Second, what do media users learn during a referendum campaign, and do all citizens gain knowledge distributed by the different media in an equal way?

Information exposure as a prerequisite for political learning

An informed electorate is considered vital for a healthy democracy because political knowledge helps citizens make rational decisions and enables them to translate their opinions into meaningful forms of participation. Information is thus essential for the process of decision-making. The information used by citizens in the decision process comes from many sources: (a) People form impressions and decide on the basis of *everyday experiences*; (b) voters also receive political cues and advice from their social environment by *political conversations* with family members or friends about the topic of a referendum, and (c) the public gets information and are influenced by *media coverage of a referendum* (free media) or by *political ads* (paid media) for or against the issue at stake. Hence voters move constantly in a *more or less information rich environment*. But citizens as media audiences also vary considerably in their habitual *exposure* and attention to mass media. The first question then is: Who has access to which media and learns what? And secondly: How is this information transformed into opinions (see Chapter 12)?

There is an ongoing debate in communication research on the extent to which the major sources of political information affect citizen learning (Chaffee and Frank 1996; Sotirovic and McLeod 2004), with the exact *role of print versus television* being debated in particular.

Print versus broadcast news

As major channels of political information studied in most election studies. Based on self-reported measures of media use, correlations of media use with political knowledge, measured, for example, as knowledge of referendum issues, pro or contra arguments or party positions on issues, are usually quite low. The average citizen's knowledge concerning public affairs in general and the issues of elections and referendums is generally limited. *Regular use of print media*, especially newspapers, was in many cases a significantly better predictor for political learning than was *use of television news* (McLeod and McDonald 1985; Robinson and Levy 1986, 1996; Delli Carpini and Keeter 1996). In general, newspaper news is much denser than television news, is visually less appealing, contains both more factual and more background information, and thus is in need of a more active user. Based on existing research, Chaffee and Frank (1996: 52) conclude: 'It is, indeed, rare to find a study in which newspaper reading is not a significant predictor of political knowledge.'

It seems not surprising that watching a lot of television and even watching television news on a regular basis does not affect political knowledge much. Television and especially television in the United States has mostly entertainment functions and television news normally contains not much relevant information about election or referendum topics. Consequently, many scholars still share Patterson and McClure's (1976) early conclusion that exposure to television news does not inform voters at all. But interestingly, Chaffee and Kanihan (1997), summarizing recent studies and new evidence, conclude that television news is becoming a major source of political information that in some respects rivals newspapers. This seems especially to be the case when knowledge measures concern personal knowledge about the candidates, rather than parties and issues. So television seems to be the preferred source for people wanting to evaluate personal qualities and candidate images. And television seems to be an effective source of passive learning, even without much involvement.

While communication research has focused on newspapers and television, not much is known about the contribution of *radio listening* to knowledge gain. Recently, Stamm et al. (1997) found evidence in the United States that radio made as large a contribution to respondents' public affairs knowledge as newspapers and television. Using U.S. National Election Study data, Young and Sung (cited in Drew and Weaver 2006: 26) found that television, radio, magazine, newspaper, and campaign news exposure were 'all significant, though rather weak, predictors of political knowledge across most of the four studied elections, but general newspaper and national television news exposure declined over time as predictors of knowledge.'

Free versus paid media

Voters do not only get more or less balanced information from news media; in addition, they seek information and are influenced by political advertising (paid media). One classical finding by Patterson and McClure (1976) is that people exposed to more political commercials on television during the 1972 US presidential campaign were more knowledgeable about the politics of the candidates McGovern and Nixon, but watching the network evening news regularly did not matter. Political ads, then, appear to actually inform the electorate. But Zhao and Chaffee (1995) concluded later, on the basis of different studies, that only in one out of six surveys advertising had a greater effect on knowledge than television news viewing. Others argue that the *effect of political advertising* on knowledge is *conditional*, advertising may be more effective especially among the less interested and less informed voters. These mixed results may be due to the vast number of methods and indicators used (Goldstein and Ridout 2004; Ridout et al. 2004).

Mass Media versus interpersonal communication

There is manifold evidence, that interpersonal communication in the form of political discussions with family members or friends functions as a channel for information diffusion in the sense that interpersonal communication networks of individuals can be understood as *social capital* (e.g. Chaffee 1982). But based only on survey data, it is difficult to clearly prove the direction of influence. *News diffusion studies* at least demonstrate that interpersonal communication is an important channel for learning about important news events. And comparative voting studies (e.g. Schmitt-Beck 2003) in Europe and the United States demonstrate that the influence of interpersonal communication in comparison to mass media is still stronger, especially in countries with a high share of floating voters or weak party identification such as the United States, East Germany, and, especially, Great Britain.

Internet

Recent studies (e.g. Sotirovic and McLeod 2004; Drew and Weaver 2006; Dalrymple and Scheufele 2007) give tentative evidence that a more active use, together with the hyperlink structure of the Internet affect learning from the Internet and, especially, from online papers, even after controlling for print newspaper and television news.

To sum up, there is vast evidence that a broad variety of information channels, like traditional print or broadcast media; new media like the Internet; interpersonal communication; and paid media in form of political advertising, are used in different combinations and with varying intensity by different segments of voters, thus contributing to political learning in manifold ways.

Differential learning: the knowledge gap hypothesis

In 1970, Tichenor, Donohue, and Olien summarized existing research demonstrating *differential learning processes*. *They* formulated for the first time the so-called *knowledge gap hypothesis:* As the infusion of information into a social system increases, not all social segments benefit equally from the media information. As a result, there is an increasing gap in knowledge between those high with social status and/or education and the less privileged segments. Later research, based on cross-sectional surveys as well as on longitudinal panel designs, supported and refined the initial knowledge gap hypothesis (Bonfadelli 1994, 2008; Viswanath and Finnegan 1996), especially by considering further mediating factors like level of issue controversy, intensity of media coverage, media used (print vs. TV) or attention paid to media.

Several authors have suggested that *television* could have a levelling influence on political knowledge gaps (e.g. Neuman 1976; Gantz 1978). However, this levelling effect holds also true for newspapers, given a high intensity of coverage on a local issue (Gaziano 1983). Intensive and controversial media coverage on a referendum campaign, may stimulate interest and the campaign may become more salient even for the less educated and politically less interested segments of society, and thus lead to a more equal flow of information. Because campaigns generate extensive media coverage, gaps that may exist at the outset of the campaign may decline as highly informed voters become saturated – so-called ceiling effects – and little-informed voters get a chance to catch up (Holbrook 2002), or existing knowledge gaps may at least stay the same and not increase over time.

Whereas the knowledge gap hypothesis became an important theoretical perspective in media effects research since the 1970s, political scientists have paid little attention paid to differences in knowledge across social segments. Although Delli, Carpini and Keeter (1996) did pay attention to identifying group differences in political knowledge, they do not focus on the differential impact of information flow or campaign information onto existing knowledge gaps.

A multifactorial cognitive model of political learning

Several researchers have criticized the widely used simple exposure measures, such as frequency of use or time devoted to television news. McLeod and McDonald (1985) early proposed to use a combination of various dimensions of media orientations like exposure time, content use, media reliance, attentiveness and media gratifications to better estimate the total media effect on political learning. Later Eveland (2001, 2002) formulated the so-called *cognitive mediation model* linking issues of motivations for media use with cognitive audience activity, and media effects. This cognitive mediation model predicts that a surveillance motive will lead to a special kind of information-processing behaviour, including attention and elaboration on news content (Eveland et al. 2003). To sum up, learning of political news and knowledge levels are not only influenced by the frequency and type of media used, but vary depending on several mediating factors, such as: (a) media use and dependency (print vs. television) in the *phase of media exposure*; (b) attentiveness to news; (c) gratification functions of media use (information and orientation vs. recreation and diversion) in the *phase of media reception*; (d) general political interest or topic specific interest on the level of individual motivation; and (e) the intensity of conflict on the level of the societal system.

Research questions

In a next step, and based on our theoretical considerations, a set of *guiding research questions* are formulated regarding the media used as information channels during the referendum campaign, information acquisition by different education levels, and the development of knowledge gaps over time.

Exposure and reception: media as channels for campaign information

First, it is of interest which channels for campaign information are the most important for Swiss voters. It is assumed that *television and newspapers* are still the main channels, and that the Internet is playing only a marginal role as source for political information. In comparison to the free media, *paid media* in the form of newspaper ads and street posters are likely to play a marginal role; however, the official government information delivered in the form of a print booklet will be recognized widely.

Differences between socio-demographic groups

Second, we test how the various channels for campaign information are used by the different social segments. It is hypothesized that the audiences for campaign media are not homogeneous, but segmented according to socio-demographic criteria. Whereas *television* is used more as information source by voters with a low educational background, *newspapers* are more important for male and older voters and those with higher educational background. However, our survey questions are a bit ambivalent insofar as 'campaign media use' was operationalized by asking citizens to estimate the various information channels in relation to 'personal importance', not by asking about the frequency of use during the campaign. In addition we asked how attentive people were for referendum information in the media.

Increasing knowledge gaps as a result of referendum campaign information flow

The third research question addresses the dynamic of knowledge acquisition and the influencing factors. According to the basic assumption of the knowledge gap paradigm it is assumed, that there will be knowledge gaps between educational segments, as well as between males and females and different age groups. Furthermore, it is assumed that increase of knowledge will be highest in the case of the corporation tax, a quite complex and new issue, but will be especially low in the two cases of asylum law and the naturalization initiative. The latter two issues have been controversially discussed for a long time in Switzerland and will be supposedly decided by voters not on the basis of differentiated knowledge but mostly on relative stable predispositions for or against foreigners and asylum seekers.

Operationalization of knowledge

Knowledge was measured with factual-knowledge questions regarding three important knowledge areas of referendum campaign: the topic at stake, the position of the important political actors, and the arguments used by those actors to evaluate and frame the topic. The topic at stake was operationalized with three questions about the consequences of the new law. These consequences are free of interpretation but can be very general or abstract. People were asked whether or not it is true that a certain consequence is imposed by the new law. The position of different political actors is important information for voters, since their party recommendations offer an easy shortcut to decision-making. People were asked about the position of the government and of the five most important parties and interest groups (in the corporate tax campaign, about the positions of the labour unions and business associations). The third aspect of knowledge refers to the arguments used by the actors. The arguments are more specific than the consequences and can include subjective interpretations. People were asked whether they had heard various arguments during the campaign. It can be argued that for an informed political decision all three aspects of knowledge are of a certain importance. Therefore, all aspects are reported separately, as well as a combined knowledge index. For our analyses, the knowledge level in each information domain (consequences, actor positions, arguments) can vary between zero and one, and indicates the proportion of correct answers. The total knowledge index is an unweighted mean of the knowledge scores of the three domains. It has to be kept in mind, that this type of measurement in the form of aided recall is likely to overestimate knowledge levels.

Results

Results are reported for all three referendum campaigns. Some measures were not included for all campaigns or only in specific survey waves. Hence, not all analysis is based on exactly the same set of variables.

Gaps in exposure and reception: Media as channels for campaign information

Respondents were asked to rate the importance of different information channels on a five-point scale from 1 to 5. The results reported in Table 11.1 show that *television* and daily newspapers still are regarded as the most important mass media for information in a referendum. The *Internet* is less

Table 11.1   Importance of information channels and content

	Asylum			Naturalization	Tax
Wave	W1	W2	W3	W1	W1
N	~1,090	~1,090	~1,090	~990	~990
Information channel					
Television	3.7	3.7	3.5***	3.8	3.8
Daily Newspaper	3.6	3.6	3.3***	4.0	3.9
Governmental information booklet	–	3.6	3.3***	3.9	3.9
Interpersonal Comm.	3.3	3.3	3.1***	3.2	3.5
Radio	3.2	3.0**	2.8***	3.5	3.4
Weekly Newspapers	–	–	–	3.2	3.0
Sunday Newspapers	–	–	–	2.6	2.5
Magazines	2.5	2.5	2.2***	2.6	2.5
Internet	2.0	2.1*	1.8**	2.4	2.4
Free Newspapers	–	–	–	–	2.3
Billboards	2.0	2.1***	1.8***	2.2	2.3
Ads in the Press	2.0	2.1***	1.9	2.3	2.3
Content					
Political-discussion programs on TV	3.7	3.7	3.4	–	–
Comments from experts	3.5	3.5	3.2	–	–
Opinion pool results	3.0	3.0	2.7	–	–
Comments from journalists	2.9	2.9*	2.6	–	–

Note: Paired-samples t-test significant differences between W1–W2 and W1–W3 respectively: *p < .05, **p < .01, ***p < .001.

important than traditional mass media channels, the official governmental information booklet, and interpersonal communication. In the survey of the two later campaigns (naturalization and tax reform) additional newspaper categories were included. The results show that primarily the paid daily newspapers are used for political information. Sunday newspapers and free newspapers are of minor importance. Billboards and ads in the press are of little importance as information channels. However, we should note that these results are based on the subjective perception of the voters and should not be equated with 'influence'. For the asylum campaign, measurements were repeated in the second and third wave. This allows observing change in the importance of different channels during the campaign. Paired-samples, t-tests between wave 1 and wave 2 and between wave 1 and wave 3 show that the retrospective evaluation of channel importance is lower for all channels with the exception of ads (which remain stable). Only slight differences can be found between the three campaigns.

For the asylum campaign, the respondents were also asked to rate the importance of different media content. According to the figures reported, the most important contents were 'political discussion programs on TV', followed by 'comments from experts', 'opinion poll results' and 'comments from journalists'.

The use of media as information channels during a referendum campaign is not the same in each social segment; so there are quite a lot of *exposure gaps* (Table 11.2). In accordance with knowledge gap theory, *newspapers* as channel for campaign information are favoured by older voters and those with higher education. In contrast *television* is favoured by female voters and by the less educated segments. *Radio* is significantly more important as an information source for elder people and in the German speaking part of Switzerland. The latter result may be explained by the greater role of private local radio stations in this language region of Switzerland. There are also exposure gaps in relation to the new medium *Internet:* Especially the young and male voters seem to use the Internet as channel of campaign information. However, compared to the other sources the Internet plays a marginal role.

In addition to this comparison of information channels, it is of interest to compare the importance of different information sources (mass media, official information of the government, important politicians, preferred parties, and perceived public opinion) and the extent to which they are used to make up one's mind (Table 11.3). *Campaign coverage by the mass media* constitutes the most important source of information for Swiss voters,

Table 11.2 Exposure gaps across social segments (asylum campaign)

Means, W3, N = 1094		Television	Newspaper	Radio	Magazines	Internet
Total		3.49	3.28	2.79	2.21	1.83
Sex	Male	3.37	3.31	2.74	2.19	1.97
	Female	3.59	3.25	2.84	2.23	1.72
Age	(1) 18–34 years	3.29	3.10	2.44	2.13	2.15
	(2) 35–49 years	3.34	3.17	2.78[a]	2.18	1.70[a]
	(3) 50–64 years	3.62[a]	3.39	2.96[a]	2.31	1.70
	(4) 65 and older	3.67[a]	3.45[a]	2.92[a]	2.21	1.85
Region	F CH	3.41	3.14	2.55	2.19	1.59
	D CH	3.51	3.33	2.88	2.22	1.91
Education	(1) Low	3.74	3.05	2.66	2.18	1.85
	(2) Medium	3.55	3.19	2.80	2.19	1.72
	(3) High	3.46	3.43[a]	2.88	2.24	1.93
	(4) Elite	3.08[a]	3.53[a]	2.72	2.28	2.04

Note: means (a = unimportant information source); sig. differences (ANOVA and t-test respectively) p<.05.

Table 11.3 Source orientations for own opinion formation (asylum campaign)

	W1	W2	W3
N	~1,080	~1,080	~1,080
Campaign coverage of mass media	3.2	3.3**	3.2
Recommendation of government	2.9	2.9	2.8
Swiss public opinion	2.7	2.8**	2.6*
Recommendations of preferred parties	2.7	3.0***	2.7
Opinion of Christoph Blocher (pro)	2.2	2.4***	2.3
Opinion of Ruth Dreifuss (contra)	2.1	2.3***	2.0**

Note: Paired-samples t-test significant differences between W1–W2 and W1–W3 respectively: *p<.05, **p < .01, ***p < .001.

followed by the official information booklet of the Swiss government and the perceived opinion of the Swiss public. Party recommendations or recommendations by the two most prominent political figures, Christoph Blocher (member of government and strongly advocating the asylum law) and Ruth Dreifuss (former member of government, and leading figure of the opposing committee) seemed to be of minor importance as reference points for the voters' decisions. The importance of the various actors increases slightly from panel wave one to wave two, but decreases again later on. In general, the rank order of these orientations remained rather stable in the course of a campaign.

Campaign information flow, voter learning and knowledge gaps

The knowledge level of Swiss citizens increased significantly in the course of all three studied campaigns and in each of the three knowledge domains (consequences, actor positions, arguments) (Figure 11.1). It is remarkable that in the asylum campaign 80 per cent of the arguments are already familiar to the Swiss citizens at the first time point. This reflects the long lasting discussion around this issue which has started before the campaigns we studied. From a normative point of view, the knowledge level with respect to consequences and actor positions is distressingly low, however. In fact the average voter knows only 40 per cent of the consequences at the beginning and around two thirds of the consequences at the end of the campaign (asylum law). Knowledge on actor positions is low as well, even though in all three campaigns the parties positions were in line with their known left-right position. In the tax campaign the knowledge of actor positions is comparably high. However, it has to be noted that this index includes more items (labour and trade associations) which might lead to a biased picture compared to the two other campaigns. The only campaign with three measurement time points indicates that knowledge

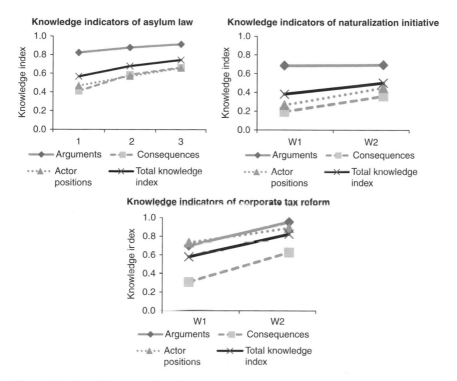

Figure 11.1 Development of total knowledge over time in the three campaigns

rises primarily in the first phase of the campaign and reaches a ceiling thereafter.

Knowledge gaps are usually operationalized in the form of *differences* between the knowledge level in the highest and the lowest educational segments or in form of a *correlation coefficient* between knowledge indicators and level of education. Tables 11.4 to 11.6 provide evidence of unequal knowledge distributions. The strength of the knowledge gaps differs substantially according to issue and knowledge type. In the case of the asylum law, the knowledge gap is initially widest for actor positions, whereas the corresponding gap for arguments is small. In the case of the corporate tax reform, the knowledge gap is widest for actor positions while the knowledge of arguments and consequences was initially more homogeneous, although rather low.

Furthermore, it is of interest whether the knowledge gaps increased or decreased over time. Tables 11.4 to 11.6 provide evidence that *existing knowledge gaps at the beginning stayed rather stable during the campaigns*. This holds true especially for the asylum campaign, whereas knowledge gaps

Table 11.4   Knowledge gaps as knowledge development over time by educational subgroups (asylum law)

Knowledge index N=1094		Arguments			Consequences			Actor positions			Total Knowledge		
		W1	W2	W3	W1	W2	W3	W1	W2	W3	W1	W2	W3
Knowledge	Diff.	0.08	0.05	0.06	0.12	0.13	0.14	0.21	0.22	0.17	0.13	0.13	0.13
gaps	Corr.	+0.12	+0.09	+0.13	+0.12	+0.14	+0.16	+0.20	+0.22	+0.22	+0.20	+0.22	+0.25

Table 11.5   Knowledge gaps as knowledge development over time by educational subgroups (naturalization initiative)

Knowledge index N = 1001		Arguments		Consequences		Actor positions		Total knowledge	
		W1	W2	W1	W2	W1	W2	W1	W2
Knowledge	Diff.	0.12	0.14	0.04	0.13	0.29	0.22	0.15	0.17
gaps	Corr.	+0.12	+0.17	+0.01	+0.12	+0.26	+0.23	+0.19	+0.25

Table 11.6   Knowledge gaps as knowledge development over time by educational subgroups (corporate tax reform)

Knowledge index N = 1001		Arguments		Consequences		Actor positions		Total knowledge	
		W1	W2	W1	W2	W1	W2	W1	W2
Knowledge	Diff.	0.00	0.05	0.01	0.18	0.25	0.29	0.09	0.18
gaps	Corr.	+0.01	+0.10	+0.04	+0.16	+0.22	+0.29	+0.14	+0.25

significantly increased in the corporate tax reform campaign. In this case, the initial knowledge levels have been rather low, but compared to the less educated citizens the better educated citizens acquired significantly more knowledge, especially concerning actor positions and consequences. As a consequence, knowledge gaps increased considerably.

Influencing and mediating factors

In a next step, we take a closer look at influencing and mediating factors besides education. This was done by multiple regression analyses (Tables 11.7–11.9) based on (1) socio-demographic factors (gender, age and education); (2) motivating factors (political interest); (3) cognitive factors (pre-existing knowledge); and (4) media influences (in the information channels used attentiveness to media information). Since knowledge acquisition is (at least

Table 11.7 Multiple regression of factors influencing different types of knowledge (asylum law)

Asylum law	Wave 1				Wave 2				Welle 3			
	Arguments	Consequence	ActorP.	Total	Arguments	Consequence	ActorP.	Total	Arguments	Consequence	ActorP.	Total
Betas												
Pre-existing knowledge	–	–	–	–	0.48	0.35	0.44	0.51	0.47	0.38	0.55	0.58
Age	0.19					-0.15		-0.11		-0.14		-0.09
Gender	-0.11		-0.19	-0.15			-0.07				-0.06	-0.05
Education		0.10	0.13	0.14		0.06				0.09	0.08	0.10
Issue interest												
Political interest	0.12	0.19	0.25	0.26	0.09	0.09	0.15	0.13	0.09		0.14	0.07
Interest in issue x education	0.09				0.09		0.11	0.08	0.09			
Interpersonal communication												
Frequency	0.10	0.12	0.08	0.13								
Opinion leader	0.11				–	–	–	–				
Opinion follower	-0.07				–	–	–	–				
Importance of sources												
Television	0.07											
Newspapers	0.06				0.06		0.08	0.11				
Radio			0.06	0.07		0.10						
Magazines												
Internet												
Billboards	-0.07	-0.06		-0.06	-0.09		-0.06	-0.06				
Print ads					0.05							
Gov't. information	–	–			0.12	0.10		0.09	0.06	-0.05	0.06	0.10
Media attention	0.12	0.13	0.14	0.14						0.12	0.06	
R^2adj.	0.17	0.13	0.17	0.26	0.33	0.21	0.35	0.43	0.30	0.21	0.42	0.46

Table 11.8 Multiple regression of factors influencing different types of knowledge (naturalization initiative)

Asylum law	Wave 1				Wave 2			
	Arguments	Consequence	ActorP.	Total	Arguments	Consequence	ActorP.	Total
Betas								
Pre-existing knowledge	–	–	–	–	0.33	0.14	0.28	0.31
Age	0.10							
Gender	-0.07			-0.08	-0.07	-0.10		-0.10
Education	0.10		0.20	0.25		0.08	0.14	0.13
Issue interest								
Political interest	0.18	0.10	0.25		0.17	0.13	0.17	0.20
Interest in issue x education				0.16			0.11	0.08
Interpersonal communication								
Frequency			0.13		0.11		0.06	0.09
Opinion leader								
Opinion follower					-0.06			
Importance of Channels								
Television								
Newspapers					0.08			
Radio								
Magazines		0.07						
Internet								
Billboards					-0.07			
Print ads			-0.07					
Gov't. information	-0.09	-0.09	0.07	-0.09		0.09	0.06	0.11
Media attention	0.18	0.08	0.07	0.17			0.06	
R²adj.	0.12	0.03	0.16	0.15	0.26	0.06	0.21	0.28

Table 11.9 Multiple regression of factors influencing different types of knowledge (corporate tax reform)

Asylum law	Wave 1				Wave 2			
	Arguments	Consequence	ActorP.	Total	Arguments	Consequence	ActorP.	Total
Betas								
Pre-existing knowledge	–	–	–	–	0.32	0.20	0.44	0.40
Age	0.28	0.09		0.15	0.13			
Gender	–0.09	–0.10	–0.22	–0.19		–0.09	–0.09	–0.08
Education			0.16	0.09	0.09		0.15	0.35
Issue interest	0.07				0.15			0.22
Political interest	0.14	0.12	0.25	0.24	0.08	0.08	0.19	0.13
Interest in issue x education						0.12		–0.25
Interpersonal communication Frequency	0.18	0.16		0.16	0.09		0.07	0.09
Opinion leader	–	–	–	–				
Opinion follower	–	–	–0.09	–		0.07		
Importance of sources								
Importance of channels								
Television								
Newspapers								
Radio	0.08							
Magazines						–0.08		–0.05
Internet							–0.05	–0.07
Billboards								
Print ads								
Gov't. information		–0.08	0.11	–0.07		0.17	0.09	0.12
Media attention	0.22	0.11		0.12				
R²adj.	0.22	0.13	0.21	0.29	0.29	0.17	0.45	0.45

to a certain extent) a cumulative process, the most important predictor for high knowledge at the end of the campaign is the knowledge at a previous time point. Compared to this parameter, all other aspects only have moderate or little explanatory power.

The results of the multiple regression analyses reveal some similarity between the three campaigns, but there are differences as well, which have to be explained by the unique features of the campaigns. With respect to *socio-demographic factors,* we find in all three campaigns and in all phases of a campaign moderate to *strong education-based knowledge gaps* and somewhat *weaker gender-based knowledge gaps.* The effect of *age* seems to be contingent on the issue at stake. Whereas older people were less informed in the case of the asylum law, they seemed to be more informed in the case of the corporate tax reform, at least at the beginning of the campaign, and in the case of the naturalization initiative, age did not influence knowledge acquisition.

With respect to interest, general political interest motivated information seeking and knowledge acquisition in all three of the studied campaigns. By contrast, issue-specific interest stimulated knowledge acquisition only in the case of the more complex and not well-known corporate tax reform issue. Issue-specific interest not only has a direct influence on knowledge, we also found moderate interaction effects in all three campaigns. However, compared to general political interest, this effect is rather unstable.

The frequency of *interpersonal communication* in the form of campaign-related discussions with family members, colleagues at work or friends is a moderate but rather stable predictor of campaign-related knowledge. However, in the case of the asylum law this only holds true at the beginning of the campaign (wave one). In addition to the frequency of interpersonal communication, the influence of different communication roles was also tested. However, the frequency of giving or receiving advice from other persons has only little explanatory power. It could be assumed that people who are asked for advice (opinion leaders) are chosen because they know more about the campaign. However, a positive effect was found only for knowledge about arguments in wave one of the asylum campaign. Asking other persons for advice can be interpreted in two distinctive ways. Either these persons (opinion followers) have higher knowledge because they receive additional information through interpersonal communication, or they could have lower knowledge, which causes them to search for information. In fact, positive as well as negative beta values are found for this parameter.

Media attentiveness, operationalized as 'having observed the issue of the campaign in the media attentively', has a modest influence on knowledge acquisition. The importance of the different information channels seems to have hardly any explanatory power at all. Campaign *ads* in the print media and posters or *bill boards* on streets and in public places have a negative impact on knowledge levels, which means that they seem to be used mostly by less informed citizens. The same holds true for the official information distributed by the government that is only modestly and in some cases even negatively correlated with campaign knowledge.

Latent growth curve model

The most important predictors identified in the multiple regressions were used to analyse the panel data with latent growth curve models a special type of structural equation model. These models have the advantage that they make use of the panel design of the data, whereas the multiple regressions only included the pre-existing knowledge as a time-dependent variable. The analysis focuses on the knowledge of consequences and analyses each of the three consequences separately for each campaign. Consequence C3 of the asylum campaign was excluded because it was not possible to obtain a sufficient model fit. This can be explained by the fact, that consequence C3 was a false statement which has probably led to many wrong and variable answers over time.

The model shows standardized estimates which can be interpreted in the same way as ordinary regression coefficients (Figure 11.2). The indices for model fit indicate an adequate level of specification.[1] The slope of the knowledge development can only be calculated for the asylum campaign because the other two campaigns only consist of two measurement time points. The unstandardized measures for slope (.55 and .52) confirm the findings of the previous analysis that there is a positive trend indicating a learning process. The fact that none of the knowledge curves starts at a value close to zero can be explained in two different ways: Either the first wave should have been conducted earlier to capture the very beginning of learning or it is a methodological artifact.

With respect to the knowledge gap hypothesis it is of special interest to analyse the influence of education on intercept and slope. Table 11.10 shows a significant positive influence of education on the intercept in five out of eight models. This confirms the findings of the previous analyses that better educated persons have higher knowledge at the beginning of the campaign. However, no significant effects were found for the slope. Hence, there is no evidence for an increasing knowledge gap between different education groups. Age seems to be of greater importance to explain different growth in knowledge. While older persons have a higher knowledge at the beginning of the campaign (significant positive effects for three consequences) there is a negative effect on slope. This means that younger persons start on a lower level but are able to learn faster than older generations. Differences between men and women are primarily found for the issue of the corporate tax reform. The negative values for the intercept indicate that women know generally less on that issue.

The findings from the multiple regression analysis that political interest and media attention are stable predictors for knowledge are confirmed.

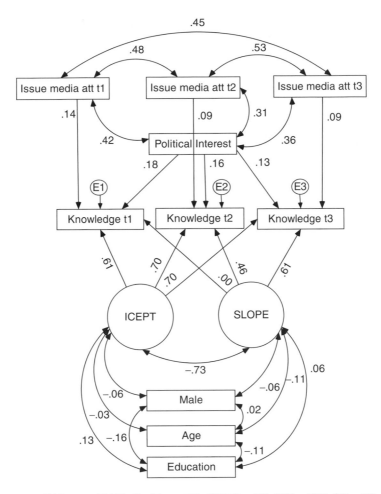

Chi Square = 59.755, df = 17, p = .000, RMSEA = .048, RMR = .0257, CFI = .973

Figure 11.2   Latent growth curve model of consequence C2 in the asylum campaign

However, this analysis reveals different issue-specific patterns. In the asylum campaign, political interest is an important predictor at the beginning of the campaign, but loses its importance over time. In the naturalization and tax campaigns, the dynamic points into the opposite direction. Political interest is less important to predict knowledge at the beginning but differentiates between the well and the poorly informed at the end of the campaign.

The models control for several additional covariances that are not displayed in the figure and not reported in the table. This includes covariance of age

Table 11.10 Parameter of the latent growth curve models for consequences

	Asylum			Naturalization			Tax		
	C1	C2	C3	C1	C2	C3	C1	C2	C3
Slope (US)	.55	.52	–	–	–	–	–	–	–
Education – intercept	–.03	.13**	–	–.02	.24**	–.01	.15**	.07	.13*
Education – Slope	.08	.06	–	–	–	–	–	–	–
Age – intercept	.17**	–.03	–	–.03	.01	.28**	.01	.07	.22***
Age – slope	.28***	–.11+	–			–	–	–	–
Male – intercept	–.03	–.06	–	.02	–.18	–.24*	–.17**	–.12*	–.26***
Male – slope	.02	–.06	–	–	–	–		–	–
Political interest – knowledge t1	.24***	.18***		–.02	.10	.01	.11***	.08**	.12***
Political interest – knowledge t2	.10***	.16***	–	.00	.36***	.20***	.15***	.11***	.12***
Political interest – knowledge t3	.02	.13***	–	–	–	–	–	–	–
Issue media attention t1	–.01	.14***	–	0.00	.10*	.07*			–
Issue media attention t2	.05	.09**	–	–	–	–	.11***	.09**	.23***
Issue media attention t3	.11*	.09**	–	–	–	–	–	–	–
Education – male	–.16***	–.16***	–	–.01***	–.01***	–.01***	–.18***	–.18***	–.18***
Education – age	–.11***	–.11***	–	–.04	–.04	–.04	–.14***	–.14***	–.14***
Chi square	44.463	59.755	–	16.852	19.779	26.337	23.942	54.248	35.283
df	17	17	–	9	7	9	9	9	9
p	.000	.000	–	.051	.006	.002	.004	.000	.000
RMSEA	.038	.048	–	.030	.043	.044	.041	.071	.054
RMR	.0131	.0257	–	.0237	.0247	.0282	.0259	.0248	.0396
CFI	.982	.973	–	.966	.962	.936	.970	.899	.955

Note: Significant covariances and regression weights: $^+p < 0.1$, $^*p < 0.05$, $^{**}p < 0.01$, $^{***}p < 0.001$.

with issue media attention at all three time points (generally positive values), covariances of age with political interest, and covariances of sex with political interest (negative). In one model (asylum C1) direct effects from issue media attention on intercept and the slope were included. Results show that issue media attention at the second and third time point have a positive effect on the intercept but media attention at the second time point has a negative effect on slope. This means that persons who report higher media attentiveness in wave two have a higher knowledge but learn slower. This combination of a positive effect on the intercept and a negative effect on slope is a typical sign for ceiling effects.

An important aspect to control for is the relation between age, gender, and education. The results show that there are important general patterns among these variables. Gender as well as age are negatively correlated with education, which means that old women are least educated and young men are best educated. It can be assumed that the negative correlation between education and age helps to scale down the knowledge gap to a certain extent. Older people are found to have both a higher knowledge and a higher political interest (both are important predictors for knowledge at the first time point). Younger people are able to limit the increase of the knowledge gap due to their better education.

Conclusion

The analyses presented in this chapter focused on the *role of media use and knowledge* acquisition in three referendum campaigns. They are based on the *knowledge gap paradigm,* which hypothesizes education-based gaps in exposure to campaign information channels and in acquiring campaign-related knowledge, and, as a consequence, increasing knowledge gaps in the course of the campaigns.

The results of our analyses clearly confirm that citizens in Switzerland still use the classical media *television and newspapers as main information channels* in direct-democratic campaigns. So far, the *Internet* as a new information source is only used by well-educated younger men and has no measurable impact on campaign knowledge. In addition, there are significant *exposure gaps* insofar as better educated citizens more heavily depend on print media, such as newspapers, whereas the less educated depend more on television as the main channel of campaign information.

With respect to *media effects in the form of knowledge acquisition* stimulated by an increase of information flow during a referendum campaign, our analyses generally confirm the existing knowledge gap research insofar as there are education- and gender-based knowledge gaps. Well educated men are better informed about the consequences, actors positions, and their arguments compared to less educated women. The detailed analysis of the consequences with latent growth curve models confirms these general patterns. The results indicate rather limited effects of mass media as information sources for knowledge acquisition. In fact, it is the *frequency of interpersonal communication, general political interest,* and *media attentiveness* which trigger knowledge acquisition.

From a normative perspective, it can be argued that the average knowledge level is rather low at the moment of the vote. For example. on the topic of naturalization, less than 50 per cent of the consequences are known on average. Knowledge of arguments seems to be generally higher than the other types of knowledge, while knowledge on actors' positions seems to be dependent on the issue.

Note

1. Root Mean Square Error of Approximation (RMSEA) of less than .07, a Comparative Fit Index (CFI) of above .92 and a Root Mean Residual of less than .05 (Hair et al. 2006: 753; Byrne 2001: 82).

12
When Campaign Messages Meet Ideology: The Role of Arguments for Voting Behaviour

Werner Wirth, Jörg Matthes, and Christian Schemer

In a seminal review of the research literature on political persuasion, McGuire (1985: 269) states that 'for half millennia rhetoricians have been analysing types of arguments, but surprisingly little empirical work has been done on the comparative effectiveness of different argument structures'. This conclusion is somewhat surprising, considering the relevance of arguments in all kinds of political debates. Especially in referendum campaigns, political parties, NGOs, and other organizations form strategic camps that hold an arsenal of arguments. At its heart, the campaign debate is centred on specific arguments in favour of or opposing a proposal. Each camp tries to promote their arguments in the debate, and the camp with the most salient and thus most compelling arguments wins the referendum. Knowing which arguments do prevail and which turn out to be less powerful in predicting the vote is therefore of central importance for the field of political persuasion.

In answering this broad question, previous research has mainly focused on the power and relative strength of positive or negative arguments (Lau 1985), the question of one-sided and two-sided argument structures (Chong and Druckman 2007), or the impact of mass-media framing on the argument repertoire of citizens (Simon and Jerit 2007). This chapter takes a different approach: We aim to answer the question of what kinds of citizens are susceptible to what kinds of arguments. It is argued that general predispositions such as left–right political ideology determine the persuasive strength of arguments. The fundamental idea is that some arguments will be more powerful in predicting voting behaviour for some kinds of individuals (e.g., left-wing citizens), while other arguments exert a stronger impact on other citizens (e.g., right-wing citizens). By doing so, we will be able to tell, first, if there is an impact of political arguments when general predispositions such as ideology are controlled for. Second, we can examine interactions of arguments and ideology, that is, that some arguments are only powerful for some people. Third and more generally, we aim at studying the dynamics of this process. In other words, the power of arguments and their interaction with ideology is analysed over time in the course of three different political campaigns.

This chapter is structured as follows: In a first step, we discuss the role of arguments for direct-democratic campaigns, especially in regard to voting behaviour. Second, we then examine the absolute weight of those arguments for each analysed campaign, that is, how strongly does the public agree with the central arguments. After that, we factor analyse all arguments in a third step. This mostly leads us to two factors for each campaign, one factor with the pro, and one with all contra arguments. At the heart of the paper, we then examine the relative weight of those argument factors for the voting decision controlling for a number of variables. The core question is whether certain arguments are more powerful in predicting voting behaviour when they meet a certain pattern of political ideology.

Arguments in political persuasion

Arguments are the key to political persuasion (Cobb and Kuklinski 1997). In every debate, two positions are pitted against each other; one side arguing in favour of a certain policy program, and the other arguing why citizens should reject it. As such, arguments are put forward by public actors, such as political figures, journalists, parties, or a camp of several actors in a referendum campaign. The higher the correlation between the arguments of a certain actor and the corresponding arguments in the media coverage, the higher is the frame building impact of that actor (see Chapter 9). Likewise, the higher the correspondence between the arguments in the media and the public salience of those arguments, the higher is the likelihood that citizens will use these arguments in their voting decisions.

Zaller (1992) theorizes that one-sided, agreed-upon argument structures are very likely to be influential to the public. However, when elites or public actors disagree in their arguments, public opinion effects are less predictable. This is important since most if not all public debates are rather ambiguous and open to different interpretations and arguments. This idea is also inherent in the framing perspective (Entman 1993; Entman, Matthes and Pellicano 2009; Matthes 2009). Frames selectively emphasize certain arguments over others as they propose a certain problem definition, treatment recommendation, causal interpretation, and moral evaluation. For the most part, these frames take the form of arguments, and a bundle of consistent arguments supporting or opposing a policy mark an entire frame.

The value of arguments for a debate can be measured by their persuasive power. This power, however, depends on various factors. There is a large body of evidence that strong arguments are more persuasive than weak arguments, especially when individuals are highly motivated and have the ability and opportunity to process those arguments (e.g., Petty and Cacioppo 1986).

Although previous research works well to explain why some arguments are more persuasive than others in general terms, the weight of arguments in the realm of politics can vary substantially with the political predispositions of citizens. This idea is in line with Zaller's (1992) model of opinion formation which states that any opinion formation process is a product of issue information (i.e. political arguments) and predispositions (such as political ideology). The extent to which predispositions are linked to the rise of arguments in a referendum debate is a key to our understanding of why some arguments turn out to be stronger than others.

The chief ideological predisposition is the left–right political orientation of individuals (see Kroh 2007). The idea is that citizens tag themselves as 'left' or 'right' when thinking about political issues. Many studies have shown that individuals act upon on that basic dimension: They derive policy views, vote for parties and candidates, and act in a way that they perceive as being close to their left–right ideological placement (e.g., Sears and Funk 1999). As Hellwig (2008: 689) states, left–right ideological orientations 'can be used as a kind of super issue dimension to access the preferences of citizens and policy makers'.

When thinking about the interplay of ideological predispositions and campaign arguments in shaping the vote, three different scenarios are possible. Each leads to a different prediction about the weight of arguments, the weight of predispositions, and the interaction of arguments and predispositions.

Argument-ideology equivalence

First, it is possible that debate arguments are essentially the same as political predispositions. That means, when controlling for political ideology, debate arguments do not explain any further variance in predicting voting outcomes. Put differently, the arguments simply reflect the political ideology of citizens. For instance, arguing for social justice is at the heart of a left-wing ideology, that is, holding this argument is essentially the same as referring oneself to be left-wing. We call this *argument-ideology equivalence*. This means that citizens do not need to know all arguments, they can derive their decision simply from their ideological predisposition (see Christin, Hug, and Sciarini 2002). This is especially likely at the beginning of a campaign, were citizens don't know that much about the content of a referendum. In such a case, predispositions would be much more powerful in explaining the vote than arguments. Whatever the specific reason for argument-ideology equivalence may be, the impact of arguments on the vote will be marginal or non-significant when a (significant) effect of ideology is controlled for.

Argument-ideology independence

Second, it is also possible that arguments and political ideology are completely independent. This would mean that arguments and ideology have a unique and independent effect on voting decisions. This does mostly occur when arguments are not completely tied to political predispositions; for instance, at the beginning of a campaign or for newly emerging political issues. Here, we would find no interaction between argument and ideology: It is not the case that some arguments are more persuasive to left-wing and some others are more powerful to right-wing individuals. Apparently, arguments stand for themselves and they are equally persuasive for all citizens. We call this *argument-ideology independence*. This reasoning is roughly in line with a simple priming account of public opinion formation. According to priming theory, the most accessible arguments will have the strongest weight for a voting decision, independent from predispositions (Mutz, Sniderman, and Brody 1996). That means that, in expressing their opinions, individuals draw on the arguments that come to their minds at the time a judgment is called for (Price and Tewksbury 1997; Valkenburg, Semetko and de Vreese, 1999; for a critique Entman, Matthes and Pellicano 2009). '[T]he theory is that information that can be more easily retrieved from memory tends to dominate judgments, opinions, and decisions' (Iyengar 1991: 130–131). According to this theorizing, it does not matter if a person can be regarded as left-wing or right-wing, the most accessible arguments will determine the vote.

Argument-ideology interaction

Third, and probably the most likely account, arguments and predispositions can interact to influence voting decisions, simply called *argument-ideology interaction*. Put differently, only those arguments that match with a certain predisposition of an individual are relevant for voting behaviour. This assumption contradicts a simple priming account of opinion formation. Lenz (2004) provides some evidence that only those pieces of campaign information are relevant to voting decisions that match with political predispositions. It follows that campaign arguments activate existing predispositions, and depending on the direction and strength of these predispositions, arguments turn out to be powerful or weak (Finkel 1993; Gelman and King 1993; Lazarsfeld, Berelson, and Gaudet 1944). This means, the existence of ideological predispositions and ideologically relevant campaign arguments does not in itself assure the predictability of the vote. Technically speaking, although there can still be a main effect of arguments, they are especially powerful when they meet certain predispositions. Some arguments are powerful when they match with a left-wing ideology; others gain great weight when they match with a right-wing ideology.

Hypotheses

We test these three possible outcomes – *argument-ideology equivalence, independence,* and *interaction* – for all three referendum campaigns, and for all waves of a single campaign. We *hypothesize that argument-ideology interaction will be more likely toward the end of the campaign, and argument-ideology independence as well as argument-ideology equivalence will be more likely at the beginning of a campaign* (hypothesis 1). The reason is that, in the course of a campaign, arguments are more and more tied to political predispositions. All involved parties or political actors take sides in a referendum and this knowledge is more and more distributed among the public. In other words, ideological bias rises toward the end of a campaign. At the beginning of a campaign, in contrast, arguments are either not known to the broad public – which could lead to argument-ideology equivalence – or they are not yet linked to ideological positions.

In addition to theorizing that argument-ideology interaction is more likely toward the end of a campaign, we also assume that this interaction may depend on the type of the campaign. In Chapter 2, we distinguished between three criteria of campaigns: their difficulty, their intensity, and the overall balance or asymmetry of the resources of the camps. It is argued that corporation tax campaign is a high difficulty-high intensity campaign with a pro balance. In contrast, the naturalization campaign is low in difficulty, average in intensity, but also with a pro balance. The asylum campaign is similar to the naturalization campaign, but here the balance is rather symmetric. When considering these characteristics of all three campaigns, especially the difficulty might play a role for predicting the matching of arguments and ideology in shaping the vote. When difficulty is high, citizens will have problems with the campaign arguments to match their ideological predispositions. Put differently, complex campaign issues are likely to promote complex arguments. In turn, when arguments are complex, individuals cannot use their ideological predispositions to understand them, as the arguments might not translate to these predispositions. Thus, we theorize that arguments and ideology are less likely to interact for difficult compared to easy-to-grasp campaigns. Therefore, we can formulate the hypothesis that there will be *a stronger argument-ideology interaction for the less difficult asylum and naturalization campaigns than for the rather difficult taxation campaign* (hypothesis 2).

Argument structures in public opinion data

Before we test our hypotheses, we examine the extent to which the public agrees with the central arguments of each campaign (see Chapter 3). For each of the three campaigns, we report survey data on the approval of those arguments. This shall provide a first overview of the absolute importance of some arguments. In order to shed light on argument structures in the course of a campaign, we then factor analyse all campaign arguments. This shall lead us to several factors that can be entered in a regression model as predictors.

Asylum campaign

Figure 12.1 shows the means of all arguments (for all three panel waves) in the first campaign. It is apparent that 'rule of law', 'humanitarian tradition' and 'abuse' are the most important arguments in terms of agreement by the public. Less important arguments are 'too many asylum seekers' or 'stronger hand is without effect'. The overall support of the arguments hardly changes over time. It is interesting to note that both, arguments in favour of and opposing the proposal are among the four most important arguments. Put differently, by looking at the simple distribution of means, we cannot predict how the final voting decision will look like. Furthermore, no argument wins much in importance in the course of the campaign; almost all of them remain at their initial level of support in wave 1. As a visual inspection of the means reveals, however, some arguments slightly lose some importance over time, especially toward the end of the campaign.

Principal component analyses[1] were conducted for each wave. The analysis for the first wave reveals two factors. The first factor, called *asylum abuse* (arguments 1, 3, and 5), embraces the idea that action must be taken against a misconduct of asylum, that asylum policy should be stricter, and that there are already too many asylum seekers in Switzerland. In short, this

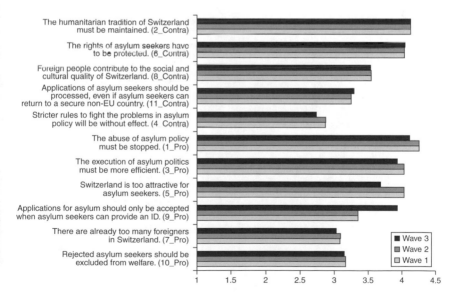

Figure 12.1 Mean distribution of asylum campaign arguments over time

argument structure poses a negative view of the whole issue of asylum policy and calls for very strict rules for asylum seekers. The focus is on negative aspects of asylum seekers. The second factor summarizes a completely different argumentation. This factor is called *humanitarian tradition* (arguments 2, 6, and 8). It stresses that the rights of asylum seekers must be protected, that the humanitarian tradition of Switzerland must be maintained, or that asylum seekers contribute to the social and cultural quality of Switzerland. This factor touches positive aspects of asylum seekers.

When conducting the same principal component analysis for wave two and wave three, the argument structure remains constant over the course of the whole campaign. Exactly the same pattern of arguments is found for both waves. The first factor, asylum abuse, can be reliably measured in all panel waves.[2] The second factor, humanitarian tradition, is less but still sufficiently reliable.[3] Reliability cannot be increased by deleting items.

Naturalization of immigrants

The distribution of means for both panel waves is depicted in Figure 12.2. It is obvious that three arguments are the most important ones in the eyes of the Swiss public. Swiss citizens largely agree with the statements that the fundamental rights of foreigners must be protected, that the process of naturalizing immigrants must be in line with the rule of law, and foreigners who want to become Swiss citizens are generally well

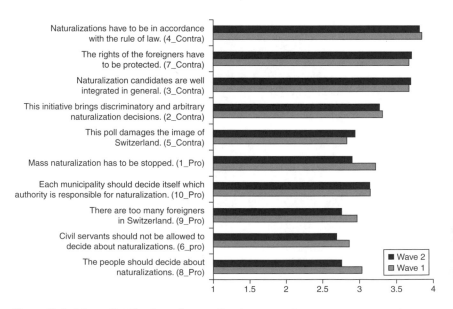

Figure 12.2   Mean distribution of naturalization campaign arguments over time

integrated. When looking at those arguments that find less agreement, we find four that are noteworthy: There are already too many foreigners in Switzerland, the Swiss public should be able to decide about naturalization applications, naturalizations by civil servants must be avoided, and the naturalization proposal harms the image of Switzerland. One of those arguments – that there are already too many foreigners in the country – was also asked with identical wording in the first study. When comparing the asylum study and the naturalization study, it becomes apparent that the public agreed with this argument to a larger extent when deciding about asylum policy. This can be explained by the fact that asylum seekers have probably a more negative image than foreigners who want to attain the Swiss citizenship. The reason is that foreigners applying for citizenship are already well integrated, and they already contribute to the wealth of the country. Thus, in the context of naturalization, foreigners are viewed in a more positive light than refugees in the context of asylum policy.

Figure 12.2 also shows that some arguments lose their importance from the first to the second panel wave. Especially those arguments that draw a negative picture of foreigners – arguments 2, 3, and 10 – find significantly less agreement in wave 2 compared to wave 1 (repeated measures analysis of variance, $p < .001$). Interestingly, there is only one argument that finds more agreement over time; that is, the argument that the proposal does harm to the image of Switzerland. All of this points to the trend that the Swiss public rejects the proposal, especially toward the end of the campaign.

When conducting principal component analysis using the same procedure as before, two factors can be found (explained variance 44%). The first factor comprises the arguments 1, 6, 8, and 10. It is argued that the Swiss public should be able to decide about who should and who should not be naturalized, or that mass naturalizations must be stopped. This factor is supportive of the naturalization reform. Thus, we call it *mass naturalization*. The second factor is made up of arguments against the naturalization proposal (arguments 2, 3, 4, 5, and 7): It is argued that the reform leads to arbitrary and discriminating naturalization decisions, that the proposal does harm to the image of Switzerland, or that all naturalizations must be in accordance with the rule of law. The factor is thus called *rule of law*. In the second panel wave, both factors can be found in precisely the same manner.[4]

Corporate taxation

Figure 12.3 depicts the distribution of means for the arguments in the corporate tax campaign. As should be apparent, four arguments can be regarded as important to the broad public. Most citizens agree that tax gifts to major stockholders are unfair, and that action needs to be taken against the high salaries of top managers. An analysis of variance with repeated

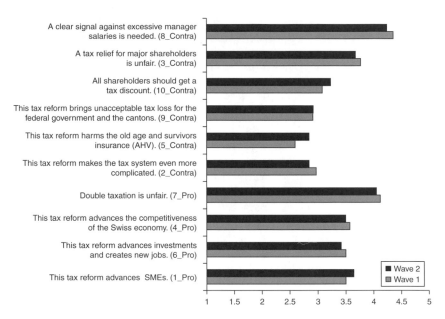

Figure 12.3   Mean distribution of corporate taxation campaign arguments over time

measures reveals that some arguments grow and others lose in importance over time. The arguments that the reform harms small and mid-sized companies, that the reform harms old and survivors' insurance contribution (AHV), and that tax cuts should be given to all stakeholders (not only the major ones) significantly (p < .01) grow in importance when comparing the first and the second wave of the panel study. In contrast, the argument that action against high manager salaries should be taken, and the argument that the new reform will further complicate the Swiss taxation system significantly decrease over time (p < .05).

We conducted a principal component analysis for both panel waves, applying the same procedure as described above (see also Chapter 14). Again, we find two factors. The first factor (arguments 1, 4, and 6) emphasizes the positive aspects of the reform. Thus, we simply call this factor *business benefits*. It is argued that the reform helps small and mid-sized companies, the competitive capability of Switzerland will be increased by the reform, or that the reform brings jobs and new investments. The second factor (arguments 5, 9, and 2) draws a completely different picture. It comprises all contra arguments, thus called *tax losses*. Here, it is argued that the reform harms the old and survivors' insurance contribution (so-called AHV), that the Swiss federation and the cantons will lose important tax money, and that the tax system will be further complicated. Again, this argument structure remains constant over the course of the whole campaign – exactly the same factors are found for the second panel wave. Reliability of both factors is lower compared to the asylum policy campaign.[5] This is certainly due to the fact that fewer items are involved in these factors.

Explaining the vote

As a result of the principal component analyses described above, we have now extracted several argument factors that can be entered in an ordinal logistic regression model to explain the vote. As the dependent variable of both waves we take voting intention ranging from 1 'strongly oppose the referendum' to 4 'strongly in favour'.[6]

We entered basic demographic variables such as sex, age, and highest education, left–right political ideology, and the argument factors. Finally, we also include the interaction term of each argument factor and the left–right ideology of our respondents. The idea behind this interaction term is that some arguments may be more powerful in explaining the vote when they meet with certain patterns of political ideology. The absence of such an interaction would imply that the arguments are equally power-ful, independent from the political ideology of our respondents. For the second and third wave of each panel study, we control for the autoregressive effect of voting intention prior to including the campaign arguments as predictors. Both, the argument factors and the ideology variable were mean centred. The interaction is analysed by plotting the effect of the focal predic-tor at the mean, one standard deviation below, and one standard deviation above the mean of the moderator. No serious threats of multi-colinearity were observed in the regression models reported below.

Asylum campaign

The results of an ordinal logistic regression analysis for the Asylum Campaign are presented in Table 12.1. In all three waves, demographic vari-ables hardly have any effects of on voting intentions. However, at wave one, higher educated individuals are less enthusiastic about the tightening of the asylum law. Not surprisingly, citizens who hold right-wing political ideolo-gies would also vote more in favour of the referendum proposal compared to voters who consider themselves as left-wing. Ideology has a very strong effect on vote choice.

However, when controlling for all those variables (including ideology) there is still a considerable amount of variance that can be explained with the approval of specific arguments in the campaign. It follows that no argument-ideology equivalence can be observed in the data. As can be seen in Table 12.1, the asylum abuse argument structure is a far stronger predictor of the voting outcome is the argument that the humanitarian tradition of Switzerland must be maintained. Obviously, the latter arguments are not as powerful as the abuse arguments. Considering the outcome of the vote,

Table 12.1   Regression coefficients for predicting the voting decision (asylum study)

Predictors	Wave 1 B	Wave 1 S_B	Wave 2 B	Wave 2 S_B	Wave 3 B	Wave 3 S_B
Demographics						
Sex	−.151	.135	−.229	.150	−.026	.142
Age	.006	.004	.003	.004	−.005	.004
Highest education	−.065**	.022	−.029	.025	−.014	.023
Political Predisposition						
Left–right ideology	.199**	.036	.161**	.040	.206**	.040
Autoregression						
Prior voting intention	–	–	.668**	.038	.768**	.079
Argument Factors						
Asylum abuse (Pro)	1.06**	.092	1.18**	.099	1.419**	.107
Humanitarian tradition (Con)	−.682**	.086	−.593**	.099	−.820**	.100
Interaction						
Asylum abuse x ideology	.057	.039	.016	.044	−.097*	.044
Humanitarian tradition x ideology	.51	.036	.025	.047	.009	.046
Total Nagelkerke Pseudo R^2	.432		.555		.668	

Note: *p < .05, **p < .001.

this is a very crucial finding. It appears that the arguments opposing the referendum proposal were weaker and therefore less effective compared to those in favour. In contrast, portraying asylum seekers in a negative light by putting forth arguments of abuse turned out to be an effective strategy. In this context, it is interesting to note that humanitarian tradition finds strong approval when we look at the absolute means of single arguments (see Table 12.1). Maybe because of this approval, its impact on the vote is comparatively small, that is, because the pros think they can safely vote for the referendum without violating the principle of humanitarian tradition. Thus, this argument structure does not perfectly discriminate between those who vote 'yes' and those who vote 'no'.

In a final step, we wanted to answer the question of whether there is an argument-ideology equivalence, independence, or interaction. As can be seen in Table 12.1, there is, in fact, an interaction effect of asylum abuse and political ideology in the third panel wave. For waves one and two, however, there is argument-ideology independence. The interaction effect for wave three is visualized in Figure 12.4. Surprisingly, this effect is negative and not positive. A positive effect would have meant that the argument structure of asylum abuse exerts a stronger impact on the vote for right-wing compared to left-wing respondents. Obviously, this is not the case. On the contrary, the abuse argument has a stronger effect on left-wing voters. The

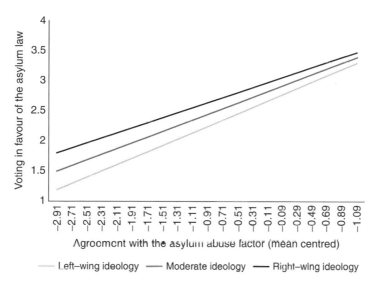

Figure 12.4 Interaction of asylum abuse argument and ideology at wave three of the asylum study

negative sign of this interaction suggests that the impact of ideology on voting choice decreases among those who agree with this argument. For those who agree with the argument, ideology makes no difference anymore, while it does make a difference for those who disagree with it: voters on the left who disagree vote more consistently against the law compared to right-wing voters who disagree. Figure 12.4 also illustrates that agreeing with the asylum abuse arguments is a very strong predictor of the vote. In explaining this interaction pattern, it is interesting to note that the regression weights for asylum abuse in predicting voting intention are on the rise over the course of the campaign (see Table 12.1). This might be a hint that the argument becomes overly powerful, thus impeding the predicted *positive* interaction effect of arguments and ideology.

Naturalization of immigrants

As Table 12.2 demonstrates, in wave one, women do oppose the referendum proposal more than men, and education is a negative predictor of voting in favour of the proposal. Age, however, has no effect on the outcome of the vote. When it comes to the political predisposition variables, left–right ideology is a significant and strong positive predictor of voting in favour in both panel waves. Also for both panel waves, the argument structure that argues in favour of the reform has a stronger impact than the *rule of law* factor. Obviously, these arguments were much more successful in shaping the vote than the contra arguments.

Table 12.2   Regression coefficients for predicting the voting decision (naturalization study)

Predictors	Wave 1		Wave 2	
	B	S_B	B	S_B
Demographics				
Sex	−.303*	.158	−.161	.185
Age	−.003	.005	−.010	.005
Highest education	−.084**	.027	−.045	.032
Political Predisposition				
Left–right–ideology	.137**	.039	.127**	.047
Autoregression				
Prior voting intention	–	–	.608**	.093
Argument Factors				
Mass naturalization (Pro)	.972**	.090	.917**	.109
Rule of law (Con)	−.428**	.089	−.525**	.104
Interaction				
Mass naturalization x ideology	−.027	.033	.078*	.040
Rule of law x ideology	−.024	.034	−.075+	.042
Total Nagelkerke Pseudo R^2	.408		.521	

Note: *p < .05, **p < .001, +p = .07.

When it comes to the question whether arguments and ideology are equivalent, independent, or interactive in their effects on vote choice, we find an interesting pattern of results. In wave one of the panel study, there is no significant interaction of ideology and both argument structures. However, for wave two, there is an interaction of political ideology and the *mass naturalization* argument structure, and a somewhat weaker interaction effect between ideology and the *rule of law* factor. The positive sign of the first interaction signals that the impact of the pro argument rises with an increase in right-wing ideology. Put differently, the more right-wing an individual is, the more powerful is the effect of this argument structure. Likewise, the negative sign of the second interaction effect suggests that the contra argument loses power the more right-wing our respondents are. In other words, contra arguments are less powerful in shaping the vote for right-wing respondents compared to left-wing respondents.

To illustrate, we visualize the interaction for the pro-reform *mass naturalization* factor in Figure 12.5. As can be seen, the line for right-wing individuals runs steeper than the line for left-wing individuals. In other words, both for left-wing and for right-wing individuals, agreement with the pro arguments leads to a vote in favour of the naturalization proposal. However, this effect is stronger for right-wing compared to left-wing individuals. Citizens varying in political ideology are thus not equally susceptible

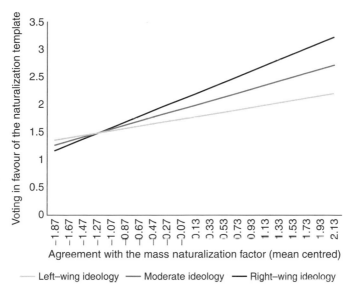

Figure 12.5 Interaction of the pro-reform argument (mass naturalization) and ideology at wave 2 of the naturalization study

to this argument structure. This is exactly what we have called argument-ideology interaction.

Corporate taxation

The results of the moderated ordinal regression are shown in Table 12.3. In wave one, there is no difference between men and women with regard to voting intention, however, in wave two, women oppose the proposal more than men. Also older voters are more opposed to the reform than younger ones, but only for wave two. When it comes to ideology, respondents who regard themselves as right-wing are more inclined to vote in favour of the proposal than those who identify with a left-wing political ideology. This effect remains constant for both panel waves.

When it comes to the effect of campaign arguments, there is a very strong impact of the *business benefits* argument structure on voting decision over the whole course of the campaign. The opposite argument structure, *tax losses*, does also have a significant effect in both waves. However, this effect is somewhat weaker. It can be concluded that both argument structures did exert an influence on voting decisions, although the ideology of our respondents was controlled for. Thus, there is no argument-ideology equivalence. As can be seen in Table 12.3, there is also no argument-ideology interaction. Put differently, for the corporate taxation campaign, the arguments turn out to be equally powerful for both, left-wing and right-wing

Table 12.3   Regression coefficients for predicting the voting decision (corporate taxation study)

Predictors	Wave 1		Wave 2	
	B	S_B	B	S_B
Demographics				
Sex	.044	.143	−.431*	.168
Age	−.002	.004	−.007	.005
Highest education	.015	.022	−.053*	.026
Political Predispositions				
Left–Right ideology	.272**	.035	.137**	.043
Autoregression				
Prior voting intention	–	–	.869**	.107
Argument Factors				
Business benefits (Pro)	.973**	.079	1.272**	1.21
Tax losses (Con)	−.622**	.075	−.621**	.092
Interaction				
Business benefits x ideology	−.003	.032	−.043	.045
Tax losses x ideology	−.039	.033	−.043	.038
Total Nagelkerke Pseudo R^2	.448		.588	

Note: *p < .05, **p < .001.

individuals. When left-wing individuals hold an argument that contradicts their ideological predisposition, this argument does nevertheless exert a powerful impact. More generally, it is not the case that some arguments work best when they match with a certain ideological predisposition. Hence, when voting in favour of or opposed to the corporate taxation proposal, ideologies and campaign arguments have an independent effect on the vote. This result is in line with our second hypothesis, predicting no argument-ideology interaction for complex campaigns.

Conclusion

We have opened this chapter by asking why some arguments turn out to be powerful predictors of the vote while others are less successful. We analysed public opinion data from all three referendum campaigns and examined the absolute and relative impact of those arguments that prevailed in the campaign. As a visual inspection of Tables 12.1, 12.2, and 12.3 reveals, the regression weights for almost all argument factors do remain on a constant level over the course of the entire campaign. Except for the *asylum abuse* factor in the asylum study, we cannot say that some factors grow and some loose in importance.

We theorized that there could be three different relationships between arguments and the political ideology of citizens. First, it could be possible that arguments simply equal ideological predispositions. This would mean that they have no unique effect on vote choice when ideology is controlled for. In all three campaigns, this has not been the case. In contrast, the argument factors explained a huge amount of variance even if ideology and the autoregressive effect of prior vote choice were controlled for. Second, we assumed that arguments and left–right ideology could exert an independent influence on the vote. In fact, we found no interaction between both variables in every single panel study. However, for the asylum and the naturalization study, this did only happen in the first panel wave. In other words, when campaign arguments are introduced to the public, citizens are convinced by them no matter whether they are left-wing or right-wing. Third, it was theorized that arguments could interact with ideological predispositions. However, this did only occur toward the end of the campaign. Especially in the naturalization campaign, some arguments were more powerful for right-wing individuals while others exerted a stronger impact on the vote for left-wing individuals. Thus, our hypothesis that argument-ideology interaction is more likely toward the end of the campaign can be confirmed.

Interestingly, and in line with our second hypothesis, no such interactions were found for the corporate taxation study. One reason is that this issue is rather difficult (see Chapter 2) and, therefore, the arguments were not as closely tied to predispositions compared to the asylum and the naturalization referendum. Moreover, this could be an explanation for the fact that the outcome of this referendum was rather close (50.5 per cent in favour).

The results are also informative about the democratic quality of direct-democratic campaigns. In all three studies, it has not been the case that citizens simply act according to their ideology. Since we found no evidence for argument-ideology equivalence, political ideology *alone* is not able to fully account for voting intentions. Direct-democratic campaigns are about arguments and, as we have seen, these arguments play a decisive role in determining the voting outcome. Especially for complex and difficult campaigns, citizens base their decisions on the campaigns arguments they find most convincing, no matter if a person is a traditional left-wing or right-wing voter. By the same token, arguments are not the one and only source of influence as ideological positions still have an impact over the course of campaigns.

In sum, we can conclude that the interaction of arguments and ideological predispositions depends on the extent to which arguments can be translated to ideological positions. When arguments do not reflect ideological positions – for instance, in campaigns with high difficulty – their impact on voting behaviour will not be moderated by ideology. In contrast, when an issue is less difficult and touches cherished ideological positions, the meeting of arguments and ideological positions will boost the vote. Taken together, the matching of campaign arguments and ideological positions does provide a reasonable explanation for the success and dynamic of referendum campaigns. This insight should serve to invite increased empirical investigations on the comparative effectiveness of different argument structures, answering McGuire's (1985) call for a deeper understanding of this key phenomenon in democratic campaigning.

Notes

1. To keep factors comparable between the chapters of this volume, campaign arguments and campaign emotions were jointly included in one factor analysis. In the course of this analysis, some arguments were excluded (see Chapter 13).
2. Cronbach's α in wave one: .72, in wave two: .75, and in wave three: .77.
3. Cronbach's α in wave one: .61, in wave two: .63, and in wave three: .66.
4. The reliability (Cronbach's α) for the first factor is .65 in wave1 and .72 in wave 2. The reliability of the second factor is lower but still reasonable: α = .56 for wave one and α = .60 in wave two. The αs do not significantly increase when single items are excluded.
5. The reliability of the first factor is α = .65 for the first wave and α = .71 for the second. For factor two, a Cronbach's α of .60 and .66 for wave 1 and wave 2, respectively is obtained. Excluding single items does not significantly increase the αs.
6. Undecided/don't knows were treated as missing values.

13
The Impact of Positive and Negative Affects in Direct-Democratic Campaigns

Werner Wirth, Christian Schemer,
Rinaldo Kühne, and Jörg Matthes

The previous chapter has convincingly demonstrated that individuals make up their minds in accordance with their issue preferences. These effects were even more pronounced when arguments matched with their ideology. We can consider these preferences to be cognition-based because the judgment is made up of arguments in favour or against a proposal. In the traditional view of political decision making and judgment, emotions are considered erratic and sometimes even dangerous responses to political life (see for an overview Marcus 2002). However, in more than three decades, political scientists (Marcus 2002; Marcus and MacKuen 1993; Marcus et al. 2000), communication scholars (Dillard and Wilson 1993; Nabi, 2002), and psychologists (Abelson et al. 1982; Isbell and Ottati 2002) have revived and rehabilitated the role of emotions for the study of political life. All these approaches state that emotions and affective reactions can have important informational functions for voters.

In their seminal study, Abelson and colleagues (1982) investigated the impact of affect on the preferences for different political candidates in presidential elections. More specifically, the authors measured voters' trait perceptions and behavioural descriptions of presidential candidates. These answers can be considered as cognition or cognitive reactions with regard to political candidates. To gauge emotional reactions towards political candidates the researchers asked their participant to indicate whether a candidate had ever made them angry or hopeful, for instance. These affective reactions were used to form a composite score of negative and positive affect towards political candidates. Finally, they asked their respondents to evaluate the candidates on a global attitude measure (i.e. feeling thermometer). This measure was thought to assess the overall preference of candidates. In their analyses, they regressed the overall evaluation of candidates on cognitions and affects. Their results demonstrated that affects of voters can have an important impact on the evaluation of presidential candidates over and above the impact of cognitions. For instance, affective reactions influenced candidate attitude in an affect-congruent way, that is, positive affect produced more positive attitudes towards a political candidate, whereas negative affect influenced attitudes negatively. Since then, these affective influences have been replicated in several studies (Granberg and Brown 1989; Marcus and MacKuen 1993; Ragsdale 1991). Subsequent studies have provided strong evidence that affective reactions do not only influence candidate evaluations, but also attitudes towards other political objects, such as social groups (Eagly et al. 1994; Esses et al. 1993; Haddock and Zanna 1993; Kuklinski et al. 1991; Stangor et al. 1991), or attitudes towards issues, such as the death penalty (Haddock and Zanna 1998), abortion (Breckler and Wiggins 1991), or the perception of the economy (Conover and Feldman 1986).

In sum, all these studies show that emotional reactions are likely to inform political preferences of voters directly. In other words, attitude objects that elicit negative (positive) affective reactions are perceived more negatively (positively). Consequently, these affective reactions influence the attitudes about the affect-eliciting object in an affect-congruent fashion. In this vein, positive affect results in more positive attitudes, and negative affect produces more negative attitudes.

In addition to such direct effects, Marcus and colleagues (1993, 2000) have demonstrated that emotions also indirectly influence political preferences. According to their theory of affective intelligence, affective reactions influence attitudes both directly and indirectly. Put simply, the theory states that positive affect influences political attitudes directly in an affect-congruent fashion. Additionally, positive affect enhances people's reliance on judgmental heuristics (e.g. party preferences). Conversely, negative affect should not directly influence political attitudes. Instead, negative affect (e.g. anxiety) makes voters leave their routines and elicits information processing and orienting behaviour. Therefore, so their argument, negative affect enhances information processing of voters in campaign and increases learning from campaign information. Although the approach of Marcus and colleagues has been questioned on theoretical (Rahn 2002) and methodological grounds (Ladd and Lenz 2008), the notion that affective reactions can influence cognitive information remains undisputed.

Previous research has provided evidence that positive and negative affect is likely to guide cognitive processing and policy reasoning (Isbell and Ottati 2002; Isbell et al. 2006; Ottati and Wyer 1993). This assumption is also in line with neuro-scientific evidence (Lieberman et al. 2003; McDermott 2004). In the realm of political judgment formation two important studies have demonstrated that affective reactions guide the reasoning about policies and proposals among ordinary citizens. Sniderman et al. (1991) assumed that ordinary citizens often do not know much about issues in the political discourse. However, they know the feelings that the political discussion elicits in them. Therefore, they argue that policy reasoning is often affect-driven. That is, emotional reactions towards a political object may motivate voters to seek and favour arguments that support their affective disposition. Empirically, they showed that positive affect towards racial minorities influences racial cognitions (e.g. support for racial equality) and these cognitions produce support for government action (Sniderman et al. 1991: 63). Put differently, when evaluating political issues, individuals tend to align cognitive arguments to their emotions towards the issue. Similar findings have been obtained by Pan and Kosicki (1996).

In sum, these studies suggest that affective reactions of citizens do not only directly influence attitudes of voters towards candidates or issues. Positive and negative emotions are likely to affect attitudes also indirectly by influencing attitude-related cognitions in an affect-congruent fashion. Depending on the theoretical framework, the interplay of cognition and emotion can be modelled as a moderated or a mediated relationship (Baron and Kenny 1986). In this chapter, we argue that emotions may have a direct or a cognitively mediated influence on voting behaviour. The interactive effects of cognition and emotion are investigated elsewhere (Kühne et al. in press). Whether affective influences on political attitudes are direct or indirect (i.e. mediated) in nature depends on the characteristics of the campaign issue. Voters are likely to know and understand the relevant arguments about familiar or easy issue, for example, from earlier debates. Therefore, voters are able to align arguments according to their emotional reactions without difficulty. They know which arguments support their emotion-induced goals. Fearful individuals, for instance, are likely to know which policies support the reduction of their fear when an issue is familiar or easy. Affective influences on voting should hence be mediated by cognitions.

Voters are likely to experience difficulties when trying to align arguments about an unfamiliar or difficult issue to their emotional reactions. Novel and difficult issues complicate the processing of arguments as the voter has probably not yet reflected the arguments and because they are more complex or abstract. Thus, the voter may be motivated to align arguments to his or her affective disposition towards the issue, but he may not be capable to do this. However, emotions may still have an impact on judgments about difficult issues. According to the affect as information approach (e.g. Schwarz and Clore 1983), individuals can use their affect as a judgment heuristic when an issue is too complex. That is, they may just ask themselves how they feel about the issue, instead of analysing all pro and contra arguments. Therefore, for issues that are high in difficulty we expect an direct effect of affective reactions on voting behaviour. The empirical findings by Sniderman and colleagues (1991) lend support to these assumptions. They found direct influences of affect on political judgments for the AIDS issue (at the end of the 70s a highly unfamiliar and difficult issue). In contrast, for the more familiar issue of racial policy they found an indirect influence of affect on political judgments. The present research aims to corroborate these assumptions further.

Theoretical assumptions and hypotheses

In line with studies demonstrating direct effects of positive and negative affect on political attitudes, we argue that political campaigns may elicit affective reactions that directly enter the judgment formation process as an informational input. Thus, positive and negative affect influences political attitudes directly in an affect-congruent fashion. In other words, the elicitation of positive affect is likely to affect attitudes positively and negative affect should result in negative attitudes. As has been previously demonstrated, these affective influences should occur independently of the effects of predispositions or cognitions.

Nevertheless, cognitions and emotions may also have a combined effect on voting. According to the indirect-effects hypothesis affective reactions motivate individuals to seek and accept affect-congruent arguments. In other words, negative affective reactions indirectly produce more negative attitudes by enhancing negative cognitions. In a similar vein, positive affective reactions indirectly result in more positive attitudes by promoting positive cognitions. However, these affect-congruent policy-reasoning processes do not operate in a vacuum. We can assume that in addition to the affect-congruent reinforcement effect of affect on attitudes inhibition effects of affective reactions are likely. Accordingly, negative affect inhibits positive cognitions in the policy-reasoning process. The same holds true for the impact of positive affect on negative cognitions. All these congruity or incongruity assumptions directly follow from theories of cognitive balance (e.g. Heider 1958; Osgood and Tannenbaum 1955; Rosenberg 1960). These theories suggest that attitudes will change in the direction of the most dominant (positive and negative) total effect of affects and cognitions on attitudes.

If and when direct or indirect effects of emotion on voting is predominant depends on the characteristics of the specific issue at stake. In Chapter 2, the campaigns were distinguished in terms of their intensity, balance and difficulty. Our hypotheses draw on the distinctions between balanced and unbalanced campaigns as well as difficult and easy campaigns. The complexity or difficulty of the campaign issue should determine whether the emotional effects on voting are direct or mediated through issue-related arguments. Difficult or complex issues should increase citizens' reliance on their feelings, as the arguments for and against the proposal may not be fully understood (e.g. Sniderman et al. 1991). Direct emotional effects on voting should thus be more pronounced for the highly complex corporate taxation policy and less pronounced for the moderately complex asylum and naturalization proposals (Hypothesis 1). In the latter cases, the voter should be able to align the arguments for and against the respective proposal with his or her issue-related emotions. That is, he or she should be able to reach the motivational goal determined by the experienced issue-related affect (e.g. a justification to vote against the restricted naturalization because one has a positive attitude towards foreigners) through the integration of goal-consistent arguments into a voting decision. Accordingly, affective influences on voting should be mediated by the arguments for and against the proposal if the issue is moderately complex (Hypothesis 2).

With regard to the differing polarization of the three campaigns, we argue that polarization should influence voters' attitude structure. More precisely, highly conflictive campaigns where many arguments for and against a proposal are primed by the news media should produce polarized attitudes. In other words, the news coverage of conflictive campaigns should raise the awareness of both pro arguments and contra arguments, which forces the recipient to align both components to generate a consistent attitude (i.e. the support of pro arguments and the refusal of contra arguments or vice versa). According to the third hypothesis, there should be a higher negative association between the pro component and contra component of an attitude in a conflictive campaign (i.e. the asylum campaign) than in a non-conflictive campaign (i.e. the corporate taxation and the naturalization campaign).

Methods

Our analyses build on three steps. First, we took a look at the changes of citizens' affective reactions to the three proposals over time. These descriptive analyses were necessary as the subsequent correlational analyses are not able to give any evidence of the emotions that were actually prevalent during the respective campaigns. Second, we conducted regression analyses analogous to the analyses reported in the previous chapter. Instead of the ideology-argument interactions, however, we included indices that measured citizens' emotional reactions to the issue at stake as we were interested in the impact of positive and negative affect on voting behaviour over and above cognitive effects (Hypothesis 1). After establishing direct effects of emotions on voting, we investigated whether affective reactions exert their effects on attitudes indirectly by influencing cognitions (Hypothesis 2). For this purpose, we conducted path analyses where emotional effects were mediated through arguments for and against the respective proposal. The path analyses were also used to test Hypothesis 3 which proposed that campaign characteristics might influence attitude structure.

In addition to the cognitive measures used in the previous chapter, we assessed positive and negative affect by relying on self-reported emotions of our respondent. In the first campaign (i.e. asylum law) our respondents were asked to what extent they experienced positive emotions like hope or pride toward asylum seekers. Conversely, for the measurement of negative affect, items like 'anger' and 'fear' were included. The emotion items were asked in three panel waves. Both scales are highly reliable in all waves.[1] The assessment of emotions in the second campaign was similar to the first one. Here, we asked our respondents to indicate to what extent they experienced positive emotions (e.g. hope, sympathy) when confronted with foreigners. Conversely, for the measurement of negative affect the items like 'anger' and 'fear' were included. Again the items formed reliable measures of positive and negative affect in both panel waves.[2]

In the final panel survey, we used a somewhat different approach to measure emotions. In the first two studies, the issues under investigation were the treatment of asylum seekers and the naturalization of foreigners. We felt that the stakeholders of the corporate taxation campaign, that is, the CEOs of small and medium-sized enterprises did not represent a homogeneous group that would elicit emotions in voters. Therefore, we did not measure citizens' emotional reactions to a certain group of stakeholders but their feelings associated with the issue at stake. For example, we asked our respondents to what extent they experience '...hope for more distributive justice when the corporate tax reform is implemented' or '...worry that the reform produces tax losses'. Similar to the previous studies, the items formed reliable indices of positive and negative affect after the exclusion of indicators with a low inter-item-correlation.[3]

Results

Descriptive results

Figure 13.1 shows the means of emotions citizens felt during the asylum campaign (measured at three points in time). It is important to note that the reported emotions do not refer to the voting issue per se but to asylum seekers. That is, positive emotions (towards asylum seekers) will probably decrease the approval of the tightening of the asylum legislation and encourage a rejection of the asylum law restriction. As can be seen in Figure 13.1, hope and unease towards foreign persons are the emotions that were evoked the most during the asylum campaign, followed by anger, joy, fear and pride (in descending order). Considering only emotions that are commonly labelled as positive (e.g. Abelson et al. 1982), it can be seen that hope was felt more often than joy and pride. Likewise, unease was the most common negative emotion, exceeding feelings of anger and fear. Over time the aggregated measures of emotion did not vary considerably. The visual inspection of Figure 13.1 reveals a slight trend towards the increase of emotional activation during the campaign. Repeated measures analyses of variance substantiate this trend, showing significant increases of fear, anger, hope

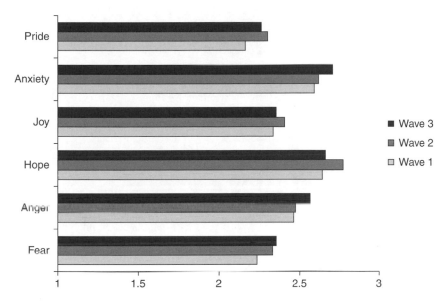

Figure 13.1 Mean distribution of emotions towards asylum seekers (asylum study)

Note: Items are preceded by the following introduction: 'When I think of asylum seekers in Switzerland I experience...'.

and pride (*p*s < .05). That is, citizens did feel more strongly about asylum seekers towards the end of the campaign.

In order to analyse the independent effects of emotions on voting intentions, we first have to show that emotions and cognitions form distinct constructs. Therefore, we submitted the items assessing emotions and items capturing cognitions (see Chapter 12) to a principal component analysis. For the asylum law campaign a four-factor structure emerges.[4] The first factor includes items like anger and fear and represents *negative emotions towards asylum seekers. Positive emotions towards asylum seekers* like hope and pride load on the second factor. Factor three and four are made up of the pro and contra arguments, respectively. Thus, the principal component analysis demonstrates that positive and negative emotions and pro and contra arguments respectively form distinct constructs.

Figure 13.2 depicts the means of emotions citizens felt during the naturalization campaign. Similar to the asylum law campaign, the reported emotions refer to a social group that was at the centre of the political debate, that is, foreigners in Switzerland. Given that the proposal aimed at a restriction of the naturalization legislation, positive (negative) emotions are likely to decrease (increase) the support of the proposal.

As Figure 13.2 shows, sympathy towards foreigners was the most pronounced emotion in the context of the naturalization campaign. Joy and

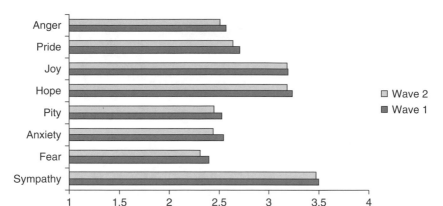

Figure 13.2   Mean distribution of emotions towards foreigners (naturalization study)

Note: Items are preceded by the following introduction: 'When I think of asylum seekers in Switzerland I experience…'.

hope are the second and third strongest emotions respectively that were evoked. The remaining emotions were at a lower level. During the naturalization campaign, positive emotions towards foreigners were thus more pronounced than negative emotions since the three strongest emotions were all positive. Analyses of variance with repeated measures showed a similar picture as in the corporate taxation study. Most emotions declined over time, although only the decrease of unease towards foreigners and the decrease of compassion gained significance ($ps < .05$). Thus, there was a slight tendency of diminishing emotions during the naturalization campaign. Similar to the asylum law campaign, the principal component analysis of the emotion measures and the arguments at wave one revealed a four-factor solution. In addition to the argument factors (see Chapter 12), we found evidence for two emotion factors, that is, *positive emotions towards foreigners* (including emotions like hope and sympathy) and *negative emotions towards foreigners* (including emotions like fear and anger).[5] The factor structure was largely reproduced on the basis of the same items measured in the second panel wave. The only difference was a problematic double loading of the emotion item 'compassion'. This item was excluded when the mean indices of positive and negative affect were computed.

Figure 13.3 shows the means of emotions citizens felt during the corporate taxation campaign. The measured emotions refer directly to the corporate taxation policy in question. That is, positive emotions toward the reform package should encourage a positive vote. Figure 13.3 demonstrates that, one the one hand, voters felt fairly happy and hopeful and, on the other hand, angry and ashamed about certain aspects of the reform package. Satisfaction and concern were less important emotions during the campaign. Analyses of variance with repeated measures show significant changes of evoked

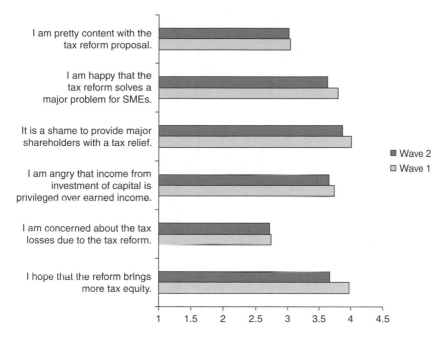

Figure 13.3 Mean distribution of emotions towards tax reform (corporate taxation study)

emotions over time. Hope for tax equity decreased significantly over time. So did anger about uneven treatment of capital and earned income, shame about tax reliefs for major stakeholders and happiness about the solution of problems for SMEs ($ps < .05$). Accordingly, voters were emotionally stronger involved in the beginning of the campaign than in the phase when corporate tax campaign unfolded.

As before, the cognitive and affective items were submitted to a principal component analysis. As a result, a four-factor structure emerges.[6] The first factor includes items referring to the *benefits for SMEs*, for example, advancing competitiveness or creation of new jobs. The second factor represents arguments concerning *tax losses* due to the reform. Factor three includes the items representing positive emotions towards the reform (e.g. '...hope for more distributive justice when the corporate tax reform is implemented'). Factor 4 represents negative emotions towards the reform (e.g. '...worry that the reform produces tax losses'). This factor structure can be found in both panel waves.

Predicting vote intentions

In order to predict voting intentions, we conduct similar ordinal regression analyses as in Chapter 12. In addition, we entered the emotional factors as independent variables to estimate the impact of emotions on voting

Table 13.1   Regression coefficients for predicting the voting decision (asylum campaign)

Predictors	Wave 1 B	Wave 1 S_B	Wave 2 B	Wave 2 S_B	Wave 3 B	Wave 3 S_B
Demographics						
Sex	–.129	.107	–.301*	.130	–.129	.142
Age	.007	.003*	.005	.004	–.004	.004
Highest Education	–.293**	.097	–.101	.012	–.060	.130
Political Predispositions						
Left–right ideology	.202**	.028	.149**	.035	.191**	.039
Autoregression						
Prior voting intention	–	–	.544**	.072	.727**	.078
Argument Factors						
Asylum abuse (pro)	.933**	.069	1.149**	.089	1.327**	.108
Humanitarian tradition (contra)	–.553**	.071	–.547**	.092	–.685**	.104
Emotions						
Positive emotions	–.106	.061	–.173*	.074	–.285**	.044
Negative emotions	.213**	.060	.248**	.074	.228**	.046
Pseudo R^2	.416		.562		.675	

Note: *$p < .05$, **$p < .001$.

intentions. The results of the regression model for the asylum law proposal are shown in Table 13.1. As can be seen, negative affect is significantly related to people's voting intentions throughout the whole campaign. Specifically, negative emotions result in higher approval of the asylum law restriction. This affective impact does not change in the course of the campaign. In contrast, positive affect does not predict people's voting intentions in the beginning of the campaign, but increased in importance during the campaign. In the second half of the campaign, positive affective reactions significantly enhanced people's opposition towards the asylum law restriction. However, in sum and in comparison to the impact of the approval of arguments (i.e. positive and negative cognitions) positive and negative affect make only a small contribution to the explanation of the variance of voting intentions.

For the naturalization issue, we found a similar pattern of results compared to the asylum law campaign. As Table 13.2 shows, negative emotions produced higher approval of democratic naturalization decisions made by the people. This affective impact does not change much in the course of the campaign. Similar to the asylum campaign, positive emotions do not predict voting intentions in the beginning of the campaign. However, in the end positive relative to negative emotions grew in importance for the prediction of people's voting intentions. For instance, when people experienced

Table 13.2   Regression coefficients for predicting the voting decision (naturalization campaign)

Predictors	Wave 1		Wave 2	
	B	S_B	B	S_B
Demographics				
Sex	−.257	.141	−.229	.188
Age	−.000	.004	−.008	.005
Highest Education	−.079**	.024	−.044	.032
Political Predisposition				
Left–right ideology	.130**	.035	.140**	.045
Autoregression				
Prior voting intention	–	–	.606**	.094
Argument Factors				
Mass naturalization (pro)	.869**	.084	.829**	.113
Rule of law (contra)	.387**	.080	−.512**	.103
Emotions				
Positive emotions	−.100	.091	−.415**	.123
Negative emotions	.254**	.076	.257**	.100
Pseudo R²	.405		.521	

Note: **$p < .001$.

positive affective reactions (e.g. sympathy, hope towards foreigners), then they were more likely to reject the proposal that was intended to restrict the rights of foreigners. Taken together, although positive and negative affects significantly predict people's voting intentions, these influences are small in size.

For the issue of the corporate tax reform we predicted stronger effects of emotions on voting intentions because of the heightened issue complexity. For the analysis, we entered positive and negative affect as the final predictors of the regression model. The results of the regression models with positive and negative emotions predicting voting intentions above and beyond the impact of demographics, ideology, and cognitions are presented in Table 13.3.

In contrast to the previous campaigns, positive and negative affect exert a stronger effect on people's voting intentions. Specifically, voters experiencing positive emotions in the context of the proposal, for example, hope or contentment, are more in favour of the corporate tax reform. In a similar fashion, those respondents who experience anger or shame are opposed to the proposal. Ten per cent of the variance of our respondents' voting intentions is explained by the impact of positive and negative affect. As the coefficients demonstrate for the first wave, the impact of positive affect on intention to vote in favour of the corporate tax proposal is significantly stronger than the impact of negative affect on the intention to reject the

Table 13.3 Regression coefficients for predicting the voting decision (corporate tax campaign)

Predictors	Wave 1		Wave 2	
	B	S_B	*B*	S_B
Demographics				
Sex	–.118	.148	–.423*	.174
Age	–.001	.004	–.008	.005
Highest Education	.050*	.024	–.013	.027
Political Predispositions				
Left–right Ideology	.177**	.038	.083*	.045
Autoregression				
Prior voting intention	–	–	.869**	.107
Argument Factors				
Business benefits (pro)	.589**	.106	.619**	.139
Tax losses (contra)	–.409**	.082	–.306**	.094
Emotions				
Positive emotions	1.077**	.097	1.183**	.127
Negative emotions	–.452**	.091	–.504**	.102
Pseudo R^2	.448		.663	

Note: *$p < .05$, **$p < .001$.

proposal. Even more important is the finding that positive affect is the single most important predictor of people's voting intentions. In other words, the hope and contentment that the tax proposal will bring about advantages is a better predictor than people's belief that the reform will produce benefits for SMCs.

From the first to the second panel wave the attitudinal influence of positive and negative emotions remain stable. Put differently, the enthusiasm about the tax reform exerts an influence on voters' attitude toward the corporate tax proposal that remains unchanged during the campaign. The same pattern of results occurs for negative emotions with respect to the tax reform. Compared to the asylum and the naturalization campaigns, emotions exert a considerable impact on voters' attitudes in the present campaign. Particularly, positive emotions played a quite important role for the formation of people's opinion about the corporate tax reform. Taken together, the results speak clearly for Hypothesis 1 that emotions mainly influence voting decisions directly if an issue is highly complex. In the demanding campaign about corporate taxation affective reactions exerted considerable direct effects on citizens' voting intentions. The topic's high complexity apparently impeded the understanding of issue-related arguments which, in turn, reduced their influence on voting and cleared the way for direct affective influences. Thus, a complex, technical issue may be accompanied by stronger direct emotional influences on voting intentions of people than familiar issues, such as policies in the context of minorities.

Direct and indirect effects of emotions on voting intentions

Apart from these direct effects of emotion on voting in the context of a complex issue (Hypothesis 1), we expected indirect effects when the issue is rather familiar. That is, we hypothesized the emotional influence on voting to be mediated by beliefs in favour and against the respective proposal. The results from the previous regressions, that is, the small size of the direct emotional effects for the asylum and naturalization campaigns, already point to this direction. To check for indirect effects we tested mediation models in which positive and negative affects influence cognitions which, in turn, have an impact on the attitudes of voters. In addition, the direct effects were estimated. The mediation models were tested in AMOS by relying on Bayesian estimation accounting for ordered categorical dependent variables.

Asylum law campaign

Figure 13.4 presents the path model[7] estimated to assess the cognitive mediation of the affective impact on voting intentions (i.e. the intention to vote) for the asylum law restriction. This analysis replicates the findings from the regression, that is, there are only small direct effects of positive and negative emotions on voting intentions. More precisely, negative emotions towards asylum seekers exert a constant impact on voting intentions during the campaign, and positive emotions became important only at the end of the campaign. In addition to these results, the figure shows that the paths from positive and negative emotions to the mediating arguments were all significant.

Specifically, negative emotions towards asylum seekers increased acceptance of the abuse argument (i.e. the argument favouring the asylum law restriction) and decreased the approval of the humanitarian argument (i.e. the argument opposing the restriction) in all three waves. Conversely, positive affect increased the approval of the humanitarian argument and decreased the approval of abuse argument. That is, the voters' feelings apparently led to affect-congruent reasoning. Interestingly, the amplification effect of emotions appears to be stronger than the inhibition effect. This becomes evident when comparing the relations between the emotions and the arguments of the same valence vs. emotions and arguments of opposing valence. Specifically, relations between emotions and arguments of the same valence were stronger than relations between emotions and arguments of opposing valence. Thus, emotions will, first and foremost, increase the generation and approval of arguments that support the initial affective state and will inhibit the creation of counter-arguments only to a lesser extent.

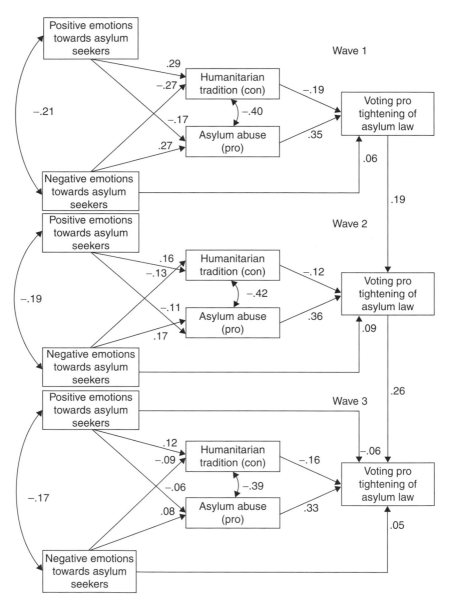

Figure 13.4   Path model of affect mediation (asylum study)

Note: Significant paths (p < .05) plus partial correlations between mediators are depicted. Autoregressive paths among cognitions and emotions are modelled but not shown. All paths were controlled for demographics and political predispositions.

In addition to the observed effects of emotions on arguments, there must also be significant relations between arguments and voting intention, to establish an indirect effect of emotions on voting intentions. These effects were replicated with our path analysis.

When we compare the coefficients across time, by and large, there is a highly stable structure of people's emotions, cognitions, and attitudes. However, we can observe that the affect-congruent influences (i.e. the influence of positive emotions on the humanitarian arguments and the influence of negative emotions on the abuse argument) decrease significantly from the first to the second panel wave. The same occurs for the inhibition or affect-incongruent influences. On the one hand, this weakening of the indirect effects may be due to the control for autoregressive effects in the second panel wave. On the other hand, this may also be due to campaign effects intervening in the voters' autonomous reasoning processes. Thus, we can assume that during the campaign, the voters' own thought generation is reduced and the influence of external information in the mass media increases. Finally, the impact of negative emotions towards asylum seekers on negative cognitions (i.e. asylum abuse) is again reduced in importance from the second to the third panel wave. Put differently, when we look at the affective influence, we can observe that, at the end of the campaign, the voting intentions of the voters are guided directly by positive emotions and indirectly by negative affect towards asylum seekers via cognitive mediation.

Taken together, for the asylum law campaign the path analysis demonstrates that emotions have a stronger indirect impact on voting intentions than direct affective influences. As has been predicted for familiar issues, the influence of emotions on voting decisions is grounded more in affect-congruent reasoning – that is, a process by which emotions enhance the activation of congruent cognitions and inhibits the activation of incongruent cognitions – than in an affect heuristic – that is, a process in which people simply rely on their feelings when forming a judgment about an issue.

Naturalization campaign

Similar to the previous analysis, we estimated a path analysis for the data gathered in the context of the naturalization study (see Figure 13.5).[8] Similar to the asylum campaign, emotions have only small direct effects on voting intentions. Negative emotions towards foreigners enhanced the preference for a restriction of naturalization procedures, both in the beginning and at the end of the campaign. In the second wave, positive emotions towards foreigner significantly decrease people's preference for a restriction of the naturalization legislation. In addition, all paths from emotions to arguments, and all paths from arguments to voting intention are significant. Again, associations between emotions and arguments of the same valence

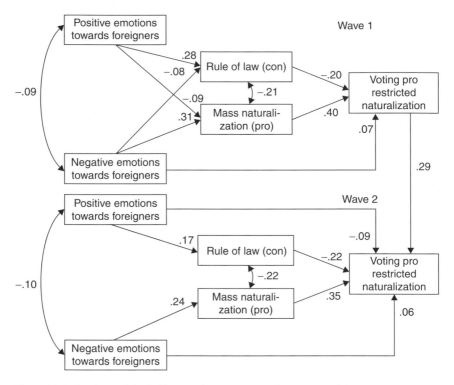

Figure 13.5   Path model of affect mediation (naturalization study)

Note: Significant paths (p < .05) and partial correlations between mediators are depicted. Autoregressive paths among cognitions and emotions are modelled but not shown. All paths were controlled for demographics and political predispositions.

are stronger than associations between emotions and arguments of opposing valence, which are only marginal. Interestingly, the affect-incongruent influences on the arguments reduce to non-significance in the second panel wave. This finding corroborates the assumption that the naturalization campaign was less polarized. Otherwise we would have expected stronger affect-incongruent effects like in the asylum campaign.

Another pattern of results also points to differences between the asylum law and naturalization campaign. The pattern of correlations between positive and negative emotions and between positive and negative cognitions (i.e. the pro and contra arguments) differs considerably in both campaigns. In the asylum law campaign, these correlations are significantly larger than in the naturalization campaign. This finding suggests that the asylum law campaign must have been more polarized than the naturalization debate, again corroborating the assumptions about differences in the campaigns in Chapter 2. In sum, we found stronger indirect effects of emotions on voting intentions than direct effects. This pattern of results confirms our hypothesis that for easy issues direct affective influences are less important than indirect effects of emotions on voting intentions.

Corporate tax campaign

Finally, the results of the path analysis for the corporate taxation campaign show a different pattern.[9] As the regression analysis has demonstrated, there are strong direct effects of emotions on voting behaviour. The path analysis replicates this result. As shown in Figure 13.6, positive emotions towards the reform support the intention to vote in favour of the proposal, and negative affect decreases the endorsement of the new tax policy. Furthermore, the influence of positive emotions on voting intentions is considerably stronger than the direct impact of negative emotions. Apart from these direct effects there is evidence for indirect affective influences on voting intentions.

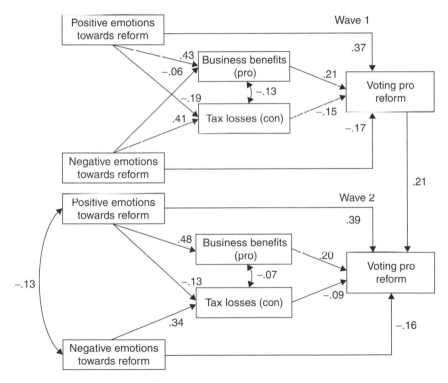

Figure 13.6 Path model of affect mediation (corporate taxation study)

Note: Significant paths (p < .05) and partial correlations between mediators are depicted. Autoregressive paths among cognitions and emotions are modelled but not shown. All paths were controlled for demographics and political predispositions.

However, the indirect effects are not very strong. Although there are considerable effects of emotions on the approval of arguments, the paths from the approval of arguments to voting intentions show only weak associations. That is, citizens approve of arguments in accordance with their emotions but, in the end, they rely on their emotions and not on their cognitions to decide. As in the path analyses for the asylum policy, voters' feelings lead to a strong amplification effect, while the inhibition of counter-arguments is weaker.

When the changes of coefficients over time are considered, two findings are noteworthy. First, the emotional impact on cognitions remained fairly stable. This also holds true for the direct emotion effects on voting intentions. Only the impact of negative emotions on the contra argument (tax losses) decreases. For instance, people experiencing negative emotions (e.g. anger about uneven treatment of capital and earned income) are more inclined to approve of the contra argument in the first wave than in the end of the campaign. Second, the significant increase in the correlation between positive and negative emotions shows that the campaign exerts a polarizing influence. In the beginning, there is no association between positive and negative emotions in the context of the tax reform. Obviously, the campaign polarizes people's affective reactions towards the tax reform, so that, in the end, people experiencing positive emotions show lower levels of negative affect and vice versa. This polarization may have helped citizens to make up their mind more easily.

Taken together, the path analyses provide strong evidence for the first hypothesis. Only when campaigns are more complex and difficult to understand (i.e. for the corporate taxation campaign) did emotions directly influence voting decision. In contrast, for more familiar and easier issues (i.e. in the asylum law and the naturalization campaign) no impressive direct effects of emotions on voting intentions occur. In addition, the path analyses support our second hypothesis, that is, affective influences on voting are mediated in campaigns about familiar or easy issues. That is, when individuals understand the arguments in favour and against a proposal, they are able to align the arguments with their affective predispositions (e.g. the liking of foreigners) and the arguments influence their voting decision. If an issue is too complex, however, citizens do not only rely on difficult arguments when making up their mind about an issue (although they are able to identify the arguments that favour their position and contradict the opposing position). In contrast, citizens listen to their emotional reactions that a certain issue elicits which informs them directly about their preference.

The path analyses also mostly support the third hypothesis. Specifically, symmetric campaigns lead to more polarized attitudes than asymmetric campaigns. As can be seen in Figures 13.4 to 13.6, in the highly conflictive asylum campaign were pro- and contra arguments more strongly negatively correlated compared to the naturalization issue and the corporate tax campaign. In other words, the more symmetric nature of the asylum law campaign polarized the electorate to a higher extent than the campaigns that were asymmetric in nature. When the naturalization initiative and the corporate taxation are considered with respect to polarization, then we can conclude that the polarization is stronger for the first compared to the latter campaign. However, the low correlation between pro and contra arguments in the corporate tax campaign may also indicate that the arguments in favour of and against the taxation reform were not fully understood. Otherwise we would have expected a higher negative correlation between pro and contra arguments because the approval of pro arguments should lead to a rejection of contra arguments.

Conclusion

Our analyses show that citizens do not exclusively rely on arguments to decide how to vote on an issue. They are also influenced by the emotions they feel when thinking about the issue. Not surprisingly, positive emotions increased support for the respective proposal while negative emotions undermined it. At the same time, the specific modality of the affective influence on voting depended on the characteristics of the issue at stake. Citizens' emotions had a stronger direct impact on voting when the issue was highly complex and difficult to understand (such as the corporate taxation reform) than when the issue was easy (e.g. for the asylum and the naturalization proposal). As the impact of arguments on voting was diminished at the same time, it is reasonable to argue that the issue-related arguments were not fully understood which guided voters' to rely on their feelings towards the proposal. This interpretation is in line with findings from social psychology that individuals can use their feelings as a heuristic both when they are not motivated to process information about a given issue or when the information are too complex for a decision to be reached (Schwarz and Clore 1983). Our results also corroborate the findings of Sniderman and colleagues (1991): They also found stronger indirect effects of emotions on attitudes for easy issues (e.g. racial policies; see also Pan and Kosicki 1996) and stronger direct effects for hard issue (e.g. AIDS policy) in the US context.

When the issue was moderately complex (as it was the case in the naturalization and the asylum campaign) emotions had only a marginal direct effect on voting. Instead, their influence on voting was mediated by issue-related arguments. That is, citizens' emotions influenced how much they approved of pro and contra arguments and the arguments, in turn, influenced their voting decision. These effects can be explained by motivated information processing within a reasoning chains model. Accordingly, the mediation of affective influence is to be understood as a more or less intentional process (e.g. Forgas 1995; Kunda 1990). Motivated processing occurs when an individual has a specific motivational goal he or she wants to obtain. Sad moods, for instance, might motivate an individual to seek positive memories to repair the negative mood (Josephson et al. 1996). In the political domain, emotions have been identified as important sources of motivational goals (e.g. Sniderman et al. 1991; Pan and Kosicki 1996). Pan and Kosicki (1996) have pointed out, for instance, that white Americans rely strongly on affective predisposition towards blacks when forming opinions about racial policies. In our studies, emotions towards foreigners influenced what arguments were approved of. Negative emotions towards foreigners, for instance, motivated individuals to approve of arguments that supported a xenophobic voting decision. That is, individuals aligned their arguments to their affective predispositions.

The cumulative evidence of previous findings and our results demonstrate that affective reactions can influence political attitudes either directly or indirectly. On the one hand, for easy or familiar issues positive and negative affect is likely to act as a predisposition exerting an indirect effect on attitude, that is, the affective impact is cognitively mediated. On the other hand, for difficult and unfamiliar issues, affective reactions also exert a direct influence on attitudes. Thus, the results of our analyses support the thesis that emotions play an important part in the realm of politics and voting, either directly or indirectly.

Notes

1. Negative affect: Cronbach's α = .73 in wave one; wave two: .76; wave 3: .78. Positive affect: α = .72 in wave one; wave two: .78; wave three: .79.
2. Negative affect: α = .75 in wave one; wave two: .79. Positive affect: α = .69 in wave one; wave 2: .68.
3. Negative affect: α = .67 in wave one; wave two: .71; Positive affect: α = .69 in wave two; wave two: .80.
4. Oblique rotation; Eigenvalue-criteria for factor extraction; 64% explained variance.
5. Oblique rotation; Eigenvalue-criteria for factor extraction; 56 % explained variance.
6. Oblique rotation; Eigenvalue-criteria for factor extraction; 63 % explained variance.
7. The model shows a perfect fit to the data, $\chi^2(43)$ = 39.9, *ns*, CFI = 1.00.
8. Again, the model fitted the data very well: $\chi^2(9)$ = 7.89, *ns*; CFI = 1.00.
9. Model fit for the path analysis: $\chi^2(18)$ = 15.1, *ns*; CFI = 1.00.

14
Conclusion

Hanspeter Kriesi

The study of political communication from an integrated perspective

In the introduction to this volume, we introduced two visions of democracy – a demand-side and a supply-side vision. For our study of direct-democratic campaigns in Switzerland, we adopted an integrated approach that combines the two visions. From such a perspective, the key question is whether, in direct-democratic campaigns, the political elites are capable of manipulating the voters in such a way as to impose their policy goals without taking the voters' preferences into account. Given the widespread lack of political knowledge on the part of the voters, and given the complexity of contemporary political decision-making, the political elites' manoeuvering space is potentially very large, opening up considerable possibilities for influencing the voters' opinion formation. Our goal was to find out the extent to which the elites make use of these possibilities and succeed in imposing their views, and to what extent the voters are enlightened or manipulated by the elites' attempts to influence them.

As we argued in the Introduction, whether or not the elites remain responsive and accountable to their voters very much depends on three conditions – the competitiveness of the political process; the independence, resourcefulness and diversity of the media; and the attentiveness of the citizen public. These three requirements define, as we have pointed out, the liberal representative model of the public space. A competitive political process implies the presence of competing political offers, opening up a real choice for the voters. To be competitive, all the adversarial camps need to be resourceful, and they need to be able to reach out to the public via the media. The media, in turn, need to be independent, resourceful and diverse enough to be able to communicate the messages from all political camps. Above all, the media need to be ready to invest in political news reporting. Ultimately, however, the manoeuvering space of the political elites crucially depends on the public. The public needs to be attentive to political news, able to follow political news reporting in different channels, and capable of independent judgement in order to assess the competing offers. An attentive public constitutes the ultimate constraint for unresponsive political elites in a democratic system because the competing elites, for their political survival, have to take into account the preferences of such a public. The political offers made by the elites have to appeal to the public's predispositions, that is, the political communication of the elites have to establish a plausible link between their 'supply' and the public's 'demands'. This is where the supply-side vision of democracy meets the demand-side vision. Or, to put it more pointedly: To the extent that the supply side is induced/constrained to take the demand side into account, the supply-side vision is dominated by the demand-side vision. By contrast, to the extent that voters' preferences are malleable, leading them to flip-flop, depending on what happens to be at the top of their minds, the supply-side vision reigns supreme.

Whether or not these conditions are fulfilled cannot be answered in the abstract but has to be studied in a given context. We have proposed to study the effect of political communication in a very specific context – Swiss direct-democratic campaigns. Such campaigns share some characteristics, which create laboratory-like conditions for the study of political communication. First, direct-democratic campaigns are of limited duration, have a clear beginning and a clear ending, and typically involve an important intensification of political communication. Second, such campaigns give rise to a bipolar pattern of competition and are focused on a specific issue, which keeps the complexity of the communication processes within manageable proportions. We have studied three issues which differ systematically with respect to their familiarity and complexity, allowing us to study the implications of some key situational conditions influencing the effect of political communications.

As we pointed out in the Introduction, the three campaigns represent three rather ideal-typical choice situations. First, the asylum campaign stands for a campaign on a familiar issue of low complexity, an easy choice situation, where most voters' minds were essentially made up before the campaign even started. Second, the naturalization campaign stands for a campaign on an unfamiliar issue of low complexity, an intermediate choice situation, where most voters' had first to familiarize themselves with the issue, but where learning about the issue was relatively easy. Third, the corporate tax campaign stands for an unfamiliar and complex issue, a difficult choice situation, where many voters even at the end of the campaign had a hard time knowing what the choice was all about.

The disadvantage of our design is obvious, too: Its natural setting implies that our three campaigns and the issues involved differ in other respects as well, which makes comparing them more complex. Thus, the asylum reform and the naturalization initiatives are issues related to immigration, while corporate tax reform is an issue of neoliberal economic reform. Accordingly, the coalitions opposing each other vary considerably, as do the resources at the disposal of the adversaries in the three campaigns. Moreover, critics may argue that we have been talking about three specific direct-democratic campaigns in Switzerland, and that our results are heavily tainted by the larger context of the Swiss media system and the Swiss political system.

We concede, of course, that the Swiss context has influenced our results, and that such a study should be replicated in other contexts to be better able to test the generalizability of our results. However, we would maintain that, even if the results of social science research in natural settings are always to some extent context-bound, they may still point beyond the narrow confines of their setting, provided the analysis succeeds in characterizing the context in general, analytical terms, and provided it succeeds in pointing out how the context conditions the results. In this summary, we shall attempt to indicate how we think that our results do not only speak to direct-democratic campaigns in Switzerland, but have something more general to say about the effects of political communication in political campaigns and about the applicability of the integrated approach of political communication.

The politicians' strategies

The institutional logic of a direct-democratic campaign is a binary, majoritarian logic that leaves little room for bargaining, does not know clearly designated leaders, and introduces a large number of potential partners. The campaign comes at the end of a protracted political process – in the Swiss case a much more protracted process than in the member states of the United States – that largely pre-structures the line-up of the competing camps and their framing strategies, as well as the outcome of the campaign. This means that the manoeuvering space of the politicians is rather limited by the preceding issue-specific political process. In addition, the politicians' control over the campaign may be limited by exogenous factors having an impact on the outcome of the campaign, but which are outside of the control by the competing camps. We have encountered two instances of such exogenous influences on our campaigns: first, the protracted conflict about the new justice minister (Eveline Widmer-Schlumpf) – who defended the government's position during the campaign for the naturalization initiative – intensely preoccupied the Swiss public in the months preceding the vote and led to a late start of the respective campaign, which has probably compromised the chances of the initiative at the polls. Second, the enormous losses of the largest Swiss bank (UBS) in the subprime crisis, which became public just before the campaign for the corporate tax reform started and resurfaced again during the campaign, seriously hurt the supporters of the reform, and are very likely to have contributed to the surprisingly close result of the vote.

In other words, politicians face great uncertainty in a direct-democratic campaign, and they are highly constrained by the issue-specific and general political context in which campaigns are embedded. Within the constraints imposed upon them, they attempt to solve above all three tasks in such campaigns: the task of forming coalitions that are as large as possible, of crafting messages that are as strong as possible, and of diffusing those messages to as large a number of voters as possible. These three tasks, we maintain, need to be solved by political actors in any referendum campaign, not only in Switzerland, but also in the United States or in referendums organized in the context of the European integration process.

Coalition formation. First of all, politicians can improve their chances of winning a contest by forging a supporting coalition that is as broad and encompassing as possible. In the event of direct-democratic campaigns, the highly fragmented, multipolar system of political actors is reduced to a bipolar configuration of coalitions as a result of the majoritarian, bipolar logic of direct-democratic institutions. As we have argued, the process of coalition formation is decisively shaped by the actors' political beliefs. These beliefs operate at the level of fundamental ideological convictions, as well as at the more down-to-earth level of policy-specific positions. Even if political actors of different persuasions do not share the same overall ideology, they may find themselves in the same camp for pragmatic reasons. This does not mean, however, that they will closely cooperate in the course of the campaign. On the contrary, as we have shown in Chapters 4 and 6, the political actors who belong to the same 'objective' coalition for pragmatic reasons are forming distinct components within that coalition, each of which primarily caters to its own constituency. Thus, in the case of the asylum law campaign, the 'third force', which was mainly made up of dissidents from the moderate right, and formed a pragmatic coalition with the left, led its own campaign, and did not cooperate with the left in a joint effort. Similarly, the moderate right did not cooperate with the left in the naturalization campaign, although the two were 'objective' allies in the battle against the conservative/populist right. Even the two component forces of the moderate right – the Liberals and the Christian Democrats – did not cooperate with each other in this particular campaign in the aftermath of their conflicts over government formation after the 2007 elections.

In other words, the formation of coalitions with separate components allows for the reconciliation of the bipolar logic of the direct-democratic campaigns with the multipolar logic of the proportional consensus democratic system that predominates otherwise in Swiss politics. This is a lesson which has wider applicability beyond the Swiss context: The majoritarian logic of the direct-democratic votes can be reconciled with the context conditions of proportional, consensus democracies that prevail on the European continent by the particular strategies of coalition formation among the political elites.

In the Swiss context, the moderate right takes a pivotal position in this process of coalition formation. In the case of immigration-related issues, where the moderate right has an intermediary position between the left and the conservative/populist right, it forms a pragmatic alliance with the one or the other, depending on the specificities of the proposal at stake. In the case of economic issues, it usually teams up in a natural alliance with the conservative/populist right in a classic left–right conflict. We have too few cases here to generalize the coalition patterns, but three aspects of what emerges here imply very important lessons which again point beyond the Swiss context. First, although there are many other actors who are part of the emerging coalitions, the parties play a key role in coalition formation. They are highly instrumental in forging coherent coalitions which provide unambiguous cues to the voters. If the parties are internally divided, their signals are no longer easy to grasp, and the voters have greater difficulty orienting themselves. Second, the cases we have selected illustrate what we know from previous studies (see Chapter 2), namely, that coalition formation in such campaigns is variable and usually ends up in either a centre-right versus left or a centre-left versus conservative/populist right configuration. The variability of the coalition formation stabilizes the system, since it makes for cross-cutting patterns of conflict and undermines the congealment of oppositions. Third, the pivotal role of the moderate right tends to have a moderating impact on the polar positions – at least with respect to cultural issues. The moderate right who also dominates the government defends the government's position and usually, although not always, prevails.

Crafting the message. Each coalition or each component of a coalition has to be able to craft a convincing message that attracts the attention of the media and the public. We found that in all three campaigns, the message was above all a substantive one, that is, the campaigns were always focused on substance, and not on the contest and the actors involved. Moreover, in all three campaigns, both camps have been able to formulate one or two strong messages to support their point of view (Chapter 5). Some chapters have used the concept of 'arguments' to refer to these messages, others have preferred to refer to 'frames' when speaking of these messages. Each camp tried to promote its own frames and to stay on message, that is, to promote the same frames throughout the campaign. The difficulty of the framing task varied, however, with the issue at stake. Thus, in the asylum campaign, where the campaigners had to deal with a familiar issue of low complexity, both sides succeeded in staying on message throughout the campaign. In the other two campaigns, the supporters of the proposals made the experience that the frames they promoted were not as successful as intended and, in one case they reacted by shifting the emphasis in framing. In the corporate tax campaign, the main frame of the supporters of the reform, the SME-frame turned out to be less effective than intended, because it was not really contested by the opposition. In the naturalization campaign, the conservative promoters' procedural argument ('people-final-say') was not as successful as intended either, which incited the campaigners in this particular case to shift to the 'mass naturalization' argument in the final stages of the campaign – especially in the paid media.

We proposed to measure the strength of a message by the amount of reactions it generates from the opposing camp. This conceptualization presupposes that messages which are ignored by the opponents are weak, while messages, which cannot be ignored by the opponents are strong. According to the conventional wisdom in political science, campaigners talk past each other, each side promoting its own themes. Even if direct-democratic campaigns do not constitute very favourable settings for the discursive quality of the public debate (see Chapter 1), it turns out that Swiss campaigners often feel constrained to react to the arguments of the opposing side, that is, the campaigns tend to have a dialogical character (Chapter 5). The degree to which a dialogue develops seems to depend a lot on the complexity of the issue at stake. Thus, we found that the extent to which the two camps referred to each other was much higher in the two immigration-related campaigns than in the highly complex case of the corporate tax campaign. Beyond this particular element of complexity, we were not able to sufficiently clarify the reasons why politicians feel compelled to react to the arguments of the other side.

The strength of a message can also be measured by its impact on the voters' choices. According to this conceptualization, the arguments of the two camps had an important effect. However, the winning camp not always had the strongest arguments. As we have shown in Chapter 13, the supporters of all three proposals always had the strongest arguments when it came to impacting the vote. But in only two of the three cases, the proponents also carried the day – in the case of the naturalization initiative, they lost, although their arguments had a stronger impact on the vote than the arguments of their adversaries. We can conclude that to have a particularly strong argument is not yet a guarantee for being able to win the contest.

Delivering the message. For Swiss politicians, just as for the Swiss media, direct-democratic campaigns are routine events which they know how to handle. The timing of the campaigns is largely determined by the established routines (Chapter 4). Thus, the campaigns start roughly two months before the ultimate voting date, and they reach their peak roughly three weeks before this date. The starting date is determined by convention, and influenced by seasonal considerations – such as the summer vacations or the Christmas break. The peak is determined by the voting behaviour of the Swiss voters, most of whom vote by mail after they have received their voting material, but quite some time before the ultimate voting date. In the case of optional referendums, opponents tend to get a first-mover advantage, because they have already mobilized to qualify the issue for the vote, and just go on to campaign for the vote itself.

The choice of the channels of mobilization is largely determined by the resources the campaigners have at their disposal. Those who have sufficient amounts of money use it for paid ads in the press and public posters – the main forms of advertising in Swiss direct-democratic campaigns, given that advertising in electronic media is forbidden. Those who do not have enough money rely more on press releases and personnel resources – organizational staff, but also on volunteers. In Switzerland, there are no disclosure laws, which means that we do not have precise information on the amounts of money spent by the opposing camps. We have, however, rough estimates for our three campaigns, based on the interviews with the campaign operatives, and we have even rougher estimates about all campaigns since the 1980s, based on the amount of published ads in some selected newspapers. In general, the Swiss right has more financial resources available than the Swiss left, which is confirmed by our three campaigns. Exceptionally, the financial resources were roughly balanced in the asylum case, because the 'third force' could count on money from parts of the business elite thanks to the connections of its leading figure, who was a businessman.

Our three cases illustrate, however, that money does not always carry the day. Thus, although the supporters of the naturalization initiative invested much more money into the campaign than its opponents, they lost the vote. Moreover, at the end of the day the relative advantage the left enjoyed in the asylum case thanks to the support by the third force did not pay off in terms of number of votes. Finally, the tremendous advantage that the supporters of the corporate tax reform had did not at the end of the day bring about a clear-cut victory for their cause. The best we can currently say in general terms about the influence of money on the outcome of Swiss direct-democratic campaigns is that money does matter, but that it does not matter a lot (Kriesi 2009).

Generally, we know that the campaign expenditures increase in both camps when the expected outcome of the vote gets close. We know this from the United States (Stratmann 2006) and from Switzerland (Kriesi 2009). The reasons behind this relationship are obvious (Erikson and Palfrey 2000): government spending is driven by the *threat* that challengers exert. The government's camp is usually, although not always, in a strong position, and it can usually be quite sure to win the direct-democratic contest. In the case of initiatives, it has virtually always won in Switzerland in the past, although this has recently been changing. But if the government's camp can count on a victory at the polls with a high probability, it has no reason to invest a lot of money. It will only invest its resources if the outcome of the vote becomes uncertain. Conversely, challenger spending is driven by the *opportunity* provided by the expectation of a close outcome. However, in the case of the challengers, spending is also driven by the intensity they often feel about their cause. Thus, challengers sometimes tend to invest the money they have, even if theirs is a lost cause. The asylum case illustrates the importance of the intensity of feelings to challengers' behaviour.

The case of the corporate tax reform is particularly intriguing against this general background. In this particular case, the challengers hardly had any money to invest at all. The government's camp, however, supported by the Swiss business community, invested large sums of money because it must have anticipated a close vote, given the exogenous events concerning the UBS and the results of its pre-electoral surveys. We do not know, of course, what might have happened if the supporters of the reform had not invested as much money as they eventually did. But given the very close outcome of the vote (50.5 percent vs. 49.5 percent), we can be quite confident that, in this particular case, money made a great difference.

The media's strategies

Campaign coverage by the mass media constitutes the most important source of information for Swiss voters, followed by the official information booklet, and by the perceived opinion of the Swiss public (Chapter 11). It is, therefore, very important to know how the Swiss media cover direct-democratic debates. We found that coverage of such campaigns is routine and ritualized business for the Swiss media. Direct-democratic campaigns routinely give rise to an intense issue-specific debate in the media, and the coverage is typically of a high level of quality. There is as of yet little evidence for a dominant market-orientation in the Swiss media (Chapter 7). The Swiss media spend an important amount of resources on the coverage of political news, and journalistic values seem to generally play an important role. Overall, the media coverage of the campaign is characterized by a high degree of intensity, diversity, and prominence (Chapter 8). The intensity and prominence of the coverage varies, however, according to the issue at stake; thus, immigration-related issues gave rise to a more intense and more prominent coverage than the more complex, unfamiliar, and highly technical corporate tax reform.

As shown in Chapter 9, campaign coverage by the media is clearly driven by politicians' input. Politicians act and the media react. The media faithfully cover the input they receive from the politicians, which results in a media output that roughly mirrors the politicians input in quantitative and qualitative terms. Although the media rely somewhat more heavily on contest frames than do politicians, they essentially take over the politicians' emphasis on substantive frames and reproduce the dialogical character of their arguments.

As a result of their overall focus on substance over contest, the debate in the media is not highly personalized (Chapter 8). Nevertheless, there are some dominant personalities and organizations in the news. Most importantly, and in line with the overall trend towards an increasing media focus on the executive, the ministers responsible for the proposal on the part of the Federal government, turn out to be the individuals with the greatest media presence in all three campaigns. In addition, the members of the Federal Parliament are also strongly represented in the media campaign. The power of the actors involved generally is a factor that increases their likelihood to make it into the media, but the input of the responsible members of the Federal government is especially attractive for the media, since they multiply their input more than that of any other source (Chapter 9).

While the prominence of the members of the Federal government is in line with the generally increasing 'presidentialization' of European democracies (Poguntke and Webb 2005), it goes against the grain of Swiss political culture. The government enjoys some important institutional advantages in the Swiss version of direct-democracy: It controls the voting agenda; it has important information tools (the official booklet, official slots for the presentation of its point of view on national TV); and its media input is, as we have seen, particularly newsworthy. But according to the Swiss political cultural tradition, the government is expected to exercise its campaigning role with a certain restraint. While entitled to provide the voters with a balanced diet of information, the authorities should, according to the traditional view, leave the opinion formation in the general public primarily to civil society, the social and political forces of the country (Kriesi 2009a).

As our results indicate, this plea for personal restraint by government representatives in campaigns is hard to reconcile with the new world of mediatized and, as far as the Swiss case is concerned, polarized politics. Personalization has not yet gone very far compared to other West European democracies (Kriesi, 2011), and the media still concentrate on the substance of the debate. But the media join the trend of the day, attribute responsibility to individual ministers, and expect them to defend the government's proposals in public.

There is another trend, which may not be dominant (yet), but which portends new problems for the future. The tabloids and free newspapers, which are significantly more market-driven than the general press, offer some coverage of direct-democratic campaigns, but do not invest in their coverage and simply report what they get out of news agencies. The free newspapers constitute a recent addition to the Swiss media system, but they already have become by far the most widely read Swiss titles. Although there is no indication that they are the only source of information for some segments of the Swiss public, to the extent that they replace the regional newspapers, which have had a very strong position in the Swiss media market, the quality of the debate in the media can be expected to suffer a serious setback.

The voters' choice

The effect of a campaign is constrained by the voters' predispositions, which are the result of the voters' previous political experiences in general, and of their exposure to the previous issue-specific debates in particular. Thus, voters who are politically interested and who generally follow political debates already have a pretty good idea about how they are going to decide an issue, before the campaign has even started. But not all the voters have already made up their minds when the campaign sets in. Depending on the familiarity and the complexity of the issue at hand, the share of voters who are still undecided or whose opinion is still malleable varies a great deal. Accordingly, campaigns may make a great difference to the outcome of the vote. Campaigns, we have argued, generally have three types of effects: They may reinforce voters' original intentions, activate their predisposition to form opinions that are in line with those predispositions, or convert them to a choice that is not in line with their predispositions. Reinforcement gives the impression of an overall lack of effect, even if it also constitutes a non-negligible effect of the campaign. Activation is indicative of an enlightening, conversion of a manipulative effect.

Overall effects. All three campaigns had massive effects on the voters' choices, which confirms the increasingly popular idea that 'campaigns matter'. They all reinforced and activated previously held intentions and predispositions. Our three campaigns, however, differ crucially with respect to the three types of outcomes. Reinforcement was paramount in the asylum law campaign. In the other two campaigns, it was the major outcome only among politically interested voters. In the naturalization campaign, activation was very prominent, especially among politically uninterested voters, no less than half of whom became activated by this particular campaign. Conversion turned out to be very important in the campaign on the corporate tax reform – our most complex and unfamiliar case. Conversions were twice as numerous in this campaign than in the two immigration campaigns. Among the uninterested voters, the share of conversions in the corporate tax campaign amounted to no less than one-third, twice the size of the corresponding share in the naturalization campaign, and almost three times their share in the asylum campaign. Among the politically uninterested, the outcome of this campaign appears to have been almost random – one-third was reinforced, one-third activated and one-third converted.

The three types of effect are less straightforward than it appears at first sight, because the voters have more than one predisposition, and the various predispositions may actually draw the voters in different directions. We analysed the effects of two key predispositions – partisan and issue-specific predispositions – in more detail (Chapter 10). According to our results, partisan activation was pervasive in all three campaigns and tended to be stronger than issue-specific activation, although both types of predispositions tended to be less decisive in the corporate tax campaign. The comparison of the behaviour of the cross-pressured, ambivalent voters in the two immigration campaigns showed that the relative importance of the two types of predispositions may vary considerably, even among proposals that initially seem closely related. Thus, ambivalent voters on the left above all followed their issue-specific preferences in the asylum campaign, while they primarily followed their party line in the naturalization campaign. The ambivalent voters on the right behaved in the exact opposite way: they followed their party line in the asylum campaign, but their issue preferences in the naturalization campaign.

We suggested two complementary interpretations for these variable priorities: on the one hand, we argued with the inherent proximity of the substance of the proposal to the issue-specific positions of both the parties and the voters. We suggested that, compared to the naturalization initiative, the asylum law was much more closely linked to the core of both the conservative/populist right's programme and the issue-specific preferences of the voters (which we operationalized by a measure for xenophobia). The naturalization initiative dealt with the question of how to integrate foreigners into the Swiss society – foreigners who have been living in Switzerland for many years – and addressed this question in a rather indirect way. Therefore, it was less obvious to link xenophobia to the naturalization case than it was to link it to the asylum case. Despite all appearances to the contrary, the conservative/populist right had greater difficulty linking the naturalization issue to its opposition to immigration, which is reflected in the modifications of its framing strategy towards the end of the naturalization campaign. On the other hand, we argued that the choice behaviour of the two types of ambivalent voters is also in line with an alternative hypothesis which posits that the voters not only take their cues from their own parties, but also from other parties – in the Swiss case most likely from the pivotal parties of the moderate right.

Learning. Among the mechanisms by which campaigns can bring about their effects, learning is certainly a very important one. Campaigns as information-rich events provide ample opportunities to learn more about the arguments of the two camps, the partisan cues, and the consequences implied by the eventual adoption of a proposal. We have found that voters learned a lot during the campaigns, the knowledge levels in all three respects significantly increased during all three campaigns (Chapter 11). At the same time, knowledge levels are unevenly distributed among the voters. Most importantly, we found indications for a knowledge gap between the more resourceful (politically interested, highly educated and committed) and the less resourceful (little interested, little educated, and uncommitted) voters. The results are of particular interest with respect to partisan learning, since partisan cues constitute the quintessential heuristic shortcut for voters' decision-making in direct-democratic campaigns. First of all, the more politically resourceful voters are significantly more likely to know about both their preferred party's position and the consequences of the proposal at the beginning of the campaign. Moreover, the more resourceful voters also learn more about the partisan cues (but not about the proposals' consequences) in the course of the campaign. That is, the knowledge gap which already exists at the outset of the campaign increases during the campaign – at least with respect to partisan learning. The exception is the naturalization initiative, where partisan knowledge was already comparatively widespread at the outset of the campaign and where individual resources do not seem to have made a difference at all.

Arguments versus emotions. We know from previous work (Kriesi 2005) that the arguments of the campaigns, or the frames used by the campaigners in their messages, have a very strong impact on the outcome of the vote. Swiss voters have previously been shown to be less minimalist than commonly expected and to rely heavily on the arguments provided by the campaigners of the adversarial camps when making their decisions. In Chapter 12, we tested the impact of arguments on the outcome of the vote, controlling for the voters' ideological predispositions. The predispositions controlled for in this chapter are not exactly the same as in the previous chapters, but correspond to self-positioning on the left–right scale. Still, the analysis in this chapter confirms the previous work by showing that arguments both of the pro camps and the con camps have a very strong impact on the individual vote at the end of the day – even if we control for the individual's general ideological predispositions.

This means that the individuals' positions on the arguments are not simply a reflection of their overall ideological stance, a result that can be interpreted in two different ways: In a positive vein, the observed independence between ideology and arguments could mean that the voters are not simply reacting to the arguments as a function of their overall ideological views, but that they reflect on the arguments and take them at their face value. In a more critical vein, this kind of independence could also be interpreted as a sign of the voters' incapacity to integrate the arguments in an overall ideological perspective. Independence between ideology and arguments could, as is argued in Chapter 12, be seen as a clear-cut case of priming: The most accessible arguments have the strongest weight. Both interpretations are, of course, compatible with the received wisdom of attitude researchers, who have known since Converse's (1964) seminal work that the attitudes of the voters are less 'constrained' by ideological considerations than the attitudes of political elites.

In addition to these independent effects, we expected to find interactive effects between the voters' overall ideology and the arguments of the campaign, which would account for the widespread activation effects of the campaigns. Activation can be thought of as a result of a match between an argument and underlying ideological predispositions. The argument that falls on fertile ground and activates latent predispositions of voters has a particularly strong effect. In line with the activation idea, we find some argument-ideology interactions at the end of the two immigration-related campaigns, but not at the end of the corporate tax campaign. The effects are strongest for the naturalization campaign, that is, for the campaign with the most widespread activation effects. Moreover, in this particular campaign, the effects are as expected: Arguments of the opposition are reinforced for voters who are generally on the left, while arguments of the supporters are reinforced for voters who are generally on the right. Surprisingly, at first sight, the activation effect for the asylum campaign implies that the misuse argument activates voters of the left more strongly than voters of the right. But on reflection, this result is quite in line with what we have found previously: It is the xenophobic voters on the left who most consistently followed their issue-specific predispositions, even if these were on the left. The great appeal of the misuse argument to those on the left explains, at least in part, why they disregarded party loyalty in this particular vote. We believe that it is possible to argue that the great appeal of this argument for voters on the left is part of the populist right's syndrome of 'welfare chauvinism', which has proven to be highly attractive to West European working class voters (Andersen and Björklund 1990).

Our analyses of the individual vote choices also show that voters do not exclusively rely on arguments to decide how to vote on an issue. They are also influenced by the emotions they feel when thinking about the issue. Chapter 13 shows that the voters' emotions had a stronger direct impact on voting when the issue was highly complex and difficult to understand (the corporate tax reform) than when the issue was easy (the immigration cases). Difficult and complex issues apparently enhance the voters' reliance on their feelings, as the arguments for and against the proposal are not fully understood. As a matter of fact, it is quite counter-intuitive that a complex technical issue such as the corporate tax reform should be accompanied by stronger emotional effects on individual voting choices than for the familiar and highly polarizing issues related to immigration. This result suggests that voters can use their feelings as a heuristic both when they are not motivated to process information about a given issue and when the information is too complex for their decision-making. Thus, the impact of ideological predispositions on the vote weakened over the course of the corporate tax campaign and was, although still significant, quite small at the end of this campaign. Similarly, the effect of the arguments, although still strong at the end of the campaign, was considerably weaker than in the immigration cases. In fact, the positive emotions proved to be by far the strongest factor in determining the final outcome of the vote in the corporate tax campaign – stronger even than the prior voting intentions at the outset of the campaign! No wonder we found such a large number of conversions in this campaign, while we could not find any system-atic media-exposure effects, nor indications for activation by matching. The impression of a random outcome in the individual decision-making process that we got in the analyses of the previous chapters is, in part at least, explained by the great importance of emotions in individuals' final decision-making in this campaign.

Direct-democratic campaigns: enlightening or manipulating?

Having assembled the evidence, we can now ask, what can we conclude from it with respect to the question that has guided our analyses: Are direct-democratic campaigns enlightening or manipulating? The answer is, it depends. In the Swiss context it mostly, but not exclusively, depends on the difficulty of the decision task, which is a function of both the familiarity and the complexity of the issue at stake.

The Swiss context provides conditions which are generally very favourable for enlightening campaigns. The political strategists and the media have developed routinized procedures with which to approach these campaigns. The political strategists provide ample input into the public debates, substantive input that focuses on the content of the issue at hand, and does not distract from substance by mainly discussing secondary aspects of the contest itself. Both camps that oppose each other in these campaigns are capable of crafting powerful messages, and both camps get a fair hearing in the media. With some exceptions, the media are not primarily market driven, but invest in political news reporting and provide intense, diverse campaign coverage of considerable quality. On average, the voters get a steady stream of arguments and voting cues, allowing them, in principle, to make enlightened choices – that is, choices which are in line with their preferences.

The overwhelming majority of the voters end up making consistent choices – up to 90 per cent of the voters in the immigration-related votes, and still roughly two-thirds in the corporate tax case. Voters learned a consider-able amount during the campaigns and, based on their enhanced knowl-edge, the campaigns mainly reinforced or activated their predispositions as should be the case in an enlightening campaign. The voters' predispositions, indeed, constitute the key constraint on their opinion formation in the course of the campaigns, which means that the supply-side manoeuvering space is generally quite limited.

This is comforting news, but not entirely so. If the vote gets close, as it did in the corporate tax campaign, the voters who cast an inconsistent vote, that is, a vote not in line with their own preferences, may become decisive to the outcome. Inspecting the corporate tax vote more closely, we find that the majority of the inconsistent voters cast a no vote. However, there is one group among the inconsistent voters who overwhelmingly cast a yes vote a group of roughly 10 per cent of all the participants in the corporate tax vote: The originally undecided voters who ended up voting inconsistently. Eighty-nine per cent of this group, or 8.6 percent of all participants in this vote, opted for a yes. This is a group largely sufficient for deciding the overall outcome of the vote in favour of the proposed reform.

For several reasons, the corporate tax campaign suggests that the manoeuvering space for politicians may not be as limited as a pure demand-side vision of democracy is making us believe. In this particularly complex case, the voters' predispositions were less constraining than in the easier immigration cases. Many voters were converted, and they voted against their predispositions. Media coverage was less intense in this particular case, and the debate in the media had less of a dialogical character than in the other two campaigns. Accordingly, exposure to campaign news did not have any systematic impact on the voters' opinion formation. At the same time, in this complex case, which left many a voter without a clue, money has been particularly asymmetrically distributed between the opposing camps. In the final analysis, the voters' emotions appear to have been the most important factor determining their voting choices in this campaign.

The crucial question is, of course, which one of our three cases is most representative of direct-democratic campaigns – the enlightening campaigns or the more dubious case of the corporate tax reform? We have comparable information on the issue complexity and the campaign balance for more than 200 proposals that have been submitted to a federal vote since 1981. As it turns out, the immigration issues resemble the typical campaigns much more closely than does the corporation tax reform. In fact, roughly only 10 per cent of proposals over the last thirty years have been of comparable difficulty for voters as the corporate tax reform, and only somewhat more than 10 per cent have given rise to such excessively imbalanced campaigns (with one side spending 90 per cent of the total or more). Only 2 per cent have been as extreme on both criteria – difficulty and imbalance, and no other case exists that has at the same time given rise to as comparably close an outcome as the corporate tax reform. In other words, the corporate tax case is quite unique in its combination of characteristics favouring a manipulated outcome.

Having come to this encouraging overall assessment, let us conclude with a few words about the ongoing trends. The share of imbalanced campaigns has been increasing more recently in Switzerland (from roughly 10 per cent in the 1980s to 16 per cent in the 2000s), as has the share of the issues that combine great difficulty of choice with an imbalanced campaign, albeit from a very low level (up from 0 per cent in the 1980s to 4 per cent in the 2000s). At the same time, the changing landscape of the Swiss press, with its shift from regional papers to tabloids and free newspapers suggests that the quality of the debate is decreasing for important segments of voters. These are two signs of deteriorating context conditions for the quality of direct-democratic campaigns. For the time being, however, we can be quite confident that, in Switzerland, the overall conditions remain such that the overall effect of these campaigns will, indeed, remain mostly enlightening.

Bibliography

Abelson, Robert P., Donald R. Kinder, Mark D. Peters and Susan T. Fiske (1982). Affective and Semantic Components in Political Person Perception, *Journal of Personality and Social Psychology* 42, 4: 619–30.

Altheide, D. L. and R. P. Snow (1979). *Media Logic.* Beverly Hills, London: Sage.

Alvarez R. Michael and John Brehm (2002). *Hard Choices, Easy Answers Values, Information, and American Public Opinion.* Princeton, NJ: Princeton University Press.

—— (1995). American Ambivalence towards Abortion Policy: Development of a Heteroskedastic Probit Model of Competing Values, *American Journal of Political Science* 39: 1055–82.

Alvarez R. Michael and Charles H. Franklin (1994). Uncertainty and Political Perceptions, *Journal of Politics* 56: 671–88.

Andersen, Jörgen Goul and Tor Björklund (1990). Structural Changes and New Cleavages: The Progress Parties in Denmark and Norway, *Acta Sociologica* 33, 3: 195–217.

Andersen Robert, James Tilley and Anthony F. Heath (2005). Political Knowledge and Enlightened Preferences: Party Choice through the Electoral Cycle, *British Journal of Political Science* 35: 285–302.

Arceneaux, Kevin (2006). Do Campaigns Help Voters Learn? A Cross-National Analysis, *British Journal of Political Science* 36: 159–73.

Arx, von Nicolas (2002). *Ähnlich, aber anders. Die Volksinitiative in Kalifornien und in der Schweiz.* Basel: Helbing und Lichtenhahn.

Asp, Kent (1983). The Struggle for the Agenda. Party Agenda, Media Agenda, and Voter Agenda in the 1979 Swedish Election Campaign, *Communication Research* 10, 3: 333–55.

Bächtiger, André, Simon Niemeyer, Michael Neblo, Marco Steenbergen and Jürg Steiner (2010). Symposium: Toward More Realistic Models of Deliberative Democracy Disentangeling Diversity in Deliberative Democracy: Competing Theories, Their Blind Spots and Complementaries, *The Journal of Political Philosophy* 18, 1: 32–63.

Baerns, Barbara (1992). *Öffentlichkeitsarbeit oder Journalismus? Zum Einfluss im Mediensystem.* Köln: Verlag Wissenschaft und Politik.

—— (1979). Öffentlichkeitsarbeit als Determinante Journalistischer Informationsleistungen, *Publizistik* 24, 3: 301–16.

Baron, Reuben M., and Kenny, David A. (1986). The Moderator-Mediator Variable Distinction in Social Psychological Research: Conceptual, Strategic, and Statistical Considerations, *Journal of Personality and Social Psychology* 51, 6: 1173–82.

Barry, Brian (1975). Review Article: Political Accommodation and Consociational Democracy, *British Journal of Political Science* 5: 477–505.

Bartels, Larry M. (2006a). Priming and Persuasion in Presidential Election Campaigns, pp. 78–112 in *Capturing Campaign Effects*, edited by Henry E. Brady and Richard Johnston, Ann Arbor: The University of Michigan Press.

—— (2006b). Three Virtues of Panel Data for the Analysis of Campaign Effects, pp. 134–63 in *Capturing Campaign Effects*, edited by Henry E. Brady and Richard Johnston, Ann Arbor: The University of Michigan Press.

Bartels, Larry M. (1993a). Democracy with Attitudes, pp. 48–82 in *Electoral Democracy*, edited by Michael B. MacKuen and George Rabinowitz, Ann Arbor: The University of Michigan Press.

—— (1993b). Messages Received: The Political Impact of Media Exposure, *American Political Science Review* 87, 2: 267–85.

Bartolini, Stefano (1999). Collusion, Competition, and Democracy, *Journal of Theoretical Politics* 11, 4: 435–70.

Basinger, Scott J. and Howard Lavine (2005). Ambivalence, Information, and Electoral Choice, *American Political Science Review* 99, 2: 169–84.

Baumgartner, Frank R. and Bryan D. Jones (2002). Positive and Negative Feedback in Politics, pp. 33–28 in *Policy Dynamics*, edited by Frank R. Baumgartner and Bryan D. Jones, Chicago: The University of Chicago Press.

—— (1993). *Agendas and Instability in American Politics*. Chicago: The University of Chicago Press.

Baumgartner, Frank R., Suzanna De Boef and Amber E. Boydstun (2008). *The Decline of the Death Penalty and the Discovery of Innocence*. New York: Cambridge University Press.

Beck, Paul Allen, Russell J. Dalton, Steven Greene, and Robert Huckfeldt (2002). The Social Calculus of Voting: Interpersonal, Media, and Organizational Influences on Presidential Choices, *American Political Science Review* 96, 1: 57–73.

Bennett, W. Lance (2009). *News: The Politics of Illusion* (8th ed.). New York: Pearson.

—— (1990a). Toward a Theory of Press-State Relations in the United States, *Journal of Communication* 40, 2: 103–29.

—— (1990b). Taking the Public by Storm: Information, Cuing, and the Democratic Process in the Gulf Conflict, *Political Communication* 10: 331–51.

Bennett, W. Lance, R. G. Lawrence and S. Livingston (2007). *When the Press Fails: Political Power and the News Media from Iraq to Katrina*. Chicago, London: The University of Chicago Press.

Bennett, W. Lance and Shanto Iyengar (2008). A New Era of Minimal Effects? The Changing Foundations of Political Communication, *Journal of Communication* 58, 4: 707–31.

Bennett, W. Lance, Viktor W. Pickard, David P. Iozzi, Carl L. Schroeder, Taso Lagos and Evams C. Caswell (2004). Managing the Public Sphere: Journalistic Construction of the Great Globalization Debate, *Journal of Communication* 54, 3: 437–55.

Bentele, Günter, Thomas Liebert and Stefan Seeling (1997). Von der Determination zur Intereffikation. Ein integriertes Modell zum Verhältnis von Public Realtions und Journalismus, pp. 225–50 in *Aktuelle Entstehung von Öffentlichkeit. Akteure – Strukturen – Veränderungen*, edited by Günter Bentele and Max Haller, Konstanz: UVK-Medien.

Bernhard, Laurent (2010). Direct Democratic Campaigning – An Empirical Analysis of the Strategies Adopted by Political Actors in Swiss Direct Democracy (2006–2008). Unpublished PhD Thesis, University of Zurich.

Betz, Hans-Georg (2004). *La droite populiste en Europe: extrême et démocrate*. Paris: Autrement.

—— (1993). The New Politics of Resentment: Radical Right-Wing Populist Parties in Western Europe, *Comparative Politics* 25, 4: 413–27.

Blum, Roger (2005). Politischer Journalismus in der Schweiz, pp. 115–30 in *Politische Kommunikation in der Schweiz*, edited by Patrick Donges, Bern: Haupt.

—— (2003). Medienstrukturen der Schweiz, pp. 366–81 in *Öffentliche Kommunikation*, edited by Günter Bentele, Hans-Bernd Brosius and Otfried Jarren, Wiesbaden: Westdeutscher Verlag.

Blumler, Jay George and Dennis Kavanagh (1999). The Third Age of Political Communication: Influences and Features, *Political Communication* 16, 3: 209–30.

Blumler, Jay George and Michael Gurevitch (2001). Americanization Reconsidered: UK-US Campaign Communication Comparisons Across Time, pp. 380–403 in *Mediated Politics. Communication in the Future of Democracy*, edited by W. Lance Bennett and Robert M. Entman, New York: Cambridge University Press.

Boehmke, Fredrick (2002). The Effect of Direct Democracy on the Size and Diversity of State Interest Group Populations, *Journal of Politics* 64: 827–44.

Boix, Carlos (2007). The Emergence of Parties and Party Systems, pp. 499–521 in *The Oxford Handbook of Comparative Politics*, edited by Carles Boix and Susan C. Stokes, Oxford: Oxford University Press.

Bonfadelli, Heinz (2008). Knowledge Gap, pp. 382–4 in *Encyclopedia of Political Communication*. Vol. 1, edited by Lynda Lee Kaid and Christina Holtz-Bacha, Los Angeles/London/New Delhi/Singapore: Sage.

—— (2000). Schweizerische Aussenpolitik als Berichterstattung in der Presse und in den Fernsehnachrichten in *Schweizerische Aussenpolitik als Gegenstand der Medienvermittlung*, edited by B. Nyffeler and R. Blum, Zurich: IPMZ.

—— (1994). *Die Wissenskluft-Perspektive: Massenmedien und gesellschaftliche Information*. Konstanz: Ölschläger.

Bonfadelli, Heinz and Marr, Mirko (2007). Journalistinnen und Journalisten im privaten Rundfunk der Schweiz. Ergebnisse einer Online-Befragung im Auftrag des Bundesamtes für Kommunikation (BAKOM). Zürich: Universität Zürich.

Bonfadelli, Heinz, Schwarb, Ursula, Widmer, Jean and Boller, Boris (2003). Publizistische Vielfalt im Lokalbereich. Teil I: Informationssendungen ausgewählter Radio- und Fernsehveranstalter im Vergleich. Studie im Auftrag des Bundesamtes für Kommunikation (BAKOM). Zürich: Universität Zürich.

Bowler, Shaun and Robert Hanneman (2006). Just How Pluralist Is Direct Democracy? The Structure of Interest Group Participation in Ballot Proposition Elections, *Political Research Quarterly* 59: 557–68.

Bowler, Shaun and Todd Donovan (2006). Direct Democracy and Political Parties in America, *Party Politics* 12, 5: 649–70.

Brady, Henry E. and Richard Johnston (eds) (2006). *Capturing Campaign Effects*. Ann Arbor: University of Michigan Press.

Brandenburg, Heinz (2002). Who Follows Whom? The Impact of Parties on Media Agenda Formation in the 1997 British General Election Campaign, *Harvard International Journal of Press/Politics* 7, 3: 34–54.

Breckler, Steven. J. and Elizabeth C. Wiggins (1991). Cognitive Responses in Persuasion: Affective and Evaluative Determinants, *Journal of Experimental Social Psychology* 27: 180–200.

Brosius, Hans-Bernd and Hans-Mathias Kepplinger (1990). The Agenda-Setting Function of Television News: Static and Dynamic Views, *Communication Research* 17: 183–211.

Buchanan, Bruce I. (2001). Mediated Electoral Democracy: Campaigns, Incentives, and Reform, pp. 362–79 in *Mediated Politics. Communication in the Future of Democracy*, edited by W. L. Bennett and R. M. Entman, New York: Cambridge University Press.

Budge, Ian (2001). Political Parties in Direct Democracy, pp.67–87 in *Referendum Democracy. Citizens, Elites and Deliberation in Referendum Campaigns*, edited by Mathes Mendelsohn and Andrew Parkin, Basingstoke: Palgrave.

—— (1996). *The New Challenge of Direct Democracy*. Cambridge: Polity Press.

Burstein, Paul (1985). *Discrimination, Jobs, and Politics: The Struggle for Equal Employment Opportunity in the United States in the New Deal.* Chicago: The University of Chicago Press.

Byrne, Barbara M. (2001). *Structural Equation Modeling with AMOS.* Mahwah/London: Lawrence Erlbaum.

Chaffee, Steven (1982). Mass Media and Interpersonal Channels: Competitive, Convergent or Complementary? pp. 57–77 in *Intermedia. Interpersonal Communication in a Media World,* edited by Gary Gumpert and Robert Cathcart, New York: Oxford University Press.

Chaffee, Steven and Frank Kanihan (1997). Learning about Politics from the Mass Media, *Political Communication* 14, 4: 421–30.

Chaffee, Steven and Stacy Frank (1996). How Americans Get Political Information: Print vs. Broadcast News, *Annals of the American Academy of Political Science* 546: 48–58.

Chambers, Simone (2004). Behind Closed Doors: Publicity, Secrecy, and the Quality of Deliberation, *The Journal of Political Philosophy* 12, 4: 389–410.

—— (2001). Constitutional Referendums and Democratic Deliberation, pp. 231–55 in *Referendum Democracy. Citizens, Elites and Deliberation in Referendum Campaigns,* edited by Matthew Mendelsohn and Andrew Parkin, Basingstoke: Palgrave Macmillan.

Chong, Dennis and James N. Druckman (2007a). Framing Public Opinion in Competitive Democracies, *American Political Science Review* 101, 4: 637–56.

—— (2007b). A Theory of Framing and Opinion Formation in Competitive Elite Environments, *Journal of Communication* 57, 1: 99–118.

—— (2007c). Framing Theory, *Annual Review of Political Science* 10: 103–126.

Christin, Thomas, Simon Hug, and Pascal Sciarini (2002). Interests and Information in Referendum Voting: An Analysis of Swiss Voters, *European Journal of Political Research* 41: 757–76.

Clark, Sherman J. (1998). A Populist Critique of Direct Democracy, *Harvard Law Review* 112: 434–82.

Cobb, M. D. and J. H. Kuklinski (1997). Changing Minds: Political Arguments and Political Persuasion, *American Journal of Political Science* 41, 1: 88–121.

Cobb, Roger W. and Charles D. Elder (1983). *Participation in American Politics. The Dynamics of Agenda-Building.* (2nd ed.). Baltimore: The Johns Hopkins University Press.

Cohen, Bernard C. (1963). *The Press and Foreign Policy.* Princeton, NJ: Princeton University Press.

Conover, Pamela J. and Stanley Feldman (1986). Emotional Reactions to the Economy: I'm Mad As Hell and I'm Not Going to Take It Anymore, *American Journal of Political Science* 30, 1: 50–78.

Converse, Philip E. (1964). The Nature of Belief Systems in Mass Publics, pp. 206–61 in *Ideology and Discontent,* edited by David Apter. New York: The Free Press.

Cook, Timothy E. (2005). Public Policy towards the Press: What Government Does For the News Media, pp. 248–62 in *The Press,* edited by G. Overholser and K. Hall Jamieson, Oxford, New York: Oxford University Press.

—— (1998). *Governing with the News. The News Media As a Political Institution.* Chicago: The University of Chicago Press.

Coombs C.H. (1964). *A Theory of Data.* New York: Wiley.

Cox, Gary W. (1999). Electoral Rules and the Calculus of Mobilization, *Legislative Studies Quarterly* 24, 3: 387–420.

Cox, Gary W. and Mathew D. McCubbins (1986). Electoral Politics As a Redistributive Game, *Journal of Politics* 48, 2: 370–89.

Cronin, Thomas (1989). *Direct Democracy: The Politics of Initiative, Referendum, and Recall.* Cambridge: Harvard University Press.

Curran, James (2007). Reinterpreting the Democratic Roles of the Media, *Brazilian Journalism Research* 3, 1: 32–54.

Curran, James (2005). What Democracy Requires of the Media, pp. 120–40 in *The Press*, edited by G. Overholser and K. Hall Jamieson, Oxford, New York: Oxford University Press.

Dahinden, Urs (2006). *Framing. Eine integrative Theorie der Massenkommunikation.* Konstanz: UVK-Verlagsgesellschaft.

Dahinden, Urs and Joseph Trappel (2005). Mediengattungen und Medienformate, pp. 389–424 in *Einführung in die Publizistikwissenschaft*, edited by H. Bonfadelli, O. Jarren, G. Siegert, Bern: UTB.

Dahl, Robert A. (1971). *Polyarchy: Participation and Opposition.* New Haven: Yale University Press.

—— (1989). *Democracy and Its Critics.* New Haven: Yale University Press.

Dalrymple, Kajsa E. and Dietram Scheufele (2004). Finally Informing the Electorate? How the Internet Got People Thinking about Presidential Politics in 2004, *The Harvard International Journal of Press/Politics* 12, 3: 96–111.

Danielian, Lucig H. and Benjamin I. Page (1994). The Heavenly Chorus: Interest Group Voices on TV News, *American Journal of Political Science* 38, 4: 1056–78.

Dardis, Frank E., Frank R. Baumgartner, Amber E. Boydstun, Suzanna De Boef and Fuyuan Shen (2008). Media Framing of Capital Punishment and Its Impact on Individuals Cognitive Responses, *Mass Communication & Society* 11: 115–40.

Deegan-Krause, Kevin (2007). New Dimensions of Political Cleavage, pp. 538–56 in *Oxford Handbook of Political Behaviour*, edited by Russell J. Dalton and Hans-Dieter Klingemann, Oxford: Oxford University Press.

Delli Carpini, Michael X. and Scott Keeter (1996). *What Americans Know about Politics and Why It Matters.* New Haven: Yale University Press.

—— (1994). The Publics Knowledge of Politics, pp. 19–40 in *Public Opinion, The Press, and Public Policy*, edited by J. D. Kennamer, Westport: Praeger.

Derks, Anton (2004). Are the Underprivileged Really that Economically Leftist? Attitudes towards Economic Redistribution and the Welfare State in Flanders, *European Journal of Political Research* 43, 4: 509–21.

Dervin, Brenda (1980). Communication Gaps and Inequities: Moving toward a Reconceptualization, pp. 73–112 in *Progress in Communication Sciences*, edited by Voigt, Marvin and Brenda Dervin, Norwood N.J.: Ablex.

De Vreese, Claes (2005). News Framing: Theory and Typology, *Information Design Journal + Document Design* 13, 1: 51–62.

De Vreese, Claes and Holli A. Semetko (2004). *Political Campaigning in Referendums. Framing the Referendum Issue.* Oxon, New York: Routledge.

—— (2002). Cynical and Engaged Strategic Campaign Coverage, Public Opinion, and Mobilization in a Referendum, *Communication Research* 29, 6: 615–41.

Dillard, James P. and Barbara J. Wilson (1993). Communication and Affect: Thoughts, Feelings, and Issues for the Future, *Communication Research* 20, 5: 637–46.

Donovan, Todd, Shaun Bowler, David McCuan and Ken Fernandez (1998). Contending Players and Strategies: Opposition Advantages in Initiative Elections, pp. 80–104 in *Citizens as Legislators. Direct Democracy in the United States*, edited by Shaun Bowler, Todd Donovan and Caroline J. Tolbert, Columbus: Ohio State University Press.

Donsbach, Wolfgang and Thomas E. Patterson (2004). Political News Journalists. Partisanship, Professionalism, and Political Roles in Five Countries, pp. 251–70 in *Comparing Political Communication. Theories, Cases, and Challenges*, edited by Frank Esser and Barbara Pfetsch, Cambridge: Cambridge University Press.

Downs, Anthony (1957). *An Economic Theory of Democracy*. New York: Harper and Collins.

Doyle, Gillian (2002). *Understanding Media Economics*. London, Thousand Oaks/New Delhi: Sage.

Drew, Dan and David Weaver (2006). Voter Learning in the 2004 Presidential Election: Did the Media Matter? *Journalism and Mass Communication Quarterly* 83, 1: 25–42.

Druckman, James N. (2004). Political Preference Formation: Competition, Deliberation, and the (Ir)relevance of Framing Effects, *American Political Science Review* 98, 4: 671–86.

—— (2001). On the Limits of Framing Effects: Who Can Frame? *Journal of Politics* 63, 4: 1041–66.

Druckman, James N. and Kjersten R. Nelson (2003). Framing and Deliberation: How Citizens Conversations Limit Elite Influence, *American Journal of Political Science* 47, 4: 729–45.

Druckman, James N., Martin Kifer and Michael Parkin (2009). *Campaign Communications in U.S. Congressional Elections*. Chicago: Northwestern University.

Eagly, Alice H. and Shelly Chaiken (1993). *The Psychology of Attitudes*. New York: Harcourt Brace.

Eagly, Alice H., Antonio Mladini and Stacey Otto (1994). Cognitive and Affective Bases of Attitudes toward Social Groups and Social Policies, *Journal of Experimental Social Psychology* 30: 113–37.

Elster, Jon (1998). Deliberation and Constitution Making, pp. 97–122 in *Deliberative Democracy*, edited by Jon Elster, Cambridge: Cambridge University Press.

Entman, Robert M. (2007). Framing Bias: Media in the Distribution of Power, *Journal of Communication* 57: 167–76.

—— (2005). The Nature and Sources of News, pp. 48–65 in *The Press*, edited by G. Overholser and K. Hall Jamieson, Oxford, New York: Oxford University Press.

—— (2004). *Projections of Power Framing News, Public Opinion, and U.S. Foreign Policy*. Chicago: The University of Chicago Press.

—— (1993). Framing: Toward Clarification of a Fractured Paradigm, *Journal of Communication* 43, 4: 51–8.

—— (1989). *Democracy without Citizens*. New York: Oxford University Press.

Entman, Robert M. and W. Lance Bennett (2001). Communication in the Future of Democracy: a Conclusion, pp. 468–80 in *Mediated Politics: Communication in the Future of Democracy*, edited by W. Lance Bennett and Robert M. Entman, Cambridge: Cambridge University Press.

Entman, Robert M., Jörg Matthes and Lynn Pellicano (2009). Framing Politics in the News: Nature, Sources and Effects, pp. 175–90 in *Handbook of Journalism Studies*, edited by K. Wahl-Jorgensen and Thomas Hanitzsch, Mahwah, NJ: Lawrence Erlbaum Associates.

Enyedi, Zsolt (2005). The Role of Agency in Cleavage Formation, *European Journal of Political Research* 44, 5: 697–720.

Epple-Gass, Rudolf (1988). *Friedensbewegung und direkte Demokratie in der Schweiz*. Frankfurt a.M.: Haag und Herchen.

Erikson, Robert S., Michael B. MacKuen and James A. Stimson (2002). *The Macro-Polity*. Cambridge: Cambridge University Press.

Erikson, Robert S., and Thomas R. Palfrey (2000). Equilibria in Campaign Spending Games: Theory and Data, *American Political Science Review* 94, 3: 595–609.

Esses, Victoria M., Geoffrey Haddock and Mark P. Zanna (1993). Values, Stereotypes, and Emotions as Determinants of Intergroup Attitudes, pp. 137–66 in *Affect, Cognition and Stereotyping: Interactive Processes in Group Perception*, edited by Diane M. Mackie and David L. Hamilton, New York: Academic Press.

Ettema, James and Gerald F. Kline (1977). Deficits, Differences, and Ceilings. Contingent Conditions for Understanding the Knowledge Gap, *Communication Research* 4, 2: 179–202.

Eveland Jr., William P. (2002). News Information Processing As Mediator of the Relationship between Motivations and Political Knowledge, *Journalism and Mass Communication Quarterly* 79, 1: 26–40.

—— (2001). The Cognitive Mediation Model of Learning from the News: Evidence from Nonelection, Off-Year Election, and Presidential Election Contexts, *Communication Research* 28, 5: 571–601.

Eveland Jr., William P., Dhavan V. Shah and Nojin Kwak (2003). Assessing Causality in the Cognitive Mediation Model, *Communication Research* 30, 4: 359–86.

Farrell, David M. and Rüdiger Schmitt-Beck (eds) (2002). *Do Campaigns matter? Campaign Effects in Elections and Referendums.* London: Routledge.

Fearon, James D. (1998). Deliberation as Discussion, pp. 44–68 in *Deliberative Democracy*, edited by Jon Elster, Cambridge: Cambridge University Press.

Ferree, Myra M., William A. Gamson, Jürgen Gerhards and Dieter Rucht (2002). *Shaping Abortion Discourse. Democracy and the Public Sphere in Germany and the United States.* Cambridge: Cambridge University Press.

Finkel, Steven E. (1995). *Causal Analysis with Panel Data.* Thousand Oakes: Sage.

—— (1993). Reexamining the Minimal Effects Model in Recent Presidential Campaigns, *The Journal of Politics* 55, 1: 1–21.

Finkel Steven E. and P.R. Schrott (1995). Campaign Effects on Voter Choice in the German Election of 1990, *British Journal of Political Science* 25: 349–77.

Forgas, Joseph P. (1995). Mood and Judgment: The Affect Infusion Model (AIM), *Psychological Bulletin* 117: 39–66.

Galtung, J. and Ruge, Marie H. (1965). The Structure of Foreign News, *Journal of Peace Research* 2, 1: 64–91.

Gamson, William A. (2004). Bystanders, Public Opinion, and the Media, pp. 242–261 in *The Blackwell Companion to Social Movements*, edited by D. A. Snow, S. A. Soule and H. Kriesi, Oxford: Blackwell Publishing.

Gamson, William A. (1992). *Talking Politics.* Cambridge: Cambridge University Press.

Gans, Herbert J. (1980). *Deciding What's News. A Study of CBS Evening News, NBC Nightly News, Newsweek and Time.* New York: Vintage Books.

—— (1979). *Deciding What's News: A Study of CBS Evening News, NBC Nightly News, Newsweek, and Time.* New York: Pantheon Books.

Gantz, Walter (1978). How Uses and Gratifications Affect Recall of Television News, *Journalism Quarterly* 55, 4: 664–72.

Gaziano, Cecilie (1983). The Knowledge Gap: An Analytical Review of Media Effects, *Communication Research* 10, 4: 447–86.

Gelman Andrew and Gary King (1993). Why Are American Presidential Election Campaign Polls so Variable When Votes Are so Predictable? *British Journal of Political Science* 23, 4: 409–51.

Gentzkow, Matthew and Jesse M. Shapiro (2006). Media Bias and Reputation, *Journal of Political Economy* 114: 280–316.

Gerber, Alan S., Dean Karlan and Daniel Bergan (2009). Does the Media Matter? A Field Experiment Measuring the Effect of Newspapers on Voting Behavior and Political Opinions, *American Economic Journal of Applied Economics* 1, 2: 35–52.

Gerber, Elisabeth R. (1999). *The Populist Paradox: Interest Group Influence and the Promise of Direct Legislation.* Princeton, NJ: Princeton University Press.

Gilens, Martin and Naomi Murakawa (2002). Elite Cues and Political Decision-Making, *Political Decision Making, Deliberation and Participation* 6: 15–49.

Golder, Sona Nadenichek (2006). Pre-Electoral Coalition Formation in Parliamentary Democracies, *British Journal of Political Science* 36: 193–212.

Goldstein, Kenneth and P. Freedman (2002). Lessons Learned: Campaign Advertising in the 2000 Elections, *Political Communication* 19, 1: 5–28.

Goldstein, Kenneth and Travis N. Ridout (2004). Measuring the Effects of Televised Political Advertising, *Annual Review of Political Science* 7: 205–26.

Gonzenbach, William J. (1996). *The Media, the President, and Public Opinion: A Longitudinal Analysis of the Drug Issue, 1984–1991.* Mahwah, NJ: Erlbaum.

Graber D. A. (2001). *Processing Politics: Learning from Television in the Internet Age.* Chicago: The University of Chicago Press.

Graber D. A. (2001). Adapting Political News to the Needs of Twenty-First Century Americans, pp. 433–52 in *Mediated Politics. Communication in the Future of Democracy,* edited by W. Lance Bennett and Robert M. Entman, New York: Cambridge University Press.

Graetz, Michael J. and Ian Shapiro (2005). *Death by a Thousand Cuts. The Fight over Taxing Inherited Wealth.* Princeton, NJ: Princeton University Press.

Gramsci, Antonio (1971). *Selections from the Prison Notebooks of Antonio Gramsci,* edited by Quintin Hoare and Geoffrey Nowell Smith, New York: International Publishers.

Granberg, Donald and Thad A. Brown (1989). On Affect and Cognition in Politics, *Social Psychology Quarterly* 52, 3: 171–82.

Greene, William H. (2008). *Econometric Analysis.* Upper Saddle River, NJ: Prentice Hall International.

Groseclose, Tim. (2001). A Model of Candidate Location When One Candidate Has a Valence Advantage, *American Journal of Political Science* 45, 4: 862–86.

Gurevitch, Michael and Jay G. Blumler (1990). Political Communication Systems and Democratic Values, pp. 269–87 in *Democracy and the Mass Media*, edited by J. Lichtenberg, Cambridge: Cambridge University Press.

Haddock, Geoffrey and Mark P. Zanna (1998). Assessing the Impact of Affective and Cognitive Information in Predicting Attitudes toward Capital Punishment, *Law and Human Behavior* 22, 3: 325–39.

—— (1993). Predicting Prejudicial Attitudes: The Importance of Affect, Cognition, and the Feeling-Belief Dimension, *Advances in Consumer Research* 20: 315–8.

Hair, Joseph F., Bill Black, Barry Babin, Rolph E. Anderson, Ronald L. Tatham (2006). *Multivariate Data Analysis.* Upper Saddle River: Prentice Hall.

Halaby, Charles. (2004). Panel Models in Sociological Research, *Annual Revue of Sociology* 30: 507–44.

Hallin, Daniel C. and Paolo Mancini (2004). Americanization, Globalization, and Secularization. Understanding the Convergence of Media Systems and Political Communication, pp. 25–44 in *Comparing Political Communication. Theories, Cases, and Challenges*, edited by Frank Esser and Barbara Pfetsch, Cambridge: Cambridge University Press.

Hamilton, James T. (2005). The Market and the Media, pp. 351–71 in *The press*, edited by G. Overholser and K. Hall Jamieson, Oxford, New York: Oxford University Press.

—— (2004). *All the News That's Fit to Sell: How the Market Transforms Information into News*. Princeton, NJ: Princeton University Press.

Hänggli, Regula (2011). Influence Factors on Frame Presence and Frame Frequency in Frame Building. Under Revision.

—— (2010). Frame Building and Framing Effects in Direct-Democratic Campaigns. Unpublished PhD Thesis, University of Zurich.

Hänggli, Regula and Hanspeter Kriesi (2009). Political Framing Strategies and Their Impact on Media Framing in a Swiss Direct-Democratic Campaign, *Political Communication* 27, 2: 141–57.

Harmel, Robert and Kenneth Janda (1994). An Integrated Theory of Party Goals and Party Change, *Journal of Theoretical Politics* 6, 3: 259–87.

Heider, Fritz (1958). *The Psychology of Interpersonal Relations*. New York: Wiley.

Heinrich, Jürgen (2001). *Medienökonomie* (2nd ed.). Wiesbaden: Westdeutscher Verlag.

Helbling, Marc (2008). *Practicing Citizenship and Heterogeneous Nationhood: Naturalizations in Swiss Municipalities*. Amsterdam: Amsterdam University Press.

Helbling, Marc and Hanspeter Kriesi (2004). Staatsbürgerverständnis und politische Mobilisierung: Einbürgerungen in Schweizer Gemeinden, *Schweiz. Zeitschrift für Politikwissenschaft* 10, 4: 33–58.

Hellwig, Timothy (2008). Explaining the Salience of Left-Right Ideology in Postindustrial Democracies: The Role of Structural Economic Change, *European Journal of Political Research* 47: 687–709.

Hillygus, D. Sunshine and Simon Jackman (2003). Voter Decision Making in Election 2000: Campaign Effects, Partisan Activation, and the Clinton Legacy, *American Journal of Political Science* 47, 4: 583–96.

Höglinger, Dominic (2008). Verschafft die direkte Demokratie den Benachteiligten mehr Gehör? Der Einfluss institutioneller Rahmenbedingungen auf die mediale Präsenz politsicher Akteure, *Swiss Political Science Review* 14, 2: 207–43.

Holbrook, Thomas M. (2002). Presidential Campaigns and the Knowledge Gap, *Political Communication* 19, 4: 437–54.

—— (1996). *Do Campaigns Matter?* Thousand Oaks, CA: Sage Publications.

Huckfeldt, Robert and John Sprague (2000). Political Consequences of Inconsistency: The Accessibility and Stability of Abortion Attitudes, *Political Psychology* 21, 1: 57–79.

Imhof, Kurt, Jens Lucht, Linards Udris, Adrian Rohner and Anna Vetsch (2008). Synthesis Report Project 8: Democracy in the Media Society: Changing Media Structures – Changing Political Communication? Zurich: NCCR-Democracy.

Isbell, Linda M. and Victor C. Ottati (2002). The Emotional Voter: Effects of Episodic Affective Reactions on Candidate Evaluation, pp. 55–74 in *The Social Psychology of Politics*, edited by Victor C. Ottati, R. Scott Tindale, John Edwards, Fred B. Bryant, Linda Heath, Daniel C. O'Connell, Yolanda Suarez-Balcazar and Emil J. Posavac, New York: Kluwer.

Isbell, Linda M., Victor C. Ottati and Kathleen C. Burns (2006). Affect and Politics: Effects on Judgment, Processing, and Information Seeking, pp. 57–86 in *Feeling Politics. Emotion in Political Information Processing*, edited by David P. Redlawsk, New York: Palgrave Macmillan.

Iyengar, Shanto (1991). *Is Anyone Responsible? How Television Frames Political Issues*. Chicago: University of Chicago Press.

Iyengar, Shanto and Adam F. Simon (2000). New Perspectives and Evidence on Political Communication and Campaign Effects, *Annual Review of Psychology* 51: 149–69.

Iyengar, Shanto and Donald R. Kinder (1987). *News that Matter.* Chicago: The University of Chicago Press.

Iyengar, Shanto, Helmut Norpoth and Kyu S. Hahn (2004). Consumer Demand for Election News: The Horserace Sells, *The Journal of Politics* 66, 1: 157–75.

Iyengar Shanto and J.R. Petrocik (1998). *Basic rule voting: The impact of campaigns on party and approval based voting.* Paper presented at conference on Political Advertising and Electoral Campaigns, American University, Washington D.C.

Jacobs, Lawrence R. and Robert Y. Shapiro (2000). *Politicians Don't Pander. Political Manipulation and the Loss of Democratic Responsiveness.* Chicago: The University of Chicago Press.

Jarren, Otfried and Patrick Donges (2006). *Politische Kommunikation in der Mediengesellschaft. Eine Einführung.* Vol. 2, überarbeitete Auflage. Wiesbaden: VS.

Jasper, James M. (2006). *Getting Your Way. Strategic Dilemmas in the Real World.* Vol. 9. Chicago: The University of Chicago Press.

Jerit, Jennifer, Jason Barabas and Toby Bolsen (2006). Citizens, Knowledge, and the Information Environment, *American Journal of Political Science* 50, 2: 266–82.

Johnston, Richard, Andre Blais, Henry E Brady and Jean Cret (1992). *Letting the People Decide: Dynamics of a Canadian Election.* Stanford: Stanford University Press.

Josephson, Braden R., Jefferson A. Singer and Peter Salovey (1996). Mood Regulation and Memory: Repairing Sad Moods with Happy Memories, *Cognition and Emotion* 10: 437–44.

Kahn, Kim Fridkin and Patrick Kenney (1999). *The Spectacle of U.S. Senate Campaigns.* Princeton, NJ: Princeton University Press.

Kaplan, Noah, David K. Park and Travis N. Ridout (2006). Dialogue in American Campaigns? An Examination of Issue Convergence in Candidate Television Advertising, *American Journal of Political Science* 50, 3: 724–36.

Keele, Luke and Jennifer Wolak (2008). Contextual Sources of Ambivalence. *Political Psychology* 29, 5: 653–73.

—— (2006). Value Conflict and Volatility in Party Identification, *British Journal of Political Science* 36: 671–90.

Kepplinger, Hans Mathias (2007). Reciprocal Effects: Toward a Theory of Mass Media Effects on Decision Makers, *Harvard International Journal of Press/Politics* 12, 2: 3–23.

—— (2002). Mediatization of Politics: Theory and Data, *Journal of Communication* 52, 4: 972–86.

Kepplinger, Hans Mathias and Marcus Maurer (2004). *Abschied vom rationalen Wähler. Warum Bundestagswahlen im Fernsehen entschieden werden.* Freiburg: Verlag Karl Alber.

Kepplinger, Hans Mathias, Gotto, Klaus, Brosius, Hans-Bernd and Dietmar Haak (1989). *Der Einfluss der Fernsehnachrichten auf die politische Meinungsbildung.* Freiburg/ München: Verlag Karl Alber.

Kepplinger, Hans Mathias, Noelle-Neumann, Elisabeth and Wolfgang Donsbach (1999). *Kampa. Meinungsklima und Medienwirkung im Bundestagswahlkampf 1998.* Freiburg: Verlag Karl Alber.

Kiefer, Marie Luise (2005). *Medienökonomik. Einführung in die ökonomische Theorie der Medien* (2. Aufl.). München: Oldenbourg.

Kinder, Donald R. (2003). Communication and Politics in the Age of Information, pp. 357–93 in *Oxford Handbook of Political Psychology,* edited by David O. Sears, Leonie Huddy and Robert Jervis, New York: Oxford University Press.

—— (1998). Communication and Opinion, *Annual Review of Political Science* 1: 167–97.

King, Gary and Langche Zeng (2001). Logistic Regression in Rare Events Data, *Political Analysis* 9, 2: 137–63.

Kiousis, Spiro, Christina Popescu and Michael Mitrook (2007). Understanding Influence on Corporate Reputation: An Examination of Public Relations Efforts, Media Coverage, Public Opinion, and Financial Performance From an Agenda-Building and Agenda-Setting Perspective, *Journal of Public Relations Research* 19, 2: 147–65.

Kiousis, Spiro, Michael Mitrook, Xu Wu and Trent Seltzer (2006). First- and Second-Level Agenda-Building and Agenda-Setting Effects: Exploring the Linkages Among Candidate News Releases, Media Coverage, and Public Opinion During the 2002 Florida Gubernatorial Election, *Journal of Public Relations Research* 18, 3: 265–85.

Kirchgässner, Gebhard, Lars P. Feld and Marcel R. Savioz 1999. *Die direkte Demokratie. Modern, erfolgreich, entwicklungs- und exportfähig.* Basel: Helbing und Lichtenhahn.

Kitschelt, Herbert in collaboration with Anthony J. McGann (1995). *The Radical Right in Western Europe.* Ann Arbor: The University of Michigan Press.

Knoke, David (1990). *Political Networks: The Structural Perspective.* Cambridge: Cambridge University Press.

Knoke, David, Franz U. Pappi, Jeff Broadbent and Y. Tsujinaka (1996). *Comparing Policy Networks: Labor Politics in the U.S., Germany, and Japan.* Cambridge: Cambridge University Press.

Koopmans, Ruud (2004). Movements and Media: Selection Processes and Evolutionary Dynamics in the Public Sphere, *Theory and Society* 33, 3–4: 367–91.

Koopmans, Ruud, Paul Statham, Marco Giugni, Florence Passy (2005). *Contested Citizenship. Immigration and Cultural Diversity in Europe.* Minneapolis: University of Minnesota Press.

Kriesi, Hanspeter (2010). *Personalization of national election campaigns.* Paper prepared for the 60th Political Studies Association Annual Conference, 29 March–1 April 2010, Edinburgh, UK.

—— (2009). Sind Abstimmungsergebnisse käuflich? pp. 83–106 in *Demokratie als Leidenschaft. Festschrift für Wolf Linder,* edited by Adrian Vatter, Frédéric Varone und Fritz Sager. Bern: Haupt.

—— (2009). The Role of the Federal Government in Direct-Democratic Campaigns, pp. 79–96 in *Rediscovering Public Law and Public Administration in Comparative Policy Analysis: A Tribute to Peter Knoepfel,* Bern: Verlag Haupt.

—— (2006).The Role of the Political Elite in Swiss Direct-Democratic Votes, *Party Politics* 12, 5: 599–622.

—— (2005). *Direct Democratic Choice. The Swiss Experience.* Lanham, Md.: Lexington Books.

—— (1994). Akteure-Medien-Publikum. Die Herausforderung direkter Demokratie durch die Transformation der Öffentlichkeit, pp. 234–60 in *Öffentlichkeit, öffentliche Meinung, soziale Bewegungen,* edited by Friedhelm Neidhardt, Opladen: Westdeutscher Verlag.

—— (1980). *Entscheidungsstrukturen und Entscheidungsprozesse in der Schweizer Politik.* Frankfurt: Campus.

Kriesi, Hanspeter and Alexander Trechsel (2008). *The Politics of Switzerland: Continuity and Change in a Consensus Democracy.* Cambridge: Cambridge University Press.

Kriesi, Hanspeter and Maya Jegen (2001). The Swiss Energy Policy Elite: The Actor Constellation of a Policy Domain in Transition, *European Journal of Political Research* 39: 251–87.

Kriesi, Hanspeter, Edgar Grande, Romain Lachat, Martin Dolezal, Simon Bornschier and Tim Frey (2008). *West European Politics in the Age of Globalization*. Cambridge: Cambridge University Press.

Kriesi, Hanspeter, Laurent Bernhard and Regula Hänggli (2009). The Politics of Campaigning – Dimensions of Strategic Action, pp. 345–65 in *Politik in der Mediendemokratie*. *PVS Sonderband 42*, edited by Frank Marcinkowski and Barbara Pfetsch, Wiesbaden: VS Verlag.

Kriesi, Hanspeter, Matteo Gianni, Pascal Sciarini and Boris Wernli (1996). *Le clivage linguistique. Problèmes de compréhension entre les communautés linguistiques en Suisse*. Berne: Office Fédérale de la statistique.

Kriesi, Hanspeter, Silke Adam and Margit Jochum (2006). Comparative Analysis of Policy Networks in Western Europe, *Journal of European Public Policy* 13, 3: 341–61.

Kroh, Martin (2007). Measuring Left-Right Political Orientation: The Choice of Response Format, *Public Opinion Quarterly* 71: 204–30.

Kühne, Rinaldo, Christian Schemer, Jörg Matthes, and Werner Wirth (in press). Affective priming in political campaigns: How campaign-induced emotions prime political opinions, *International Journal of Public Opinion Research*.

Kuklinski, James H., Ellen Riggle, Victor C. Ottati, Norbert Schwarz and Robert S. Wyer Jr. (1991). The Cognitive and Affective Bases of Political Tolerance Judgments, *American Journal of Political Science* 35, 1: 1–27.

Kunda, Ziva (1990). The Case for Motivated Reasoning, *Psychological Bulletin* 108: 480–98.

Lachat, Romain and Pascal Sciarini (2002). When Do Election Campaigns Matter, and to Whom? Results from the 1999 Swiss Election Panel Study, pp. 41–57 in *Do Political Campaigns Matter?* edited by David M. Farrel and Rüdiger Schmitt-Beck, London: Routledge.

Ladd, Jonathan and Gabriel S. Lenz (2008). Reassessing the Role of Anxiety in Vote Choice, *Political Psychology* 29, 2: 275–96.

Ladner, Andreas and Michael Brändle (1999). Does Direct Democracy Matter for Political Parties? An Empirical test in the Swiss Cantons, *Party Politics* 5, 3: 283–302.

Lau, Richard (1985). Two Explanations for Negativity Effects in Political Behavior, *American Journal of Political Science* 29: 119–38.

Laumann, Edward O. and David Knoke (1987). *The Organizational State. Social Choice in National Policy Domains*. Madison: The University of Wisconsin Press.

Laumann, Edward O. and Franz U. Pappi (1976). *Networks of Collective Action: A Perspective on Community Influence Systems*. New York: Academic Press.

Lawrence, Regina (2000). *The Politics of Force: Media and the Construction of Police Brutality*. Berkeley: University of California Press.

Lazarsfeld, Paul F., Bernard Berelson and Hazel Gaudet (1968)(1944). *The Peoples Choice. How the Voter Makes up his Mind in a Presidential Campaign*. New York: Columbia University Press.

Lenz, Gabriel S. (2004). *A reanalysis of priming studies finds little evidence of issue opinion priming and much evidence of issue opinion change*. Paper presented at the annual meeting of the Midwest Political Science Association, Chicago.

Lieberman, Matthew D., Darren Schreiber and Kevin N. Ochsner (2003). Is Political Cognition Like Riding a Bicycle? How Cognitive Neuroscience Can Inform Research on Political Thinking, *Political Psychology* 24, 4: 704–881.

Lipset, Seymour M. and Stein Rokkan (1967). Cleavage Structures, Party systems, and Voter Alignments. An Introduction, pp. 1–64 in *Party systems and Voter Alignments: Cross-national Perspectives*, edited by Seymour M. Lipset and Stein Rokkan, New York: Free Press.

Lindbeck, Assar and Jörgen W. Weibull (1987). Balanced Budget Redistribution and the Outcome of Political Competition, *Public Choice* 52, 3: 273–97.

Long, Scott J. and Jeremy Freese (2006). *Regression Models for Categorical Dependent Variables Using Stata*. Lakeway Drive: Stata Press.

Lupia, Arthur and John G. Matsusaka (2004). Direct Democracy. New Approaches to Old Questions, *Annual Review of Political Science* 7: 462–83.

Lupia, Arthur, Mathew D. McCubbins and Samuel L. Popkin (2000). *Elements of Reason: Cognition, Choice and the Bounds of Rationality*. New York: Cambridge University Press.

MacManus, John (1995). A Market-Based Model of News Production, *Communication Theory* 5, 4: 301–38.

Manin, Bernard (1987). On Legitimacy and Political Deliberation, *Political Theory* 15: 338–68.

—— (1995). *Principes du gouvernement représentatif*. Paris: Calman-Lévy.

Manweller, Mathew (2005). Coalition Building in Direct Democracy Campaigns, *American Politics Research* 33: 246–82.

Marcinkowski, Frank (2006). Mediensystem und politische Kommunikation, pp. 394–424 in *Handbuch der Schweizer Politik*, 4th ed., edited by Ulrich Klöti, Peter Knoepfel, Hanspeter Kriesi, Wolf Linder, Yannis Papadopoulos, Zürich: NZZ-Verlag.

Marcus, George E. (2002). *The Sentimental Citizen: Emotion in Democratic Politics*. University Park: Pennsylvania State University.

Marcus, George E. and Michael B. MacKuen (1993). Anxiety, Enthusiasm, and the Vote: The Emotional Underpinnings of Learning and Involvement during Presidential Campaigns, *American Political Science Review* 87, 3: 672–85.

Marcus, George E., W. Russel Neuman and Michael MacKuen (2000). *Affective Intelligence and Political Judgment*. Chicago: The University of Chicago Press.

Marr, Mirko, Vinzenz Wyss, Roger Blum und Heinz Bonfadelli (2001). *Journalisten in der Schweiz. Eigenschaften, Einstellungen, Einflüsse* (Reihe: Forschungsfeld Kommunikation, Bd. 13). Konstanz: UVK Medien.

Matthes, Jörg (2009). What's in a frame? A Content Analysis of Media-Framing Studies in the World's Leading Communication Journals, 1990–2005, *Journalism and Mass Communication Quarterly* 86: 349–67.

—— (2007). *Framing-Effekte. Zum Einfluss der Politikberichterstattung auf die Einstellungen der Reizipienten*. München: Verlag Reinhard Fischer.

Mazzoleni, G. (1987). Media Logic and Party Logic in Campaign Coverage: The Italian General Election of 1983, *European Journal of Communication* 2, 2: 81–103.

Mazzoleni, Gianpietro and Winfried Schulz (1999). Mediatization of Politics: A challenge for Democracy? *Political Communication* 16, 3: 247–61.

McClosky, Herbert and Dennis Chong (1985). Similarities and Differences between Left-Wing and Right-Wing Radicals, *British Journal of Political Science* 15, 3: 329–63.

McDermott, Rose (2004). The Feeling of Rationality: The Meaning of Neuroscientific Advances for Political Science, *Perspectives on Politics* 2, 4: 691–706.

McGuire, William J. (1985). Attitudes and Attitude Change in *Handbook of Social Psychology*, edited by G. Lindzey and E. Aronson, New York: Random House.

McLeod, Jack M. and Daniel G. McDonald (1985). Beyond Simple Exposure. Media Orientations and Their Impact on Political Processes, *Communication Research* 12, 1: 3–33.

McLeod, Douglas M., Gerald M. Kosicki and Jack M. McLeaod (2009). Political Communication Effects, pp. 228–251 in *Media Effects. Advances in Theory and Research*, 3rd ed., edited by Jennings Bryant and Mary Beth Oliver, London: Routledge.

McManus, John H. (1995). A Market-Based Model of News Production, *Communication Theory* 5, 4: 301–38.

—— (1994). *Market-Driven Journalism: Let the Citizen Beware?* Thousand Oaks, London/ New Delhi: Sage Publications.

McNair, B. (2003). *An Introduction to Political Communication* (3rd ed.). London: Routledge.

McQuail, Dennis. (1992). *Media Performance: Mass Communication and the Public Interest.* London: London.

Meffert, Michael F., Michael Guge and Milton Lodge (2004). Good, Bad, and Ambivalent: The Consequences of Multidimensional Political Attitudes, pp. 63–92 in *Studies in Public Opinion Attitudes, Nonattitudes, Measurement Error, and Change,* edited by Willem E. Saris. Princeton, NJ: Princeton University Press.

Meier, Werner A. and Michael Schanne (1994). *Medien-,Landschaft Schweiz.* Zürich: Pro Helvetia.

Meier, Werner A. and Otfried Jarren (2001). Ökonomisierung und Kommerzialisierung von Medien und Mediensystem. Einleitende Bemerkung zu einer (notwendigen) Debatte, *Medien & Kommunikationswissenschaft* 49, 2: 145–58.

Merton, Robert K. (1968). The Matthew Principle in Science. The Reward and Communication System of Science Considered, *Science* 59, 3810: 56–63.

Meyer, Thomas (2002). *Media Democracy. How the Media Colonize Politics.* Cambridge: Polity Press.

Moe, Terry M. (1980). *The Organization of Interests: Incentives and the Internal Dynamics of Political Interest Groups.* Chicago: The University of Chicago Press.

Morris, Dick (1999). *The New Prince. Machiavelli Updated for the Twenty-First Century.* Los Angeles: Renaissance Books.

Mutz, Diana C., Paul M. Sniderman and Richard A. Brody (1996). Political Persuasion: The Birth of a Field of Study, pp. 77–99 in *Political Persuasion and Attitude Change,* edited by Diana C. Mutz, Paul M. Sniderman, and Richard A. Brody, Ann Arbor: University of Michigan Press.

Nabi, Robin L. (2002). Anger, Fear, Uncertainty, and Attitudes: A Test of the Cognitive-Functional Model, *Communication Monographs,* 69: 204–216.

—— (1999). A Cognitive-Functional Model for the Effects of Discrete Negative Emotions on Information Processing, Attitude Change, and Recall, *Communication Theory* 9, 3: 292–320.

Nadeau, Richard, Neil Nevitte, Elisabeth Gidengil, and André Blais (2001). *Election Campaigns As Information Campaigns: Who Learns What and with What Effect?* Working Paper, Montréal.

Neidhart, Leonhard (1970). *Plebiszit und pluralitäre Demokratie.* Bern: Francke.

Neuman, Russell W. (1976). Patterns of Recall among Television News Viewers, *Public Opinion Quarterly* 40, 1: 115–23.

Nimmo, Dan D. (1970). *Political Persuaders. The Techniques of Modern Election Campaigns.* Englewood-Cliffs: Prentice Hall.

Norris, Pippa, John Curtice, D. Sanders, Margret Scammell and Holly Semetko (1999). *On Message – Communicating the Campaign.* London: Sage.

Oliver, Pamela (1984). If You Don't Do It, Nobody Else Will: Active and Token Contributors to Local Collective Action, *American Sociological Review* 49: 601–10.

Oliver, Pamela E. and Gregory M. Maney (2000). Political Processes and Local Newspaper Coverage of Protest Events: From Selection Bias to Triadic Interactions, *American Journal of Sociology* 106, 2: 463–505.

Osgood, Charles E. and Percy H. Tannenbaum (1955). The Principle of Congruity in the Prediction of Attitude Change, *Psychological Review* 62: 42–55.

Ossipow, William (1994). Le système politique suisse ou lart de la compensation, pp. 9–56 in *Elites politiques et peuple en Suisse. Analyse des votations fédérales: 1970– 1987,* edited by Yannis Papadopoulos, Lausanne: Réalités Sociales.

Ottati, Victor C. and Robert S. Wyer Jr. (1993). Affect in Political Judgment, pp. 296–315 in *Explorations in Political Psychology,* edited by Shanto Iyengar and William J. McGuire, Durham: Duke University Press.

Page, Benjamin I. (1996). *Who Deliberates? Mass Media in Modern Democracy.* Chicago, London: The University of Chicago Press.

Page, Benjamin I. and Marsahll M. Bouton (2006). *The Foreign Policy Disconnect. What Americans Want From Our Leaders but Don't Get.* Chicago: The University of Chicago Press.

Pan, Zhongdang and Gerald M. Kosicki (1996). Assessing News Media Influences on the Formation of Whites Racial Policy Preferences, *Communication Research* 23, 2: 147–78.

—— (1993). Framing Analysis: An Approach to News Discourse, *Political Communication* 10: 59–79.

Papadopoulos Yannis (1991). Quel rôle pour les petits partis dans la démocratie directe? *Annuaire suisse de science politique* 31: 131–50.

Patterson, Thomas E. (1998). Political Roles of the Journalist, pp. 17–32 in *The Politics of News. The News of Politics,* edited by Doris Graber, Denis McQuail and Pippa Norris, Washington DC: CQ Press.

Patterson, Thomas E. and R.D. McClure (1976). *The Unseeing Eye.* New York: Putnam.

Peake, Jeffrey S. and Matthes Eshbaugh-Soha (2008). The Agenda-Setting Impact of Major Presidential TV Addresses, *Political Communication* 25: 113–37.

Petrocik, John R. (1996). Issue Ownership in Presidential Elections, with a 1980 Case Study, *American Journal of Political Science* 40, 3: 825–50.

Petty, Richard E. and John T. Cacioppo (1986). The Elaboration Likelihood Model of Persuasion, pp. 123–205 in *Advances in Experimental Social Psychology,* edited by L. Berkowitz, New York: Academic Press.

Picard, Robert G. (2005). Money, Media, and the Public Interest, pp. 337–50 in *The Press,* edited by G. Overholser and K. Hall Jamieson, Oxford, New York: Oxford University Press.

—— (2002). *The Economics and Financing of Media Companies.* New York: Fordham University Press.

—— (1998). Media Concentration, Economics and Regulation, pp. 193–217 in *The Politics of News. The News of Politics,* edited by Doris Graber, Denis McQuail and Pippa Norris, Washington DC: CQ Press.

Poguntke, Thomas and Paul Webb (eds) (2005). *The Presidentialization of Politics: A Comparative Study of Modern Democracies.* Oxford: Oxford University Press.

Powell, G. Bingham Jr. (2004). The Chain of Responsiveness, *Journal of Democracy* 15, 4: 91–105.

Price, Vincent and David Tewksbury (1997). News Values and Public Opinion: A Theoretical Account of Media Priming and Framing, pp. 173–212 in *Progress in Communication Sciences: Advances in Persuasion.* Vol. 13, edited by G. A. Barnett and F. J. Boster, Greenwich, CT: Ablex.

Protess, David L., Fay Lomax Cook, Thomas R. Curtin, Margaret T. Gordon, Donna R. Leff, Maxwell E. McCombs and Peter Miller (1987). The Impact of Investigative Reporting on Public Opinion and Policymaking, *Public Opinion Quarterly* 51, 2: 166–85.

Przeworski, Adam (1998). Deliberation and Ideological Domination, pp. 140–60 in *Deliberative Democracy,* edited by Jon Elster, Cambridge: Cambridge University Press.

Rabe-Hesketh, Sophia and Anders Skrondal (2008). *Multilevel and Longitudinal Modeling Using Stata*. (2nd ed.). College Station, TX: Stata Press.

Ragsdale, Lyn (1991). Strong Feelings: Emotional Responses to Presidents, *Political Behavior* 13, 1: 33–65.

Rahn, Wendy M. (2002). Book Review of Affective Intelligence and Political Judgment, *Journal of Politics* 54, 1: 262–64.

Ridout, Travis N., Dhavan V. Shah, Kenneth M. Goldstein, and Michael M. Franz (2004). Evaluating Measures of Campaign Advertising Exposure on Political Learning, *Political Behavior* 26, 3: 201–25.

Riker, William H. (1996). *The Strategy of Rhetoric. Campaigning for the American Constitution*. New Haven: Yale University Press.

—— (1986). *The Art of Political Manipulation*. New Haven: Yale University Press.

—— (1984). The Heresthetics of Constitution-Making: The Presidency in 1787, with Comments on Determinism and Rational Choice, *American Political Science Review* 78: 1–16.

—— (1962). *The Theory of Political Coalitions*. New Haven: Yale University Press.

Robinson, John P. and Mark R. Levy (1996). News Media Use and the Informed Public: A 1990's Update, *Journal of Communication* 46, 2: 129–35.

—— (1986). *The Main Source: What People Learn from Television* News. Beverly Hills, CA: Sage.

Rohrschneider, Robert (2002). Mobilizing Versus Chasing: How do Parties Target Voters in Election Campaigns? *Electoral Studies* 21, 3: 367–82.

Rosenberg, Milton J. (1960). A Structural Theory of Attitude Dynamics, *Public Opinion Quarterly* 24, 2: 319–40.

Rudolph Thomas J. (2005). Group Attachment and the Reduction of Value-Driven Ambivalence, *Political Psychology* 26: 905–28.

Rudolph Thomas J. and Elizabeth Popp (2007). An Information Processing Theory of Ambivalence, *Political Psychology* 28: 563–85.

Russ-Mohl (1994). Symbiose oder Konflikt: Öffentlichkeitsarbeit und Journalismus, pp. 313–26 in *Medien und Journalismus 1. Eine Einführung*, edited by Otfried Jarren, Opladen: Westdeutscher Verlag.

Sabatier, Paul A. and Christopher M. Weible (2007). The Advocacy Coalition Framework: Innovations and Clarifications, pp. 189–220 in *Theories of the Policy Process*, 2nd ed., edited by Paul A. Sabatier, Boulder, Col: Westview.

Saffarnia, Pierre A. (1993). Determiniert Öffentlichkeitsarbeit tatsächlich den Journalismus? *Publizistik* 38, 3: 412–25.

Saris, Willem E. and Paul M. Sniderman (2004). Introduction, pp. 1–13 in *Studies in Public Opinion Attitudes, Nonattitudes, Measurement Error, and Change*, edited by Willem E. Saris, Princeton, NJ: Princeton University Press.

Sartori, Giovanni (1968). The Sociology of Parties. A Critical Review, pp. 1–27 in *Party Systems, Party Organizations, and the Politics of New Masses*, edited by O. Stammer, Berlin: Institut für politische Wissenschaft an der Freien Universität Berlin (reprinted in Peter Mair (ed.) (1990). *The West European Party System*. Oxford University Press).

Saxer, Ulrich (1998). Was heisst Kommerzialisierung? *Zoom Kommunikation und Medien* 11: 10–17.

Scammell, Margaret (1999). Political Marketing: Lessons for Political Science, *Political Studies* 47, 4: 718–39.

Scarrow, Susan E. (2001). Direct Democracy and Institutional Change: A Comparative Investigation, *Comparative Political Studies* 34, 6: 651–65.

Schattschneider, E.E. (1975) (1960). *The Semisovereign People*. New York: Wadsworth Thomson Learning.

Scheufele, Dietram A. (1999). Framing As a Theory of Media Effects, *Journal of Communication* 49, 1: 103–22.

Schmitt-Beck, Rüdiger (2003). Wirkungen politischer Kommunikation: Massenmedial und interpersonale Einflüsse auf die Wahlentscheidung, pp. 337–68 in *Politische Kommunikation im internationalen Vergleich. Grundlagen, Anwendungen, Perspektiven*, edited by Frank Esser and Barbara Pfetsch, Wiesbaden: Westdeutscher Verlag.

Schudson, Michael (1998). *The Good Citizen. A History of American Civic Life*. Cambridge, Mass.: Harvard University Press.

Schulz, Winfried (1976). *Die Konstruktion von Realität in den Nachrichtenmedien*. Freiburg/München: Verlag Karl Alber.

Schumpeter, Joseph A. (1962) (1942). *Capitalism, Socialism and Democracy*. London: Allen and Unwin.

Schwarz, Norbert and Gerald L. Clore (1983). Mood, Misattribution, and Judgments of Well-Being: Informative and Directive Functions of Affective States, *Journal of Personality and Social Psychology* 45: 513–23.

Sciarini, Pascal and Alexander H. Trechsel (1996). La démocratie directe en Suisse: Lélite politique victime des droits populaires? *Revue suisse de science politique* 2, 3: 201–32.

Sears, David O. and Carolyn L. Funk (1999). Evidence of the Long-Term Persistence of Adults Political Predisposition, *Journal of Politics* 61: 1–28.

Selb, Peter, Hanspeter Kriesi, Regula Hänggli and Mirko Marr (2009). Partisan Choices in a Direct-Democratic Campaign, *European Review of Political Science* 1, 1: 155–72.

Shaw, Daron R. (1999a). The Effect of TV Ads and Candidate Appearances on Statewide Presidential Votes, 1988–1996, *American Political Science Review* 93, 2: 345–61.

—— (1999b). A Study of Presidential Campaign Event Effects from 1952 to 1992, *Journal of Politics* 61, 2: 387–422.

Shen, Fuyuan (2004). Effects of News Frames and Schemas on Individuals Issue Interpretations and Attitudes, *Journalism and Mass Communication Quarterly* 81: 400–16.

Sides, John (2006). The Origins of Campaign Agendas, *British Journal of Political Science* 36, 3: 407–36.

Siegert, Gabriele (2001). *Medien Marken Management: Relevanz, Spezifika und Implikationen einer medienökonomischen Profilierungsstrategie*. München: Reinhard Fischer.

Sigal, Leon (1973). *Reporters and Officials*. Lexington, MA: D.C. Heath.

Sigelman, Lee, and Emmett H. Jr. Buell (2004). Avoidance or Engagement? Issue Convergence in Presidential Campaigns, *American Journal of Political Science* 48, 4: 650–61.

Simon, Adam F. and Jennifer Jerit (2007). Toward a Theory Relating Political Discourse, Media, and Public Opinion, *Journal of Communication* 57: 254–71.

Singer, Judith B. and John B. Willett (2003). *Applied Longitudinal Data Analysis: Modeling Change and Event Occurrence*. New York: Oxford University Press.

Sinnott, Richard (2002). Cleavages, Parties and Referendums: Relationships between Representative and Direct Democracy in the Republic of Ireland, *European Journal of Political Research* 41: 811–26.

Smith, Daniel A. (1998). *Tax Crusaders and the Politics of Direct Democracy.* New York: Routledge.

Smith, Daniel A. and Caroline J. Tolbert (2004). *Educated by Initiaive. The Effects of Direct Democracy on Citizens and Political Organizations in the American States.* Ann Arbor: The University of Michigan Press.

—— (2001). The Initiative to Party. Partisanship and Ballot Initiatives in California, *Party Politics* 7, 6: 739–57.

Sniderman, Paul A. (2000). Taking Sides: A Fixed Choice Theory of Political Reasoning, pp. 67–84 in *Elements of Reason: Cognition, Choice, and the Bounds of Rationality,* edited by Arthur Lupia, Mathew D. McCubbins, and Samuel P. Popkin. Cambridge, UK: Cambridge University Press.

—— (1993). The New Look in Public Opinion Research, pp. 219–45 in *Political Science: The State of the Discipline II,* edited by Ada W. Finifter, Washington, DC: The American Political Science Association.

Sniderman, Paul A. and John Bullock (2004). A Consistency Theory of Public Opinion and Political Choice: The Hypothesis of Menu Dependence, pp. 337–57 in *Studies in Public Opinion. Attitudes, Nonattitudes, Measurement Error, and Change,* edited by Willem E. Saris and Paul M. Sniderman, Princeton, NJ: Princeton University Press.

Sniderman, Paul M. and Louk Hagendoorn (2007). *When Ways of Life Collide.* Princeton, NJ: Princeton University Press.

Sniderman, Paul M., Louk Hagendoorn and Markus Prior (2004). Predisposing Factors and Situational Triggers: Exclusionary Reactions to Immigrant Minorities, *American Political Science Review* 98, 1: 35–50.

Sniderman Paul M. and M. Levendusky (2007). An Institutional Theory of Political Choice, pp. 437–56 in *Oxford Handbook of Political Behavior,* edited by Russell Dalton and Hans-Dieter Klingemann, Oxford: Oxford University Press.

Sniderman, Paul M., Perangelo Peri, Rui J.P. de Figueiredo, jr., and Thomas Piazza (2000). *The Outsider. Prejudice and Politics in Italy.* Princeton, NJ: Princeton University Press. Sniderman, Paul M., Philip E. Tetlock and Laurel Elms (2001).Public Opinion and Democratic Politics: The Problem of Nonattitudes and the Social Construction of Political Judgement, pp. 254–88 in *Citizens and Politics. Perspectives from Political Psychology,* edited by James H. Kuklinski. Cambridge University Press.

Sniderman, Paul M., Richard A. Brody and Philip E. Tetlock (1991). *Reasoning and choice: Explorations in Political Psychology.* Cambridge: Cambridge University Press.

Sniderman, Paul M., and Sean M. Theriault (2004). The Structure of Political Argument and the Logic of Issue Framing, pp. 133–65 in *Studies in Public Opinion: Attitudes, Nonattitudes, Measurement Error and Change,* edited by Willem E. Saris and Paul M. Sniderman. Princeton, NJ: Princeton University Press.

Snow, David A. and Robert D. Benford (1988). Ideology, Frame Resonance and Participant Mobilization, pp. 197–218 in *From Structure to Action: Social Movement Participation across Cultures,* edited by Bert Klandermans, Hanspeter Kriesi and Sidney Tarrow, Greenwich, CT: JAI Press.

Soroka, Stuart N. (2002). *Agenda-Setting Dynamics in Canada.* Vancouver, B.C.: UBC Press.

Sotirovic, Mira (2008). Political Knowledge, pp. 593–600 in *Encyclopedia of Political Communication.* Vol. 2, edited by Kaid, Lynda Lee and Christina Holtz-Bacha, Los Angeles/London/New Delhi/Singapore: Sage.

Sotirovic, Mira and Jack McLeod (2004). Knowledge as Understanding: The Information Processing Approach to Political Learning, pp. 357–94 in *Handbook of Political Communication Research*, edited by Kaid, Lynda Lee, Mahwah, NJ: Erlbaum.

Stamm, Keith, Michelle Johnson and Brennon Martin (1997). Differences among Newspapers, Television, and Radio in Their Contribution to Knowledge of the Contract with America, *Journalism and Mass Communication Quarterly* 74, 4: 687–702.

Stangor, Charles, L. A. Sullivan and Thomas E. Ford (1991). Affective and Cognitive Determinants of Prejudice, *Social Cognition* 9, 4: 359–80.

Steenbergen, Marco (2008). *Event Count Models*. Berne: University of Berne.

Steenbergen Marco R. and Paul R. Brewer (2004). The Not-So-Ambivalent Public: Policy Attitudes in the Political Culture of Ambivalence, pp. 93–129 in *Studies in Public Opinion Attitudes, Nonattitudes, Measurement Error, and Change*, edited by Willem E. Saris, Princeton, NJ: Princeton University Press.

Stimson, James A. (2004). *Tides of Consent. How Public Opinion Shapes American Politics*. Cambridge: Cambridge University Press.

Stimson, James A, Michael B. MackKuen and Robert S. Erikson (1995). Dynamic Representation, *American Political Science Review* 89, 3: 543–65.

Stokes, Susan C. (1998). Pathologies of Deliberation, pp. 123–39 in *Deliberative Democracy*, edited by Jon Elster. Cambridge: Cambridge University Press.

Stratmann, T. (2006). Is Spending More Potent For or Against a Proposition? Evidence from Ballot Measures, *American Journal of Political Science* 50, 3: 788–801.

Strömbäck, J. (2008). Four Phases of Mediatization: An Analysis of the Mediatization of Politics, *The International Journal of Press/Politics* 13, 3: 228–46.

Strömbäck, J., and L.W. Nord (2006). Do Politicians Lead the Tango? A Study of the Relationship between Swedish Journalists and their Political Sources in the Context of Election Campaigns, *European Journal of Communication* 21, 2: 147–64.

Swanson, David L. und Paolo Mancini (1996). Patterns of Modern Electoral Campaigning and their Consequences, pp. 247–76 in *Politics, Media, and Modern Democracy. An International Study of Innovations in Electoral Campaigning and Their Consequences*, edited by David L. Swanson und Paolo Mancini, London: Praeger.

Swiss Federal Chancellery (2006). *Briefliche Stimmabgabe: Analyse der eidgenössischen Abstimmung vom 27. November 2005*. Bern.

Tichenor, Phillip, George Donohue and Clarice Olien (1970). Mass Media Flow and Differential Growth in Knowledge, *Public Opinion Quarterly* 34, 2: 159–70.

Tillie Jean (1995). *Party Utility and Voting Behavior*. Amsterdam: Het Spinhuis.

Tilly, Charles (1978). *From Mobilization to Revolution*. Indianapolis: Addison Wesley.

Tomz, Michael, King, Gary, und Langche Zeng (1999). *Relogit. Rare Events Logistic Regression*, Version 1.1 for Stata, Cambridge, MA: Harvard University, October 1, <http://gking.harvard.edu/>

Trechsel, Alexander and Pascal Sciarini (1998). Direct Democracy in Switzerland: Do Elites Matter? *European Journal of Political Research* 33, 1: 99–123.

Tresch, Anke (2009). Politicians in the Media: Determinants of Legislators Presence and Prominence in Swiss Newspapers, *The International Journal of Press/Politics* 14, 1: 67–90.

—— (2008). *Öffentlichkeit und Sprachenvielfalt. Medienvermittelt Kommunikation zur Europapolitik in der Deutsch- und Westschweiz*. Baden-Baden: Nomos.

Underwood, Doug (2001). Reporting and the Push for Market-Oriented Journalism: Media Organizations as Businesses, pp. 99–116 in *Mediated Politics. Communication in the Future of Democracy*, edited by W. Lance Bennett and Robert M. Entman, Cambridge: Cambridge University Press.

Valkenburg, Patti M., Holli A. Semetko and Claes de Vreese (1999). The Effects of News Frames on Readers Thoughts and Recall, *Communication Research* 26: 550–69.

Van Aelst, P., B. Maddens, J. Noppe and S. Fiers (2008). Politicians in the News: Media or Party Logic? Media Attention and Electoral Success in the Belgian Election Campaign of 2003, *European Journal of Communication* 23, 2: 193–210.

Van der Brug, Wouter and Meindert Fennema (2003). Protest or Mainstream? How the European Anti-Immigrant Parties Developed into Two Separate Groups by 1999, *European Journal of Political Research* 42, 1: 55–76.

Van der Brug, Wouter, Meindert Fennema and Jean Tillie (2005). Why Some Anti-Immigrant Parties Fail and Others Succeed: A Two-Step Model of Aggregate Electoral Support, *Comparative Political Studies* 38, 5: 537–73.

—— (2000). Anti-Immigrant Parties in Europe: Ideological or Protest Vote? *European Journal of Political Research* 37: 77–102.

Van der Eijk, Cees, Wouter Van der Brug, W., Martin Kroh and Mark Franklin (2006). Rethinking the Dependent Variable in Voting Behavior: On the Measurement and Analysis of Electoral Utilities, *Electoral Studies* 25, 3: 424–47.

Van Kempen, H. (2007). Media-Party Parallelism and Its Effects: A Cross-National Comparative Study, *Political Communication* 24, 3: 303–20.

Van Schuur Wijbrand H. (1993). Nonparametric Unfolding Models for Multicategory Data, *Political Analysis* 4: 41–74.

Van Schuur Wijbrand H. and W.J. Post (1998). MUDFOLD. A Program for Multiple Unidimensional Unfolding. Version 4.0. Groningen: iec ProGAMMA.

Viswanath, K. and John Finnegan (1996). The Knowledge Gap Hypothesis: Twenty-Five Years Later, pp. 187–227 in *Communication Yearbook*. Vol.19, edited by Brant Burleson and Adrienne Kunkel, Thousand Oaks / London / New Delhi: Sage.

Vuong, Q. H. (1989). Likelihood Ratio Tests for Model Selection and Non-Nested Hypotheses, *Econometrica* 57: 307–33.

Walder, Andrew G. (2006). Ambiguity and Choice in Political Movements: The Origins of Beijing Red Guard Factionalism, *American Journal of Sociology* 112, 3: 710–50.

Wassermann, Stanley and Katherine Faust (1994). *Social Network Analysis. Methods and Applications.* Cambridge: Cambridge University Press.

Weaver, David, Maxwell McCombs and Donald L. Shaw (2004). Agenda-Setting research: Issues, Attributes, and Influences, pp. 257–82 in *Handbook of Political Communication Research*, edited by Lynda Lee Kaid, Mahwah, NJ: Lawrence Erlbaum.

Weaver, David H., Randal A. Beam, Bonnie J. Brownlee, Paul S. Voakes and G. Wilhoit Cleveland (2007). *The American Journalist in the 21st Century. US News People at the Dawn of a New Millennium.* Mahwah, NJ: Lawrence Erlbaum Associates.

Weischenberg, Siegfried, Armin Scholl and Maja Malik (2006). *Die Souffleure der Mediengesellschaft. Report über die Journalisten in Deutschland.* Konstanz: UVK.

Wirth, Werner (1997). *Von der Information zum Wissen. Die Rolle der Rezeption für die Entstehung von Wissensunterschieden.* Opladen: Westdeutscher Verlag.

Wolfsfeld, Gadi. (1997). *Media and Political Conflict. News from the Middle East* (Reprint ed.). Cambridge, Mass: Cambridge University Press.

Wooldridge, Jeffrey M. (2002). *Econometric Analysis of Cross Section and Panel Data.* Cambridge, Massachusetts: MIT Press.

Zaller John R. (2003). A New Standard of News Quality: Burglar Alarms for the Monitorial Citizen, *Political Communication* 20: 109–30.

—— (2003). The Statistical Power of Election Studies to Detect Media Exposure Effects in Political Campaigns, *Electoral Studies* 21, 2: 297–329.

—— (1999). *Market competition and news quality.* Paper prepared for presentation at the 1999 annual meetings of the American Political Science Association, Atlanta, GA. Paper präsentiert.

—— (1996). The Myth of Massive Media Impact Revisited, pp. 17–78 in *Political Persuasion and Attitude Change*, edited by D. C. Mutz, P. M. Sniderman, and R. A. Brody, Ann Arber: University of Michigan Press.

—— (1992). *The Nature and Origins of Mass Opinion.* New York: Cambridge University Press.

Zhao, X. and Steven H. Chaffee (1995). Campaign Advertisements Versus Television News as Sources of Political Issue Information, *Public Opinion Quarterly* 59, 1: 41–65.

Zuckerman, Alan S. (1975). Political Cleavage: A Conceptual and Theoretical Analysis, *British Journal of Political Science* 5, 2: 231–48.

Index